Learning to Become a Professional in a Textually-Mediated World

Linguistic Insights

Studies in Language and Communication

Edited by Maurizio Gotti,
University of Bergamo

Volume 139

PETER LANG
Bern · Berlin · Bruxelles · Frankfurt am Main · New York · Oxford · Wien

Ken Lau

Learning to Become a Professional in a Textually-Mediated World

A Text-Oriented Study of Placement Practices

PETER LANG
Bern · Berlin · Bruxelles · Frankfurt am Main · New York · Oxford · Wien

Bibliographic information published by die Deutsche Nationalbibliothek
Die Deutsche Nationalbibliothek lists this publication in the Deutsche Nationalbibliografie; detailed bibliographic data is available on the Internet at ‹http://dnb.d-nb.de›.

British Library Cataloguing-in-Publication Data: A catalogue record for this book is available from The British Library, Great Britain

Library of Congress Cataloging-in-Publication Data

Lau, Ken
Learning to become a professional in a textually-mediated world : a text-oriented study of placement practices / Ken Lau.
p. cm. – (Linguistic insights: Studies in language and communication v. 139)
Thesis (Ph.D.)–Lancaster University, 2009.
Includes bibliographical references and index.
1. Discourse analysis–Data processing. 2. Functional discourse grammar.
3. Computational linguistics. I. Title.
P302.3.L38 2012
401'.410285–dc23

2012004554

ISSN 1424-8689
ISBN 978-3-0343-1016-1

Hochfeldstrasse 32, CH-3012 Bern, Switzerland
info@peterlang.com, www.peterlang.com, www.peterlang.net

Printed in Switzerland

Contents

Acknowledgements

The support of a number of people gave me the strength and energy to complete this book. I would like to thank them wholeheartedly:

First and foremost, Greg Myers, my PhD supervisor at the Lancaster University, UK who offered extensive constructive feedback on my thesis drafts and inspired me throughout my PhD journey. This book is based on my PhD thesis, so without him, it would not have come to fruition.

All my other teachers and course mates at the Lancaster University who made my life there so fruitful and intellectually-stimulating.

My current and former colleague-friends from the Centre for Applied English Studies, the University of Hong Kong who always give me moral support and are there for me when I need them. David Gardner and Agnes Lam, in particular, not only always value my work and offer encouragement, but also act as my mentors and role models showing me how to work professionally.

The series reviewer and editor for their valuable comments on the manuscript.

My research assistant Jacqueline Lai who helped edit the book chapters and did all the typesetting work so meticulously.

Cambridge University Press (CUP) and American Spinal Injury Association (ASIA) for their permission to reprint Figure 1 on p.30 (CUP), Figure 2 on p.33 (CUP) and Figure 3 on p.121 (ASIA).

Last but not least, my family for their patience and love – my parents, two elder brothers, sister-in-law and nephew have created an ideal 'learning context' for me to pursue my dream!

1 Rethinking Learning

A vignette after dinner
Eight of us gathered around the table: we inquired about the recipes for various dishes, shared the experience of juggling among work, family and study, recalling the 'daunting' yet fruitful experience of having the PhD confirmation panel, teased about a 'reminder' t-shirt printed with the name of a street in Japan (the one who wore it lived there and it was bought by his wife!)... *After all, I learn.* (July 2005)

The vignette above highlights some of the main events at a dinner party organised and attended by a group of graduate students pursuing a PhD degree in Applied Linguistics at the same university in the United Kingdom. At the end of the vignette the dinner guest claimed that he had learnt something from the party, yet the episode depicted stark contrasts with a traditional learning scene. Broadly speaking, there are five learning events involved in the vignette, namely, learning the recipes for dishes, learning time management, learning about a critical moment and stage in the PhD study, learning about a street located in Japan and learning that a classmate has a 'thoughtful' wife. If we compare these learning events with those that we have in schools (particularly in the old days), several distinct differences can be identified. Firstly, the setting within which learning takes place is different. Learning in schools is always institutionalised and takes place in a formal setting: desks and chairs are lined up neatly; a whiteboard, markers, a projector, a computer, textbooks and handouts are teaching and learning necessities. Secondly, the participants involved are usually a teacher and a group of students, with the former mainly imparting knowledge and the latter as passive recipients. Thirdly, knowledge is often acquired through examples taken out of real-life contexts, for example, learning English grammar through completing mechanical tasks in a grammar book. Fourthly, the ultimate goal of learning in academic institutions is to gain a pass in the end-of-term examinations, in which students' performances are quantified and/or tested against criteria and subsequently compared.

With multiple learning options in perspective, Lave and Wenger (1991) propose a new conception of learning which ties in with various social practices in our daily lives. Learning comes out of interactions within an informal setting and although goal-directed, it is set within the realm of our physical needs (e.g., eating) and human nature. There is no formal assessment mechanism; and yet knowledge produced is socially validated based on participants' contributions. Knowledge transfer is not top-down, although participants at the dinner come with diverse academic/professional backgrounds and are at various stages on the PhD programme. Participants take on multiple roles at the dinner gathering: chefs who prepare the meal, somebody's husband and wife, a 'tour guide' introducing Japan, etc.; yet what is shared among the participants is the identity as a graduate student on an Applied Linguistics programme in the Linguistics and English Language Department at a British university. Meanings negotiated in the interactions among participants are not merely confined to experiential (Halliday/Matthiessen 2004) but also interpersonal (Martin/White 2005) to maintain solidarity. Such a view implies that learning is a social practice rather than seeing it just as an end to institutionalised teaching. This thus puts learning "in the context of our lived experience of participation in the world" (Wenger 1998: 3) and suggests that students on a PhD applied linguistics programme conform to Lave and Wenger's (1991: 89) conception of a 'Community of Practice' (CoP). Table 1 compares the view of learning in school and learning in a CoP.

Variable		*Learning in School*	*Learning in a CoP*
	Setting	Formal – usually classroom contexts	Informal – as lived experience of participation in the world
	Goal	To warrant a successful progression (e.g. study)	Social interactions to maintain solidarity and as a response to human needs
	Knowledge transfer	Usually top-down; largely passive knowledge receiving	Usually peer-to-peer; active contributions and participation required

Table 1. A comparison between two views of learning.

1.1. Motivation of the current study

In response to the growing trend of professionalisation of academic disciplines (Leydens 2008) and heightened awareness of professional competence, 'placement' or similar terms as internship/practicum has been widely integrated into the academic curriculum in many universities worldwide; Hong Kong is no exception. Placement provides an intermediate platform where novices learn to become professionals through engaging in tasks central to the running of and valued by an institution. One major task that these novices need to grapple with is writing. In social work placement, for instance, over 60% of student workers' (STWs') time is devoted to writing (Storey/Tsang/Dora 2003). Although writing may not account for such a significant proportion of the work in the placement of other fields, STWs engaging in various writing activities sustains and continues the institutional practice. Another rhetorical function of writing specific to the context of placement is to convince the stakeholders that the novice has attained the level of professional competence which warrants a progression to the next stage of the learning trajectory.

Although there have been research studies investigating placement writing or alike (e.g., Dias *et al.* 1999, Dias/Paré 2000, Schneider/Andre 2005), the focus is often placed on its social context. Studies that look into the linguistic aspects of writing in placement are lacking. Such studies are nonetheless necessary given the fact that writing is often socially situated and goal-oriented which pose limitations to the writers' linguistic choices.

Another complication of the picture is related to the provision of English enhancement programmes. In Hong Kong, most of the university English enhancement courses are academic-oriented (Flowerdew 2005), i.e., English for Academic Purposes (EAP), targeted at helping students grapple with the English demanded in their academic study. There are 'professional' courses but most of them are prone to teaching generic skills in business communication: writing memos, proposals, conducting simulated business negotiation meetings. Very few courses are specifically designed based on the genuine language needs in the workplace. Insufficient understanding of disciplinary knowledge, technical terminologies/jargon and the workplace's language requirements may deter curriculum developers from introducing discipline-specific English for Occupational Purposes (Dudley-Evans/St John 1998) courses. Also, the development of such courses is often very time consuming and involves a close collaboration between content experts and language instructors, which may pose a lot of challenges and difficulties along the way. In this respect, novices often acquire institutional genres without going through a relevant and targeted language training programme prior to placement.

1.2. Scope of the current study and research questions

Using CoP as an overarching framework, this study investigates how novice writers learn to write various documents required in the workplace during their placements in their course of reading for a degree. I deliberately avoid using 'professional' or 'workplace' as the modifier of 'document' in the previous sentence because my data suggest that the documents these STWs accomplished in the workplace are often modified and restructured, which makes them slightly different from the documents completed by the professional/experienced members even in the same organisation. Texts consumed and produced in placement are presumably very much hybrid in nature, bearing both academic and professional features. In addition, the use of reflective writing in professional training has gained recognition and a critical understanding of how reflection is facilitated through writing is needed. The first focus of this study is to investigate how all these features are blended into the placement genres and their rhetorical functions in aiding novices' enculturation.

As novices often receive insufficient workplace writing training at the university, expert members in the profession play a significant role in novices' genre acquisition. The second focus of this study therefore is to explore how novices are inducted into the CoP with the help of expert members.

The informants in this study are undergraduates who have to undertake placements during their course of studies. In other words, they are on the one hand acquiring disciplinary knowledge in an academic context, while on the other they are learning to practice like professionals in the workplace. Their identities are therefore in a state of flux and hybridised (student and professional). This seemingly conflicting identity renders them a special status and role (Sarangi/Roberts 1999) in the workplace. The textually derived interpretation of the roles of these professionals-to-be remains as a largely unexplored area in applied linguistics and the investigation of which constitutes another research focus of my study.

The research foci outlined above are developed into the following research question that guides the current study: *In what way do novice writers adapt to the discourse practices in professional contexts during placements, and how do their roles exert an influence on their discourse practices in relation to their identities?*

The question is further specified as a series of questions and sub-questions:

1. How do novices learn to adapt to the discourse practices during their placement?
   1a. What kind of texts are produced in placement?
   1b. What are the roles of genres and practices in placement?

1c. What social forces are imposed and how do they influence novices' dis course practices?

1d. How do novice writers revise their texts and how are they drawn into disciplinary practices via making use of feedback from expert members?

2. How do informants' roles influence their discourse practices in relation to their identities?

2a. How are roles operationalised in placement?

2b. What linguistic devices are found and how are they manipulated in constructing and reflecting the roles of the informants in texts?

The above research questions highlight the textual orientation of this study. More specifically, the connection between writing and practice is realised through linguistic analysis of texts with respect to genre and lexico-grammar. Data elicited will present a comprehensive view of placement at the level of conceptualisation as well as internal operations which involve textual products and human interactions with them.

1.3. Significance of the current study

This study makes a number of contributions to illuminating our understanding of discourse aspects of the placement, a relatively novel epistemological site which deserves more attention from applied linguists. The following is a list of contributions:

- This study offers a useful lens for us to look at the specific linguistic repertoires demanded of STWs in the workplace and how these novice writers reconcile possible tensions generated from the transition from the academia to the workplace and deal with the "ethical dilemma posed by the need to support institutional goals which may be at odds with personal values" (Parks 2001: 406).
- As for the contributions to theories, this study contextualises a general social theory of learning (CoP) within a linguistic framework to understand a phenomenon drawing on both interview and textual data. The present work also contributes to the current discussions of two overlapping yet distinct theoretical

concepts – identities and roles – and understanding of how they are operationalised and exert influence on STWs' discourse practices in the placement contexts. Although identity in CoP is considered entirely as a social phenomenon and category, this thesis sheds light on the ways this concept can be treated as a linguistic entity (see also Ivanič 1997).

- This study also aims to illustrate an interface that draws pedagogical, professional, and discourse practices together, with the emphasis placed on how genres mediate among these three practices.
- From a pedagogical perspective, this thesis provides important empirical ground for the design of relevant placement and language support programmes for novices, a basis that will encourage collaboration between disciplinary experts and language instructors.

1.4. Organisation of the book

This chapter forms the backdrop to the research study, providing a context of investigations and motivation behind the current study in response to the need to rethink the concept of learning. The research niche, the research questions and the significance of this study were then described.

Chapter 2 starts off with a historical account of writing across the curriculum (WAC) movement and the related writing research development from the 1970s. Then a detailed explanation of various views of learning and the theoretical underpinning of the major concepts, particularly Communities of Practice, will be provided. Related terminologies will be defined within the context of use in this book. A critical reading of previous work on workplace writing, feedback research and writing and identities will be provided with a view to positioning the current study.

Chapter 3 offers a review of the research design and my theoretical position in relation to the methodologies adopted. The adoption of the relatively new qualitative terminology 'crystallization' will be explained and its operationalisation will be discussed with respect to the data generation methods, data collected, findings and interpretation. How the concept of reflexivity is taken into serious account at various stages of my research will be delineated. This chapter will end with a discussion of trustworthiness checks.

Chapter 4 has two main purposes: offering a conceptual contribution and acting as a bridge between the first three background chapters and the next three main analysis chapters. The term 'placement' is problematised and theorised in relation to the aspects of CoP. A working definition of placement will be provided. The conceptualisation justifies the setting up of the subsequent chapters with each of them working around a theoretical aspect of placement.

Chapter 5 takes a genre-based perspective to investigate the interactions among three practices, namely, discourse practice, pedagogical practice and professional practice. The ways these practices mediate and facilitate placement learning are analysed with reference to the lexico-grammatical choices, rhetorical organisation and the associated social context of the placement texts.

Chapter 6 analyses the role of feedback and revision in drawing a novice writer towards disciplinary practices. I attempt to trace the writing journey of one of the informants during his placement in a social work agency by having a close reading of the proposal drafts and session reports he wrote and his use of the teacher's feedback and revisions. This chapter will analyse various types of feedback and revision (broadly language-related ones and content-related ones) and their interactions in detail.

Chapter 7 aims at problematising the concepts of roles by examining its operationalisation in relation to identities in discourse practices. The chapter begins with a linguistic analysis of transitivity, through which the roles played by the STWs associated with the social context are understood. The second half of the chapter goes from the other direction: the social context within which roles are realised will be highlighted in order to understand its impact upon STWs' discourse practices.

The final chapter will first summarise the main findings of this study followed by the limitations. Implications for future research will then be stated.

2 Positioning the Study

> Writing is a complex act, integrally related to learning and knowing, and performs a variety of functions. (Dias *et al.* 1999:9)

This study is aimed at investigating undergraduates' enculturation into professional contexts during placement, with a primary focus on their adaptation to various discourse practices. Fundamental to the enculturation is the occurrence of learning concomitant with the construction of informants' intermediate hybrid identities, i.e., as student-professionals. In this chapter, I therefore broadly position the current study within the realms of *learning*, *writing* and *identities* in relation to previous academic literature. The analytical perspectives taken on board in the current work have also been informed by genre studies, the Writing-Across-the-Curriculum (WAC) movement and Systemic Functional Linguistics (SFL).

Since the previous research work pertinent to these areas of concern is abundant, I have to be restrictive regarding the selection of the literature for discussion. First and foremost, the belief that writing is a learning tool forms the crux of the first part of this chapter. This is delineated firstly by situating learning within a historical account of the learning-to-write and WAC movements presented in Section 2.1, highlighting the paradigm shift from considering writing as solely a means of communication to valuing it as an essential tool conducive to learning (Tynjälä/Mason/Lonka 2001). This is relevant to the current study as writing in placement is an important indicator of STWs' learning. The different theoretical conceptions of knowledge and learning, which cut across the development of various writing research paradigms (see Section 2.2) will then be introduced. A more focused attention will then be devoted to the justification of the adoption of Lave and Wenger's (1991) Communities of Practice (CoPs) as the overarching theoretical framework guiding the current study (see Section 2.3). The associated identity and role transitions will be discussed with reference to the social identities theories.

My orientation towards writing as a socio-cognitive situated activity shapes the second part of the chapter. Section 2.4 begins by reviewing writing research, mainly conducted in North America, which will enhance our understanding of the different discourse practices between academia and workplace engaged by novice writers. Previous work on the interaction between writing and identities is also reviewed in order to justify the need to differentiate identities from roles in this project. Section 2.5 outlines research on genre and its acquisition in a professional context. Bhatia's concept of 'genre integrity' will form the basis of the analysis of placement texts as these texts by default feature the hybrid characteristics of academic and professional discourses. Further, I have taken into consideration his advocacy that one should go beyond the analysis of linguistic resources when conducting genre analysis to integrate the socio-cognitive factors that essentially play a role in the "construction, interpretation, use and exploitation to achieve non-linguistic ends in real life professional contexts" (2005: 112). The role of genre acquisition with respect to professional practice is also discussed.

Another aspect that constitutes the theoretical framework is to consider language function at the discourse-semantic level in functional terms. Section 2.6 will provide an overview of systems of construing experiential and interpersonal meanings together with their implications on the textual data analysis. A summary of key arguments concluded from the review of literature will be given in the last section of this chapter.

2.1. From writing-to-learn to learning-to-write

The traditional distinction between writing across the curriculum (WAC) and writing in the disciplines (WID) lies in their different orientations, with the former often conceptualised as 'writing-to-learn' while the latter 'learning-to-write' (Carter/Ferzli/Wiebe 2007). 'Writing-to-learn' views writing as a learning tool and problem-solving, which is "cognitively based" (McLeod 1989: 342). 'Learning-to-write' sees writing as a way to socialise into disciplinary communities, which is "rhetorically based" (McLeod 1989: 342). Though based on different theoretical assumptions, 'writing-to-learn' and 'learning-to-write' do not stand against but complementary to one another in the tertiary educational context where novices use writing to construct domain-specific knowledge and at the same time, to enculturate into the respective CoP. A historical development of these related concepts is provided below.

2.1.1. Writing-to-learn and WAC movements

Writing had long been solely considered as a means of communication, without having connection with learning domain-specific knowledge. The major emphasis then was therefore placed on the accurate use of the language. This has been considered, in Russell's terms (1991: 2002), writing 'outside' the disciplines. Quinn (1995) noted that even today, there seems to be a lack of collaboration between disciplinary experts and language teachers which can be seen from their lack of understanding of each other's pedagogy and research. The failure in such interdisciplinary collaboration may stem from a lack of commitment (to time) to work together, the open attitude of both sides (Lee 2008), and/or the ideology of protecting one's 'professional turf'.

The roots of dovetailing learning and writing can be traced back to the process writing movement and cross curricular writing program in the 1970s in North America (Nelson 2001; Carter/Ferzli/Wiebe 2007). Two important pioneers in these movements were James Britton and Janet Emig. Britton (1970) found from his study of schools in Britain that writing was treated as no more than just a means for information transfer. Three functional types of writing were later identified, namely, transactional, poetic and expressive. It was the expressive type of writing that was considered instrumental to the concept of writing-to-learn in the sense that it encouraged "exploring and reflecting upon ideas" (Bazerman *et al.* 2005: 57). Following a similar line of thought, Emig (1977) published an article titled 'Writing as a Mode of Learning' advocating the fact that writing should be the agenda of the whole school instead of being confined to language teachers. This article paved the way for the later development of WAC programs which involved educating and training teachers about the role of writing in content-area learning.

Central to the belief that writing can assist the learning of disciplinary subjects is the impact generated by the popularisation of cognitive paradigm of writing research, which shifted the attention of the researchers and practitioners from the end-product to the processes that shape a piece of written work. There have been various attempts to capture the process of writing; the earliest model is probably Rodman's Pre-Write/Write/Re-Write one but such a stage-description linear model was criticised for its inability to capture the inner process of a writer (Flower/Hayes 1997). With the use of think-aloud protocols, Flower and Hayes (1980) developed an influential cognitive model of writing, highlighting the recursive nature of the operation of subprocesses subsumed into the three main processes: planning, translating and revising. The emphasis on the recursive, non-linear progression of writing processes underlies writing as a problem-solving activity. Bereiter and Scardamalia (1987) also consider writing as problem-solving and make the distinction between 'knowledge telling' and 'knowledge transforming'. Knowledge telling is often employed by novice writers who simply write down everything they know about the subjects. Knowledge transforming requires higher cognitive skills including the interaction between what to write (content) and how to write (rhetoric). These two concepts have implications on how we conceptualise the writing activity of tertiary writers who are inducted into moving from knowledge telling to knowledge transforming.

Langer and Applebee (1987) further ascertain the role of writing in thinking and learning, claiming that (1) writing activities promote learning better than other types of activities such as reading, (2) various writing activities focus students' attention on different forms of information, and (3) analytic writing promotes more thoughtful and complex inquiry into the subject matter in question.

To sum up, the core of writing-to-learn movement is premised on the belief that writing is a problem-solving activity controlled mainly by the cognitive faculty of the brain.

2.1.2. Learning-to-write and WID

Although considered primarily as a cognitive model, Flower and Hayes' conceptualisation appears to have also considered the broader context of writing by taking into account the different needs of readership (embedded in the writer's long-term memory), an aspect that is seen as a fundamental basis of later sociology of writing (e.g., Myers 1989, 1990). In the 1990s, along with the mainstream writing research paradigm switching from cognitive to social, writing-to-learn also entered a new WAC's phase, Writing-in-the-Disciplines (WID), focusing on writing as an act of socialising into a discipline and bridging writing and knowing (Carter 2007). Previous studies of learning to write seem to have focused on general academic text types such as the essay, the term paper, etc. which lack the core element of 'discipline'. In the first instance, WID may seem to downplay the role of learning in a discipline but this has been challenged by Carter, Ferzli, and Wiebe (2007: 280):

> Students do not learn to write the discourses of the disciplines simply to master those discourses; rather, they write to learn, in addition to the subject matter of the discipline, the ways of knowing and doing that define the discipline.

In brief, WID foregrounds learning as social. In their work analysing the function of writing for the secondary science laboratory work, Keys *et al.* (1999: 1080) suggested that "students linked their experiences […] to their understanding of the nature of science. They developed detailed and specific understanding about the nature of scientists' everyday work". In this respect, WID is best understood as "writing to learn by learning to write in the disciplines" (Carter/Ferzli/Wiebe 2007: 280). However, Russell (1991: 95) criticises the fact that scientific writing (e.g. laboratory report) was used "as a means of exclusion, a means of setting and enforcing disciplinary standards, rather than as a means of introducing students to the scientific community through meaningful participation in its activity". This comment is grounded in his observation of school based writing (see for example Russell 1991; Lerner 2007; Paretti 2006 for the case in engineering) for which he considered it often lacks the awareness of real-world demands. This is in line with Jolliffe's (1994) concern with the myth of transcendence; i.e., how transferrable the writing skills acquired at school are to the workplace? This study, nevertheless, attempts to investigate how novice writers learn to write 'professional' documents in the workplace and what they learn through writing in the placement context, even without systematic workplace writing training at the university.

The above discussion has summarised two important phases of the WAC movements. The theoretical underpinning of this study is built up by drawing on aspects from these two phases: the cognitive orientation from the WAC phase and the socio-rhetorical orientation from the WID initiative.

2.2. Views of knowledge and learning

After reviewing previous work on 'writing-to-learn' and 'learning-to-write' movements, this section takes a step back to consider various conceptions of learning that have cut across the history of the two movements and beyond. Table 1 summarises the different conceptions of learning and their relevance to the present study.

Proponent(s)	*Major concept/ theories developed*	*Description of major concept/ theory developed*	*Relevance to this study*
Jerome Bruner	Constructivism	Learning is a dynamic process where learners construct new ideas by reinterpreting prior knowledge so as to reconcile them with the new	Informants have to reconcile the different schemas of writing and requirements between school and workplace
John Dewey	Social constructivism Experiential learning	Learning is a social activity and it is important to gain knowledge from experience	Informants learn through various experience (e.g. documentation) in the placement context
Lev Vygotsky	Zone of proximal development	Scaffolding of knowledge depends on two conditions which are through self- construction and social interaction with 'capable peers'. Emphasis is laid on social context of learning.	Informants work and engage in social interaction with 'capable peers' during placement
Jean Lave and Etienne Wenger	Situated Learning Legitimate Peripheral Participation Communities of Practice	Learning is essentially a social practice which results from our active participation and engagement in the pursuit of various enterprises, and experiences it as meaningful, premised on the assumption that human beings are social beings	Informants participate in various practices (including discourse practices) within the context of placement, where they learn through observation, peripheral participation and various informal encounters

Table 1. Summary of literature on various approaches to learning.

The debate in regard to the theoretical basis of knowledge influences an individual's perception of learning. The different beliefs can broadly be classified into two main categories: subjectivism and objectivism, as to whether knowledge and truth are based on subjective judgments or objective facts. Proponents of objectivism hold that knowledge is hard, real and tangible (Cohen/Manion/Morrison 2001) which can be transferred, premised on the belief that social reality has an objective truth 'out there' to be discovered. Those who subscribe to subjectivism, on the other hand, consider that knowledge is personal and unique that "what is learnt by an individual is founded on his or her own construction" (Wiredu 2005: 39), suggesting that people's perceptions, experiences, interactions, perspectives are meaningful properties of social reality (Mason 2002). These fundamentally different philosophical assumptions of nature of knowledge bring with them theories of learning and instruction/educational practices. Constructivists challenge and reject the objective assumptions of learning (proposed in behaviourism and cognitivism) and homogeneity of learners, advocating instead "a more open-ended learning experience where the methods and results of learning are not easily measured and may not be the same for each learner" (Mergel 1998). Proponents of constructivism include Bruner (1986) whose theoretical framework encompasses social and cultural aspects of learning, suggesting that learning is a dynamic process in which learners construct new ideas by reinterpreting prior knowledge so as to reconcile them with the new. In other words, learners no longer take up a receptive role in the discourse of learning but actively engage in negotiation of meaning with the world (Wenger 1998; Henri/Pudelko 2003).

John Dewey, an influential writer of educational thought and practice in the 20th century, argues for the importance of interaction, reflection and experience (Kember/Wong/Yeung 2001; Smith/Jeffs 2005). Dewey's constructivism stresses the importance of social context and individual's own construction of knowledge (Wiredu 2005). His works, mainly based on philosophical pragmatism, have shed light on later educational methods such as experiential learning (Smith/Jeffs 2005) and reflective practice (e.g., Boud/Keogh/Walker 1985; Boyd/Fales 1983 and Section 2.6). Following Bruner and Dewey, Piaget's constructivism again lays emphasis on the role of the individual while, unlike his antecedents, he has bridged the gap between social and cognitive and has developed a highly influential model of child learning and development, weaving four primary cognitive structures (namely, sensorimotor, preoperations, concrete operations and formal operations) attesting that the cognitive structure of a child increases in sophistication with development, and cognitive development makes adaptation to the environment through the process of assimilation and accommodation. Social constructivist Vygotsky criticises Piaget's theoretical framework and his stress on the role of the individual, claiming that social interaction comes into play before the development of cognition. He states (1978: 57) that

> every function in the child's cultural development appears twice: first, on the social level, and later, on the individual level; first, between people (interpsychological) and then inside the child (intrapsychological). This applies equally to voluntary attention, to logical memory, and to the formation of concepts. All the higher functions originate as actual relationships between individuals.

Vygotsky argues for a socio-historical (or socio-cultural) approach to learning which primarily involves interaction among people, events happening around the world and the use of cultural tools (e.g. semiosis), altogether shaping a social and cultural context that facilitates learning, and ultimately leads to cognitive development within the zone of proximal development (often abbreviated as ZPD):

> The distance between the actual developmental level as determined by independent problem solving and the level of potential development as determined through problem solving under adult guidance or in collaboration with more capable peers. (Eysenck 2001: 374)

In brief, ZPD is the difference between a child's performance when tested on their own and tested in a social context provided by someone with the necessary knowledge. If we extend this notion a bit further, we can see that the scaffolding of knowledge depends on two conditions: through self-construction as well as social interaction with 'capable peers'. The notion of ZPD coincides with the epistemological site investigated in this current project where newcomers work closely with expert members. Undeniably, Vygotsky's idea of social development is complementary to the social learning theory developed by Bandura (1977) and the situated learning theory by Lave and Wenger (1991). The social learning theory emphasises the importance of imitation and modelling of behaviour, which fits well with placement learning as STWs needs to model the way expert members perform not only in terms of rendering professional services to clients but also written documentation.

2.2.1. Communities of practice

More recently, the concepts of situated learning and communities of practice proposed by Lave and Wenger have become influential in various fields; to name a few, applied linguistics (e.g., Sarangi/van Leeuwen 2002), education (e.g., Tsui/Edward/Lopez-Real 2006), and business and management (e.g., Wenger/McDermott/Synder 2002). Lave and Wenger (1991) emphasise that social interaction is a key component in learning, which is "an integral part of generative social practice in the lived-in world" (1991: 35). They (see also Wenger 1998) criticise traditional institutionalised teaching that takes knowledge out-of-context; instead they promote the idea of 'legitimate peripheral participation' (LPP), suggesting that novices move gradually from a peripheral position in a 'community of practice' towards fuller participation by engaging with expert members. They documented the observation of anecdotes of novice midwives, tailors, quartermasters, butchers and nondrinking alcoholics in order to exemplify the concept of "cognitive apprenticeship" (Lave/Wenger 1991: 62; Lau 2008) and illustrate the fact that 'instruction' very often takes place unintentionally.

Wenger (1998) further expands the concept of situated learning, premised on the fundamental assumption that humans are social beings – placing "learning in the context of our lived experience of participation in the world" (1998: 3). Learning is essentially a social practice which results from our active participation and engagement in the pursuit of various enterprises, and experiences it as meaningful. His social theory of learning encompasses four main components characterising social participation as a process of learning: learning as doing, as belonging, as becoming and as experience (Figure 1).

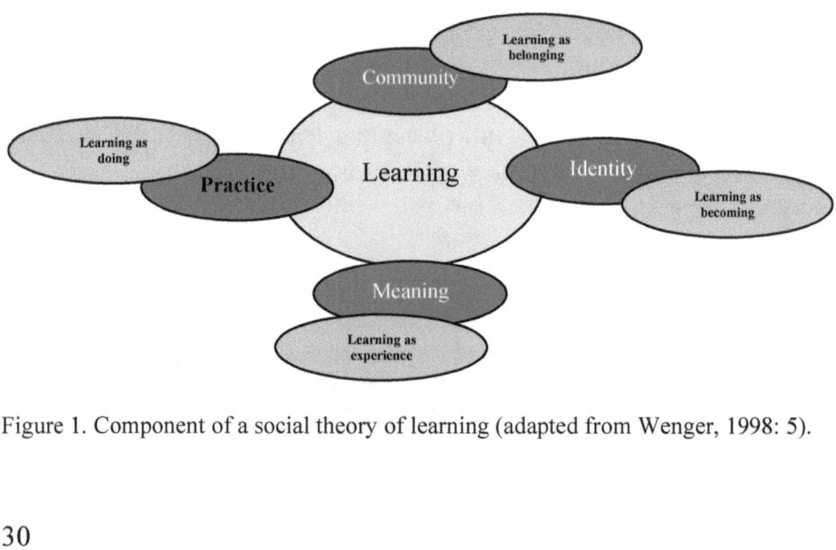

Figure 1. Component of a social theory of learning (adapted from Wenger, 1998: 5).

The concepts of 'community', 'practice', 'meaning' and 'identity' are mutually defined and inter-related. For instance, Candy, the informant of this study, is a novice student worker (*identity*) who had to socialise with the veteran social workers in the community youth centre (*community*) in order to learn to become a full participant by engaging in and making sense (*meaning*) of various professional practices, e.g. documentation (*practice*). Wenger (1998: 45) therefore defines CoP as follows:

> collective learning results in practices that reflect both the pursuit of our enterprises and the attendant social relations. These practices are thus the property of a kind of community created over time by the sustained pursuit of a shared enterprise.

2.2.1.1. Concept of practice

The term 'practice', which appears twice in the previous quote, needs to be clarified and discussed in a more elaborate manner because it constitutes the main theme of the study. Etymologically, *practice* originally means "to do, act, or perform habitually" and only after the mid-16th century did the term begin to connote "expert" (Harper 2001). According to the 100-million-word BYU-British National Corpus (1980s-1993) (Davies 2004), *practice* has a strong connotation with 'professions', reflected in its being preceded by vocation-oriented determiners such as 'professional', 'medical', 'clinical', 'classroom', 'legal' and 'management'. Researchers have also attempted to define *practice* in specific fields: for instance, Bartlett (2003) defines social work practice as "being recognised by a constellation of values, purpose, sanction, knowledge and method" whereas Eribes (1997) focuses on the inherently directive nature of the term claiming that "practice assumes a special role in our (architectural) profession". While most definitions mainly relate *practice* to the act of doing in terms of giving it structure and meaning, Orlikowski (2002: 256) highlights it with reference to the individual and institutional levels:

> [...] defined as recurrent, materially bounded, and situated social action engaged in by members of a community [...] Practices are engaged in by individuals as part of the ongoing structuring processes through which institutions and organizations are produced and reproduced. This is thus both individual

> (because performed by actors in their everyday action) and institutional (because they shape and are shaped by organizational norms and structures).

This view is consistent with Wenger's position in the sense that *practice* is considered as social practice. Although 'social', the concept does not exclude the cognitive and individual aspect but is merely a shift from mental entities towards an external reality such as artefacts, skills, shared knowledge and understanding, habitual actions, etc (Jones 2008). Based on the discussion above, the use of *practice* in this book therefore has the following qualities:

- Practice is concerned with both the process and outcome
- Practice ties in with professionalism, giving it a legitimate status
- Practice relates to both individual and community
- Practice is about engagement and experience to make meaning

These four ways of thinking about *practice* shape the conceptualisation of the informants' learning experience and hence the analytical units adopted. For example, the fact that practice is concerned with both the process and outcome directs my attention to seeing writing-to-learn from both the process (e.g., revision process) and product (e.g., finished texts) point of view.

2.2.1.2. Practices as the source of coherence

A CoP defines itself along three dimensions (Figure 2), all of which are related to practice as the source of coherence. The first component is mutual engagement. Practice does not start in a historical vacuum or geographical proximity but resides around people who engage in some common actions or ideas. This is of paramount importance as it means that CoPs can be formed by members of different social categories. Homogeneity is neither a result of nor something we seek for in a CoP. Expert-novice mutual interactions and engagements form an important basis of the placement structure. The foregrounding of the existence of such an apprenticeship relationship is a major condition which distinguishes a *community of practice* from a *discourse community* (Pogner 2005).

Joint enterprise is the second component. Wenger claims that an enterprise is always negotiated by participants through which they move beyond the stated goals and reach the "communal regime of mutual accountability" (1998: 81). Placement, although the immediate context within which it is located is the professional workplace, cannot attain an ontological status without being co-constructed and granted legitimacy by the academic departments of the professional studies at a university. The overarching goal of such an enterprise is to train competent and qualified professionals to continue the practice; to achieve this, novices have to take courses at the university, undertake placements in various institutions or various departments within an institution and struggle through the process of learning to write, speak and act like their professional counterparts. As for the professional bodies, their official status is maintained partly through sharing the social responsibilities to provide on-the-job learning opportunities by taking on interns and having them trained by the experts in the organisation to the acceptable standard in accordance with the professional ethics. In addition, on the basis of what informants told me, it seems that the immediate personal goal of the STWs is to get the placement over with by taking up an active role in the enterprise and engaging in organisation's tasks as 'semi-professionals'.

Last but not least, shared repertoire (including routines, words, tools, gestures and concepts), which only belongs to the participants of a respective CoP, is developed as a resource to reflect the history of mutual engagement. These communicative tools or shared repertoires need to be appropriated by newcomers in order for them to function effectively within this community.

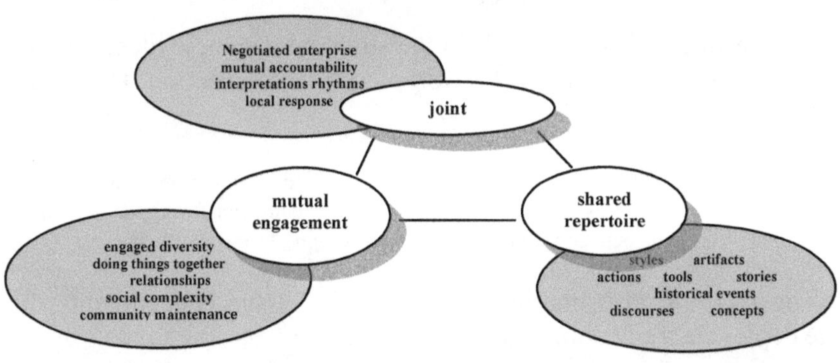

Figure 2. Dimension of practice as property of a community (adapted from Wenger 1998: 73).

2.2.1.3. Participation and reification

The fundamental elements sustaining an informal CoP are participation and reification with a duality nature. Participation, according to Wenger, refers to "social experience of living in the world in terms of membership in social communities and active involvement in social enterprise" (1998: 55). He reiterates the temporal and on-going nature of the concept which describes both the active engagement in the enterprises and the forging of the identities. Extended participation in CoP results in the creation of abstractions which members congeal into things – reification – an ontological perspective reflecting the social construction of reality. Wenger (1998: 58) states that "we project our meanings into the world and then we perceive them as existing in the world, as having a reality of their own". The significance of reification lies in the fact that it shapes our experience and acts as a reflection of practices.

Both participation and reification are crucial to the understanding of STWs' learning in placement. STWs need to *participate* in various textually-mediated (Smith 1999) activities in the workplace, for example, treating a client with a musculoskeletal problem, which is eventually *reified* as a consultation report or other forms of documentation. Their work may need to be supervised by an expert member because of their lower status and level of competence than that of their professional counterparts.

2.2.1.4. CoP, identities and roles

It is noteworthy that the STWs in the study take on new identities and roles when participating in the workplace communication. Dias *et al.* (1999: 21) point out

> the potentialities of genres for creating spaces for forming and realizing new versions of self as one discovers new motives and transforms the self in response to the new communicative needs and opportunities.

Wenger (1998) also highlights the 'identity' issue concomitant with the deployment of community resources:

> It [the repertoire] includes the discourse by which members create meaningful statements about the world, as well as the styles by which they express their forms of membership and their identities as members (1998: 83).

The above quote has theoretical bases on both the social identity theory (Tajfel/Turner 1986) and the self-categorisation theory which underlie the expression of a personal self with regard to certain social categories as well as personal attributes or competence (Ashforth 2001). Bjorklund (2002), for example, found that those occupational therapy trainees who almost finished the fieldwork placed their focus on their role as the practitioners in practice while those who just began the clinical placement emphasised their own abilities. In the case of the informants of this study, who were all at the early stage of their placement, they had to recognise how their student-professional hybrid identities legitimise and at the same time restrict their professional practice and hence discourse practice in the placement (see Chapter 7).

The above discussions provide an important ground for the inclusion of identity aspects in this study since identity exists *within* discourse and comes into play during discourse practices. This view, however, is not able to fully account for the reality in placement as identity is not a fixed entity (see Chapter 4). Rather, the representation of identity in this book will be extended to incorporate a more interactionist and functional perspective, and the adoption of the term 'role', in my view, can better capture the essence.

2.2.1.5. Enculturation

Another crucial dimension embedded in this study is enculturation. Enculturation has long been the research interest in anthropology and social psychology. These studies focus mainly on identity formation of immigrants (e.g., He 1998; Weinreich 2009) and child development (e.g., Tseng 2001). Of the various definitions of the term, Hesselgrave's (2008) is among the most relevant to this study. He defines enculturation as "the process by which individuals acquire the knowledge, skills, attitudes, and values that enable them to become functioning members of their societies". The repertoires mentioned are also crucial to STWs' enculturation into professional CoP. In addition, they need to assimilate and embrace the work "practices, language, viewpoints and behaviors" (Gray 2004: 23).

2.3. Theoretical framework and research niche

CoP is a workable theoretical framework for this study in two ways. First, CoP deconstructs the social context of enculturation in terms of joint enterprise, mutual engagement and shared repertoire. Second, through participating in various tasks in a professional workplace, novices realise, develop and consolidate their identities along the way. These social aspects of enculturation have been investigated in many previous studies; yet the linguistic dimension to it seems to have been left largely unexplored. Tusting (2005) attempts to address the role of language in a CoP but her use of Fairclough's critical discourse analysis framework in reinterpreting Wenger's vignette does no more than just making apparent the power issue underlying the social structure, which was not treated in depth by Wenger (Fox 2000). Analysis of texts produced in the organisation is still lacking. In this study, the linguistic aspect is intertwined with the social aspect, i.e., not treating them as separate aspects *per se,* because of the belief that language constructs reality. Texts produced in placement is analysed with reference to its social context.

2.4. Communities of practice and writing

The discussion so far has focused the attention on 'learning' in general. This has paved the way for setting out the connection among ways of knowing, doing and writing in the disciplines. This section reviews research studies on workplace discourse practices that have informed the current study.

2.4.1. Discourse and discourse practices

This piece of research investigates workplace discourse practices and so the phrase 'discourse practice' needs to be defined within the context of use in the study. As a point of departure, the modifier 'discourse' needs to be scrutinised first, as it has been defined in many different ways. The distinction between a big 'D' Discourse and small 'd' discourse proposed by Gee (2001) is the most useful for my purpose. In the first instance, the broadest definition of discourse points to the practices of talking and writing (e.g., Woodilla 1998), which is language-in-use, a small 'd' in Gee's definition. Although *discourse* covers both written and oral communication, the former will be the focus of this study. For the sake of convenience, unless otherwise specified, all the relevant discourse studies cited and analyses undertaken are concerned with writing, even though the word 'written' is not used before discourse practice.

As Gee (2001) highlights, language use is not simply about getting the words right. *Discourse* embodies shared knowledge and is a representation of world view, which is the Big 'D'. This ties in with the regulatory property of discourse in the sense that it restricts the way the language is used and the way to construct knowledge. For instance, physiotherapy discourse presupposes certain ways of making meaning, such as the prevalent use of quantitative data and vocabulary items specific to physiotherapy consultations.

Similar to practice, another essential property about D/discourse is that it cannot be studied directly. It has to be examined through systematic analysis of texts (Phillips/Lawrence/Hardy 2004; Fairclough 1992). For instance, to gain an understanding of social work discourse, one will need to collect a body of relevant texts social workers have to accomplish in their daily work, such as proposals, evaluation reports, administrative documents, etc. When analysing these texts, it is important to consider them in relation to other relevant texts. The analysis of a social work proposal may involve the analysis of social welfare policy documents to gain insight into the socio-political contexts that shape the written texts.

Based on the above discussion of discourse and that of *practice* in section 2.2.1.1, 'discourse practice' in this study, to put it simply, refers to those textually-mediated activities which are recognised by the institution and bear a rhetorical function. This can be illustrated by the example of the completion of consultation reports by physiotherapy student workers. Such a discourse practice is recognised by the hospital as a professional activity and by the university as a pedagogical activity. Accordingly, the rhetorical functions of this activity are to propose treatment options to clients as well as demonstrate knowledge to expert members.

2.4.2. Workplace discourse studies

There has been abundant research on workplace's discourse practices covering professions such as social work (e.g., Hall/Slembrouck/Sarangi 2006), law (e.g., Bhatia 2005; 2008a), business (e.g., Louhiala-Salminen 2002), architecture (e.g., Dias *et al.* 1999), pharmacy (e.g., Askehave 2002) and health care (e.g., Cook-Grumperz/Messerman 1999). The discourse analytic approaches these studies adopt are notably conversation analysis, socio-pragmatic analysis, genre analysis and lexico-grammatical (functional) analysis. The first two types of analyses typically work around spoken data featuring linguistic strategies such as turn-taking, adjacency pair and sequencing. For example, in doctor-patient consultations, turn-taking analysis may go from simply 'How are you' and the subsequent replies at the very beginning stage, "to history taking questions and answers, to diagnostic announcements and their receipts, to treatment proposal" (Maynard/Heritage 2005: 429).

The latter two analytical approaches work with both spoken and written data. Genre analysis aims to find out a staged pattern by identifying the obligatory and optional moves in a text and the discourse function associated with each 'move'. Lexico-grammatical analyses place emphasis on smaller grammatical units such as word choices and how these units are built up to shape the discourse meaning. Combining these two analytical approaches, Forey and Lockwood (2007), for instance, identify the generic structure of inbound call centre transactions and the communication problems associated with choices of interpersonal, intercultural and discourse nature.

Studies related specifically to the professional contexts in Hong Kong are also starting to grow. Representative examples include work done in land surveying (e.g., Cheng/Mok 2008), tax accounting (e.g., Flowerdew/Wan 2006), banking (e.g., Chew 2005), textile and clothing (e.g., Li/Mead 2000) and building services engineering (e.g., Evans 1999). This growing interest in professional communication can also be reflected in the growing number of English in the workplace/English for Occupational Purposes courses available at the universities in Hong Kong, which have always been dominated by EAP-type courses. One common concern that comes out of these studies appears to be the local workers' insufficiency in 'discursive competence', which involves the ability to produce as well as understand discourse in a concrete situation, for example, in a professional workplace (Capucho/Oliveira 2005; Bhatia 2005). Given the sociolinguistic dichotomisation of Hong Kong that English is invariably used in written documentation for "important business meant for external destinations" (So 1998: 164) whereas Cantonese Chinese is used mainly in verbal communication, the emergence of discursive 'incompetence' is understandable. For example, Chew (2005) found that new local banking entrants had difficulties in using English in drafting memos. A similar sentiment was expressed in Flowerdew and Wan's study (2006). It was found that when drafting tax computation letters, "delving outside of the standard format could prove to be a challenging task" (2006: 148) for tax accountants.

In addition to focusing on the texts *per se*, Dias *et al.* (1999) present a good case to highlight the fact that workplace writing is more than just an asocial, formulaic organisation of texts but involves a complex intertwining of social relationships, tools, historical, cultural, temporal and physical dimensions. Adopting mainly Lave and Wenger's theoretical framework, they attempt to show that literacy skills of student apprentices are scaffolded through engaging in various practices, gradually moving from observation to legitimate peripheral participation. This process engenders the development of "socially distributed cognition" (1999: 31), a schema which is essential to accomplishing a group activity. This underscores the social component embedded in the discourse production.

2.4.3. Discourse practices, identities and roles in workplace

Much of the recent research on identity and workplace discourse has shifted from a deterministic, fixed, and stabilised position to a more open-ended, negotiated, and constantly emerging one. With the existence of what Gee, Hull and Lankshear (1996) term as "the new work order", professional boundaries become blurry; hierarchical structures are destabilised (Sarangi/Roberts 1999); workers can no longer be committed to a single role but have to take on various "repertoires of identities" (Kroskrity 1993 as cited in Garzone 2010: 17). Such changes have engendered discourse studies on various sites: Iedema and Scheeres (2003) found from their study of a game machine factory (see also Scheeres 2003) and a teaching hospital that the work was heavily textualised and workers manifested language to enact and manage self in the socio-political arena. Using focus group interviews, Axford (2005) realised how 19 Australian novices in three distinct fields (teaching, nursing and engineering) made sense of the way of doing things during their placements. Her study revealed that novices nowadays had to come to grips with a number of complexities and at times contradictions in the modern work environment, amalgam of established and new practices, an emphasis on performance and accountability over practice, preference for team work over solitary efforts, to name a few. The change in work practice thus also comes with re-defining professionalism and constructing new forms of identities and roles.

The new work order is also faced with challenges. For instance, Bathmaker and Avis (2005) investigated how trainee teachers in the UK learnt to build up their professional identities. Surprisingly, the subjects found themselves marginalised rather than being drawn to fuller participation, which was contrary to what was expected in a CoP.

While most of the discourse studies on the impact of a new work order focus on institutional talks, limited research seems to have been undertaken on aligning professional practice, identities and roles with *written* discourse practices. Such kind of work has nevertheless started to receive attention recently with Bhatia's advocacy of a *critical genre analysis* (Bhatia 2008b), i.e. a multi-dimensional approach to textual analysis integrating the socio-cognitive factors that essentially play a role in the "construction, interpretation, use and exploitation to achieve non-linguistic ends in real life professional contexts" (Bhatia 2005: 112). In his study of the production of corporate annual reports, Bhatia went beyond the textual level in order to "understand the nature, function and execution of this corporate practice embedded in business culture" (2005: 172) through the understanding of the private intention of an individual writer, often enacted by the contextual conditions. The issues of power, multiple role-shifting, audience, etc. all contribute to the integrity of the genre.

Parks (2001) also found that status of members within a CoP shapes the genre, tying in with their level of competence associated with their roles. In the school she observed, nurses were taught not to write a medical diagnosis (or simply medical terms); instead they had to use plain English to describe the patients' signs and symptoms, corresponding to what they can act on. For example, they should write 'burning when voiding' (nursing diagnosis) instead of 'urinary tract infection'. If the patient has obvious symptoms of diabetes, nurses are not allowed to write 'diabetes' but an awkward, less common phrase like 'poor circulation'. The current study also delves into how the status of these STWs, situating between learners and practitioners, affects the linguistic choices they have.

2.4.4. Expert-novice exchanges in workplace

In the workplace, expert-novice exchanges are important to ensure continuity of good practice (Wenger 1998). One important aspect of such mutual engagement in the workplace is feedback. Woodward-Kron (2004), in her research on undergraduates' enculturation into the academic discourse community, suggests that "providing marker feedback (on writing) is an opportunity for the experienced members of the discourse community to frame the discipline's discursive practices for novice participants" (2004: 142). In other words, novices learn to socialise into the community through negotiating meaning with experienced workers via feedback. This apprenticeship or dyadic approach to learning-to-write is prevalent in workplace. Pogner (2003) analysed the text production in an engineering community involving feedback-revision cycles between professional engineers (of different roles). He claims that text production is a way of showing "writers' expertise and professionalism in the technical sphere" and "their legitimate membership in the discourse community of engineers" (2003: 857). In his research, he discovered that writing is a form of action itself; through revising texts, professional engineers negotiate and realise their professional standard and roles while at the same time maintaining solidarity with discourse members. While his work investigates the interactions between professionals of similar status, I am interested to know the role feedback plays in negotiation of meaning between novices and experienced workers in the process of enculturation, taking into account a more obvious power difference.

The underlying assumption of many feedback studies (e.g., Hyland/Anan 2006; Lee 2003; Ferris/Roberts 2001) is that feedback can benefit writers; yet the fundamental question – 'how' writers, the ultimate users, make the most of the feedback in the revision process – has not been fully addressed. Such a research niche can best be filled by undertaking diachronic studies in which writers' engagements and interactions with assessors' feedback are factored into the equation. Adopting a diachronic perspective implies that analyses shift from a single-draft context to a multiple-draft one. Research has shown that teacher feedback is more effective and conducive to students' learning if they are placed in a pedagogical setting where multiple drafting is required. Ferris (1995: 36) further explains:

> Because students must rethink and revise previously written essay drafts, they are more likely to pay more attention to their teachers' advice on how to do so than in a situation in which they are merely receiving a graded paper with comments and corrections to apply to a completely new essay assignment.

Literature on the diachronic study of the use of feedback in writing, however, is scarce. Myers' study (1990) on biologists' writings is one of the most oft-cited pieces of research in this area. His study challenges the traditional cognitive paradigm of writing research, which was dominant in the 1980s, by showing that the two scientists' personae as well as their writing and revision processes are constantly being shaped by the ideologies of the knowledge-community to which they belong:

> I argue that the process of writing a scientific article is social from the beginning, because it involves compromises between opposing rhetorical demands and opposing goals [...]. On the one hand the researcher tries to show that he or she deserves credit for something new, while on the other editors and reviewers try to relate the claim to the body of knowledge produced by the community (1990: 67).

Studying revision processes can thus usefully reveal the fact that text production depends on many external factors; to put it in another way, what counts as 'knowledge' is socially validated via discursive practices within a respective community. Following a similar fashion, Berkenkotter and Huckin (1995) trace the journey of publication of two scientists, in which they documented in detail how the two writers have to position their work within a large body of existing knowledge by means of intertextuality and wrestle with the rhetorical demands from the reviewers to create a "phony story" (1995: 55). Going through the revision processes not only underlies a text-mediated social action, but more importantly, a move from epistemologically subjective claims to epistemologically objective ones (Searle 2003). In Chapter 6, in order to understand the roles of teacher feedback in placement learning, a close reading of all the written comments on the drafts of an informant was conducted. Complemented with in-depth interviews, this case study can better reveal the STW's learning pathway by understanding how he made sense of the comments and reacted to them.

2.4.5. Reflective writing and reflective practice in workplace

Different institutions feature different types of workplace writing but one genre is typical of the professional training stage: reflective writing (Campell-Evans/Maloney 1998). Previous research has recognised the instrumental values of reflective writing in professional development (Luk 2008; White 2008); and yet the inherently dynamic nature of its construction and the wide range of lexical choices at writers' disposal have made it impossible to apply the restricted definition of genre to this kind of writing. Having said that, however, reflective writing also bears what I call 'genre quality' and its construction needs to be best understood with inter-contextual references. For instance, my informants' reflective writings always involve the recount of experience mediating between the past and present, the academia and professional organisation, as well as theory and practice. Based on the above, it can be seen that while analysing the prescriptive, schematic structure of texts has proven to be useful for investigating textual products, genre analysts now realise and discourage the over-simplification of the text construction, which nevertheless neglects writer's 'private intentions', as suggested in section 2.4.3 of this chapter.

The term "reflective practice", being popularised by Schön (1983), points to the ability of the practitioner to go beyond the technical knowledge required to complete a task and bring novelty and insight into the job in terms of skills such as framing and reframing problems and solutions. The ability to reflect on action was seen as a defining characteristic, among others, of professional practice. The value of reflective practice in professional development in various fields has well been documented, such as education (e.g., Osterman/Kottkamp 1993) and those relevant to this study, for instance, nursing (e.g., Connor 2008), physiotherapy (e.g., Kember *et al.* 2001) and social work (e.g., Swindell/Watson 2006).

Schön's idea of reflective practice is in fact what he termed 'reflection-in-action', which is the spilt-second decision-making process. Nevertheless, for the purpose of this study, the definition of reflective practice will be 'reflection-on-action', which is by and large a post-mortem form of reflection. A wide range of discursive forms is available for reflective practice, for example, reflective essays, journals, post-mortem meeting notes, verbal articulation, or even just a piece of paper documenting the learning processes. For the placement contexts I analysed, reflective essays, self-evaluation reports and self-reflection forms are the textual artefacts of reflection. It is common to see reflective writings being integrated into a structured curriculum, yet they do not always contribute to the assessment of a course. This implies that reflection is embedded in, integral to and an underlying construct of the design of a course rather than being treated as a separate or add-on component. More specifically, it will be shown later that the tasks STWs accomplish are inherently reflective in nature.

2.5. Genre studies

Our understanding of society has become more complicated than before, and therefore it is necessary to expand our understanding of how genre works for it "develops within, embodies, and establishes society's values, relationships, and functions" (Devitt 2004: 33). In professional contexts, genres are the conduit through which members communicate with their peers. Berkenkotter & Huckin (1995: 1) highlight the role of genres in achieving professional success:

> Genres are intimately linked to a discipline's methodology, and they package information in ways that conform to a discipline's norms, values and ideology. Understanding the genres of written communication in one's field is, therefore, essential to professional success.

In line with this belief, a genre-based perspective is taken to investigate the interactions among three practices in this study, namely, pedagogical practice, professional practice and discourse practice within the context of placement. The interaction between professional practice and discursive practice has been discussed by Bhatia (2005, 2008a) with reference to the concept of genre integrity, as explained in an earlier section in this chapter. Pedagogical practice, not discussed by Bhatia, is nevertheless particularly relevant to this project as genre acquisition of newcomers along the boundary of the professional community, to a large extent, involve external inputs from expert members and reflection on the learning experiences.

There have been mainly three traditions of genre theories and analytical approaches, namely, the ESP, the North America New Rhetoric and the Australian Systemic Functional Linguistics (SFL) (Hyon 1996). The ESP approach highlights the connection between the formal characteristics of texts (such as organisational patterns, choices of verbs) and the communicative purposes. Such approach has been deployed to analyse a wide range of genres, such as applied linguistics research articles (Yang/Allison 2003), editorial letters (Flowerdew/Dudley-Evans 2002), and weblogs (Herring *et al.* 2004). The approach also gives rise to a range of variationist/specificity studies involving a comparison of certain linguistic features of the same genres across several disciplines (see for example Hyland/Hamp-Lyons 2002; Huckin 2003; Hyland 2009).

The North American notion of genre is consistent with the Australian Hallidayan view in the sense that they both link specific features of texts with the social practice (Russell 1997b). Going beyond merely a broad generalisation of common textual features, the North American approach focuses genre more on "local and dynamic terms" (Russell 1997b: 226). Instead of looking at the commonalities of one genre (e.g. proposal) across various institutions, the attention is paid to the local, specific "activity system" (Dias/Paré 2000: 3; Dias 2000) and how people interact in that system to give rise to the regularities in the ways people accomplish the writing in that particular activity system (Russell 1997a, 1997b). This important theoretical (re-)conceptualisation is to consider genre as a social action (Miller 1984) in response to exigence, a term introduced by Bitzer (1968 qt in Dias *et al.* 1999) and later reinterpreted by Miller (1994) as a typified rhetorical response to a situation that is socially defined.

Proponents of SFL such as Jim Martin define genres as staged, goal-oriented social processes (Martin/Christie/Rothery 1987). Genres are staged because they are sequenced to allow for the building up of meanings to eventually reach the writer's desired goal. They are social processes because participants of a culture have to interact in order to achieve them. In addition to linguistic features, SFL also pays attention to how other semiotic modes contribute to meaning potentials, e.g. diagrams. The next section will detail the SFL system and how it is used in my study.

2.6. Systemic-functional perspectives

The review of literature in the previous sections has laid the theoretical foundation and provided an essential context to the development of the current work. A research niche identified from the review is the lack of systematic treatment of the linguistic aspect of enculturation. The following sections will thus present how language is conceptualised and analysed with respect to the present study, emphasising the function of language in shaping meaning and effecting actions.

The major linguistic tool adopted in this research is Systemic Functional Linguistics (SFL). The adoption of the SFL perspective highlights the inextricable connection among language, context and function (Butt *et al.* 2000; Thompson 2004). SFL underlies the fact that language is modelled as a social semiotic, which is therefore a meaning-making resource (Halliday/Matthiessen 2004). Eggins (1994) suggests that language as a semiotic system involves making meaning by choices and during that process, choices from a linguistic system are encoded or interpreted against the background of what could have been meant in that particular context.

In the SFL model, there are two levels of language, extralinguistic and linguistic (Figure 3). The extralinguistic level of language can further be divided into CONTEXT OF CULTURE[1] and CONTEXT OF SITUATION. CONTEXT OF CULTURE, often labeled as 'genre' in traditional terms, places language use in a broader context which is always backgrounded (e.g. workplace) while CONTEXT OF SITUATION, often termed as 'register', points to a more immediate context (e.g. writing a consultation report). CONTEXT OF SITUATION further specifies three parameters as FIELD, TENOR and MODE OF DISCOURSE. These three aspects are defined simply the following way (Butt *et al.* 2000: 13):

> Field: what is to be talked or written about; the long and short term goals of the text;
> Tenor: the relationship between the speaker and hearer;
> Mode: the kind of text that is being made.

These three parameters affect one's language choices which in turn reflect the three main functions of language: ideational, interpersonal and textual. To describe them in a more technical way, meaning is metafunctionally theorised as "simultaneously construing ideational 'reality', an interpersonal 'reality' and a textual 'reality'" (Hood 2004:

1 Small caps are often used in SFL to differentiate its own use of terms from other types of grammar.

11). This view of conceptualisation underlies the fact that ideational and interpersonal meanings are what language is instead of what language does.

The linguistic levels of language delineate a tri-strata system, embedding a two-level content plane of discourse semantic (systems of meanings) and lexico-grammar (systems of wordings/systems of signing), as well as the expression plane of expression (including systems of sound, writing and gesture). The different levels of language are presented in Figure 3.

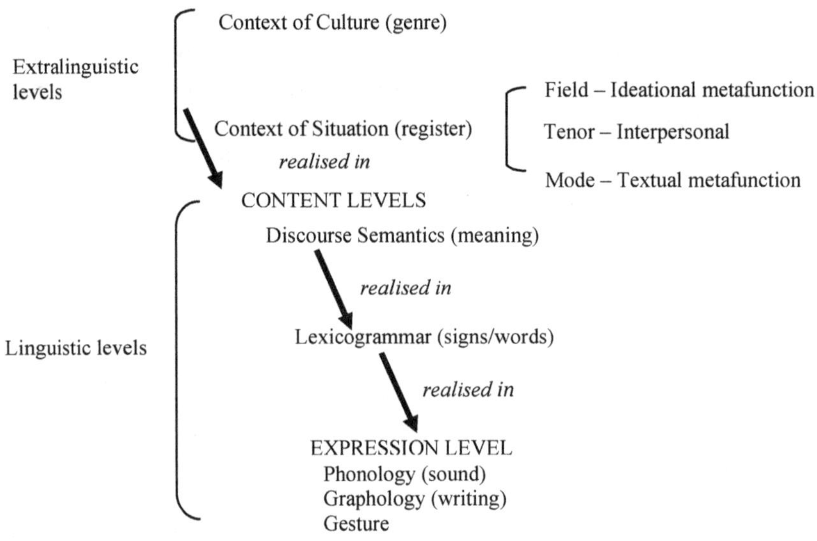

Figure 3. Levels of language (adapted from Butt *et al.* 2000: 15).

Figure 3 illustrates a very important point: each level of language is realised in choices available at the level under it. For example, discourse semantics is realised in the choices of lexico-grammar which is in turn expressed through the various resources available at the expression level. Discourse semantics is more abstract than lexicogrammar in terms of meaning making and allows a wider range of resources to encode the meaning. Hoods (2004: 12) cited Martin (1992: 19) to explain this:

> [S]etting up a level of discourse semantics stratified with respect to lexico-grammar on the content plane [...] permit[s] generalisations to be made across structural and non-structural textual relations. [...] [S]tratification [...] gives rise to a model in which the discourse semantics both generalises across grammatical resources and accounts for relations between as well as within clause complexes. The discourse semantics is therefore more abstract than, and deals with larger units than, lexicogrammar.

The aim of presenting an overview of the SFL model is to highlight SFL's concern over the function of language and the emphasis on choices. In placement, language plays a key role in constructing a case, often in the form of an assessment, whereby follow-up actions need to be taken. Different choices of lexico-grammar can exert very different effects on the readers (e.g., the supervisor, the clients). During the professional training period, novices need to learn the appropriate discipline-specific language to communicate with other members in the CoP. Mastery of such language is not confined to the use of disciplinary vocabulary items; being attentive to discourse semantics is equally important. The following two sections will take a closer look at the grammatical resources in construing the experiential and interpersonal meanings to illustrate how discourse-semantic meaning is being realised by lexico-grammatical choices.

2.6.1. Ideational/experiential meaning

From the ideational perspective, language consists of a variety of resources for making reference to entities in the world and how those entities act on and relate to one another (Thompson 2004). In this respect, the first metafunction expressed concerns primarily the propositional content of a message, representing, at the simplest level, what is going on (verbs), who/what things are involved (nouns) and under what circumstances (adverbials). Take the following sentence extracted from Candy's reflective report as an example:

> The student worker assisted the social worker to accompany the students of XX to visit YY.

The above sentence is a typical English sentence with distinguishable components: doers of the action (the student worker, the students of XX), the 'done-to' (the social worker, YY) and the actions involved (assisted, to accompany, to visit). Using the SFL categories, the above sentence can be represented simply in the following way:

The student worker	assisted	the social worker	to accompany the students of XX to visit YY
Participant	*Process*	*Participant*	*Circumstance (purpose)*

If this sentence is taken out of the context (CONTEXT OF SITUATION), it does not seem to be intriguing enough and warrants a further analysis in any sense. This sentence, nonetheless, is extracted from a self-reflection report which is a type of personal narrative. The fact that the subject position is realised by 'the student worker' instead of the first person pronoun (I) is contrary to what is presumably expected to appear in this kind of reflective genre. This, therefore, provides a good reason to go through a more systematic analysis with reference to parameters external to that of textual levels, e.g. CONTEXT OF CULTURE, writer's perception of the genre, etc.

From the ideational perspective, the action, or process in SFL terms, is central to the meaning constructed in the clause. The process is often realised by the verbal group in the clause. In the example cited above, the process *assisted* implies an attenuated role assumed by the STW. However, what deserves our attention is not just the grammatical resources of the verbal group *per se*, but also the way it links the participants in the subject and object positions, i.e. *the student worker* and *the social worker* in the example. *Transitivity*, which concerns chiefly the "configuration of participants associated with different processes" (Lock 2005: 73), is brought into play in the textual analysis, precisely because a different choice of process (e.g., *experience*) and participants (e.g., *client*) provide important traces of how the whole discourse is being shaped and constructed in terms of identities and roles (to be explained in Chapter 7).

2.6.2. Interpersonal meaning

The second metafunction which is of concern in this study is the interpersonal. To consider language from an interpersonal perspective recognises the interactional nature of discourse. There are many kinds of exchanges in the human world such as offers, rejections, confirmations, description and so on. Four basic speech roles are identified, namely giving information (statement), demanding information (question), giving goods-and-services (offer) and demanding goods-and-services (order). Except for offers which mainly give rise to non-linguistic ends as a result of a pragmatic interpretation, the other three roles are associated with a particular grammatical structure: statement by declarative clauses, question by interrogative clauses and order by imperative clauses. Similar to the role of process in construing the experiential meaning, mood choices are crucial to the realisation of the interpersonal metafunction. Mood choices are realised by the Subject-Finite relationship. For example, the sentence 'They will continue to adopt a passive and non-productive role'.

They	will	adopt	a passive and non-productive role.
Subject	*Finite Modal*	*Predicator*	*Complement*
Mood		Residue	

This sentence construes a declarative mood realised typically by the subject (*They*) followed by the finite modal (*will*) with a positive polarity. In interrogative statements, the position of the subject and finite will be swapped, i.e., *Will they adopt a passive and non-productive role?* As for imperative clauses, either or both of the two elements may be omitted, i.e., *Adopt a passive and non-productive role.*

Among the different exchanges, evaluation/assessment is the most archetypical linguistic context of the professional world. Evaluation/assessment aligns the roles of the professional and the client through linguistic means, for example, a consultation report. In SFL, evaluative meaning is analysed by the APPRAISAL system and this has been the main analytical device used to analyse the social work texts, mainly because of its more complete discourse structure (as opposed to medical documentation which is mainly in a point form).

The first and foremost question to be asked in this section is 'why is EVALUATION chosen as an analytical device?' The most straightforward answer to this question is that evaluative meaning is embedded in the texts I am studying, both explicitly and implicitly. Take the social work field as an example, the main responsibility of a social worker is to undertake various assessments. As Hall, Slembrouck and Sarangi (2006: 15) point out:

> [T]he everyday processes of social work inevitably involve setting in motion processes which aim to produce assessments of what type of case this is or what is going on here. Furthermore, such activities will involve paying attention to concerns about how such assessments are presented and justified.

A social worker has to *assess* the needs of a client, *assess* the expected outcome of the proposed counselling sessions and *assess* the techniques being used. When it comes to assessments, *evaluation* is always part of the package at any time. Such a view in fact implies that EVALUATION constitutes part of the social practice (Linde 1997). This, however, only partly accounts for the adoption of EVALUATION in this study. To gain a full picture regarding its usefulness in analysing the professional discourse in question, we need to turn to EVALUATION as lexis, which is still a relatively unexplored research area. Taking on such a perspective means evaluation of entities via lexical choices (Hood 2004, 2006). Most of the previous studies on EVALUATION as lexis centre on what functional linguists called FOCUS under the system of GRADUATION, or *hedging* in traditional terms, signaling the commitment of epistemic stance (Kärkkäinen 2003) of the writers (e.g., Salager-Meyer 2000). While these studies attempt chiefly to understand the 'toning down' of claims in a text, the system of graduation offers a much wider lens for us to understand also the 'toning up' and 'objectifying' claims via categories such as INTENSIFICATION and QUANTIFICATION. In addition to GRADUATION, this study will also place a strong emphasis on strategic lexical choices realised in the combination of AFFECT, JUDGMENT and APPRECIATION for they have significant roles to play in culminating rhetorical power in such a persuasive text.

2.6.2.1. EVALUATION framework

There are three sub-systems under EVALUATION: ATTITUDE, ENGAGEMENT and GRADUATION. ATTITUDE refers to values by which the writers pass judgment, make assessment and associated emotional responses. It is graded in terms of positive or negative evaluation and it shows the stance the writers are explicitly adopting. Attitudinal terms may express AFFECT to describe feeling and emotions (e.g., love, fear, like), or JUDGMENT to assess the human behaviour (e.g., insightful), or APPRECIATION to evaluate the aesthetic qualities of entities (e.g., important, profound). These attitudinal categories are represented in the following diagram (see Figure 4):

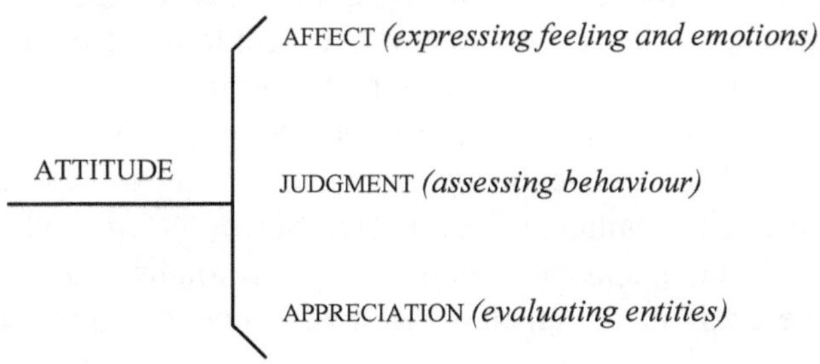

Figure 4. ATTITUDINAL system.

In Chapter 6, the ATTITUDINAL system will be further explained with reference to the evaluative elements in a proposal.

GRADUATION points to the grading of meanings (see Figure 5). Meanings are scaled within the appraisal system to indicate writer's attitude towards what is written. FORCE is used to quantify and qualify the attitudinal meanings expressed (e.g., *much* emphasis, *very* important). Apart from enhancing the attitudinal meanings, experiential meanings can also be graded in terms of amount, temporal dimension and frequency (e.g., the study involves a *small sample* of written texts; *more recent* research on hedging; such phenomenon is *rarely* reported in ....)

Focus, on the other hand, "has to do with the sharpening or softening of boundaries around categorical meanings" (Hood 2006: 40). To sharpen the boundaries, one may say *real* research or otherwise 'the *kind of* research' to serve a softening function. The categorical boundaries around processes, according to Hood, can also be softened by "encoding a lack of completion or realization". For instance, "*attempts* to explore", "a *plausibly* underscore".

Figure 5. GRADUATION system.

The last subtype under the system of APPRAISAL is ENGAGEMENT, which has to do with the alignment of speaker's/writer's voice to the propositions put forward. It points to the interpersonal space within which a speaker/writer negotiates with respect to diverse view-points or opinions (White 2003). This can be realised through the use of modals of probability (e.g. it may ….), attributions (e.g., A group of researchers report that …), counter-expectancy markers (e.g., unexpectedly), distancing (e.g. she claims that …), etc. Since ENGAGEMENT is more commonly found in spoken discourse (e.g., Arkoudis 2005) or academic writing, there will not be an elaborate analysis on this in my study.

2.7. Concluding remarks

In this chapter, I have positioned the current study at the intersection of education and applied linguistics. In educational terms, I have been trying to argue for the importance of a study that traces the social context of transition from an academic learning environment to a professional one, especially at the early stage of enculturation. The discussions on WAC and WID have helped to justify the value of undertaking a study which investigates the real-world demands in terms of discursive competence in the workplace. The present study, which can be classified as 'discipline in English' in nature points to the role played by content experts and the STWs themselves in moving into the community of practice of a specific discipline, by means of learning the discourse practices.

In applied linguistics terms, I have illustrated how the studies of genre, workplace writing and identities form the theoretical underpinning of the present study. Previous genre studies direct my attention to the social action brought about by genre; workplace writing research reveals the discourse challenges faced by novice and/or ESL writers; research on workplace identities always ties in with the competence of the workers.

This chapter has also justified the use of SFL as the analytic tool for the placement texts collected. The major reason is its emphasis on the dovetailing of language and function. SFL not only changes the way we view language, it provides useful analytical categories for discourse analysis, for example, the APPRAISAL framework. Figure 6 shows the building blocks of this study.

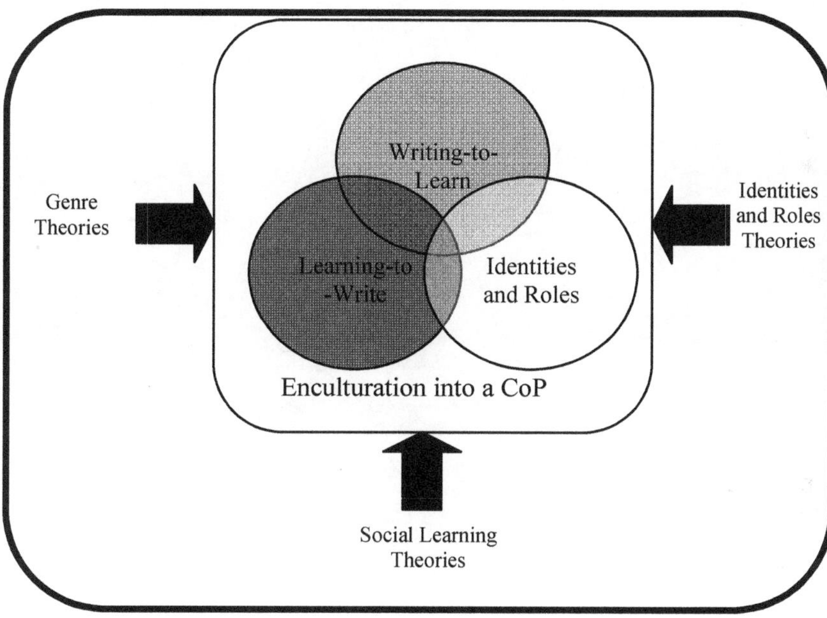

Figure 6. Building blocks of the current study.

In the following chapter, I will outline the research design of the study, drawing attention to the research paradigm that influences the choice of methodologies adopted for this study.

3 Methodology and Research Design

> In postmodernist mixed-genre texts, we do not triangulate, we *crystallize* [. . .]. I propose that the central image for "validity" for postmodern texts is not the triangle – a rigid, fixed, two-dimensional object. Rather, the central imaginary is the crystal, which combines symmetry and substance with an infinite variety of shapes, substances, transmutations, multi-dimensionalities, and angles of approach. (Richardson 2000: 934)

This chapter describes the methodology used for collecting and analysing the data for this study. I will first review the recruitment of informants of the main study and outline their academic background and information necessary for the analysis. The nature of the academic/professional disciplines in question is then presented. Next there is a description of the epistemological sites which have helped to generate fruitful data. Since qualitative interviews and informants' writings are the two main data sources, the process of data generation (Mason 2002) will then be substantiated, followed by an overview of the research schedule and design.

With a view to capturing the multiple perspectives needed for understanding the complex nature of placement, "postmodernist crystallization" (Richards 2006: 771; see also Richardson/St. Pierre 2005) is a methodological metaphor that helped me conceptualise the whole research approach. A section will thus be devoted to the explanation of this metaphor and to showing how it became a viable option in light of the practical constraints of this research. Trustworthiness checks associated with the concepts as validity and reliability situated within the post-positivist paradigm will then be illustrated.

In the last section of this chapter, the concern of transferability of research findings (Miles/Huberman 1994; Flick 1998) beyond the context of the current study will be delineated.

3.1. Purposive sampling

Since this research investigates, in broader terms, the acquisition of and the adaptation to the discourse practices in placements, it is of utmost importance to have informants that are engaged in learning taking place in such settings. The university where I collected my data is known for its orientation toward practical applications in professional fields. Placement training, or what the university calls 'work-integrated education' is integral to the curriculum of their courses and has made it a graduation requirement. This explains why I chose this university to conduct my fieldwork. It is specified on the university homepage (HKPolyU 2011) that

> With the aim to help students to be 'all-round students with professional competence' and to produce 'preferred graduates', all students taking undergraduate degree programmes should complete a mandatory *Work-Integrated Education* component as part of the curriculum requirement. Work-Integrated Education (WIE) is 'work-based learning experiences which take place in an organizational context relevant to a student's future profession, or the development of generic skills that will be valuable in that profession.' It offers students the opportunity to learn to connect classroom theory with practical workplace applications through on-the-job work placements.

3.2. The informants

Out of the 13 students expressing interest, nine from five disciplines eventually were recruited in the project, namely, social work (Candy and Wayne), physiotherapy (Carl and Simon), radiography (Paul and Joyce), occupational therapy (Vincy) and nursing (Pamela and Zoe). The wide range of disciplines covered was built into the research design, as this could make the research more illuminating and a wider disciplinary perspective could be obtained. With at least two informants within the same discipline except for Occupational Therapy because of its smaller number of intake (46) every year, cross-checking of data which could enhance the reliability and credibility of the research findings was made possible (see later section on the discussion of reliability and credibility, also Cohen/Manion/Morrison 2001; Golafshani 2003). Recruiting a greater number of informants was also due to the possibility of withdrawals which could happen at any stage of the research.

Among the nine informants recruited, two of them (Zoe and Vincy) lost interest and so decided to withdraw from the study midway through the data collection stage. As for Paul, Joyce, and Pamela, it was found that they did not engage in substantial writing activities during their placement. During their first placement, in addition to learning how to operate various medical equipment, their major task was to understand the structure and terminologies used in different documentation forms. For instance, Joyce learnt how to fill out a form detailing the dosage of radioactive material applied, angle of application (e.g., the Wedge angle), distance, and the representation of the applied area. Although data regarding their discourse practices was lacking, their observation and reflection on their placement learning still contributed a lot to the understanding of the enculturation process. In this respect, the data generated by Candy, Wayne, Carl and Simon was analysed in depth for this study. Supplementary data support from Paul, Joyce and Pamela was provided and the symbol ^ will be used in the analysis chapters to indicate data from these three informants. The depth thus takes the priority yet without sacrificing the breadth of the data too much.

During the period this research was carried out, Wayne and Candy were completing their first year study in social work and had undertaken their placement in two youth centres. Carl and Simon[2], in their second year of physiotherapy course, had clinical placement in the in-patient ward of the hospitals. Although they were studying at an English-medium university, they struggled with using English in their academic studies. This can be reflected from the lexico-grammatical errors they made in their writing and interviews[3]. Table 1 presents the demographic information of the nine informants.

---

2 Simon withdrew from the university after having completed his second year.

3 Both Candy and Wayne admitted to me frankly in the interview that English was the biggest challenge for them in the academic study.

Informants / gender / initials	*Course of study* (year)*	*Venue of placement work*	*Placement work*	*Written discourse practices during placement*	*Other relevant information*
Wayne/M/WW	BA in Social Work (Year 1)	Social service centre in mainland China	Observation, individual assessment of clients, design and evaluate clients	Proposal, session report, reflective writing	Graduated from the higher diploma program from the same university, very weak in English
Candy/F/CD		Social service centre in Hong Kong	Observation, individual assessment of clients, design and evaluate clients	Proposal, session report, reflective writing	Graduated from a Chinese- medium secondary school, limited exposure to English apart from academic settings
Carl/M/CL	BSc in Physiotherapy (Year 2)	Ward visit	Observation, clients' consultation	Science clinical teaching report, consultation record, reflective writing	Performed well academically in science subjects – yet English was a struggle for him
Simon/M/SN		Ward visit	Observation, clients' consultation	Science clinical teaching report, consultation record, reflective writing	Lacked motivation for completing his study
Paul/M/PM	BSc in Radiography (Year 1)	Ward visit	Mainly observation, understanding structure of forms	Not engaging in substantial writing activities	Fluent English but weak in his major subjects, studied in the UK before
Joyce/F/JL		Ward visit	Mainly observation, understanding structure of forms	Not engaging in substantial writing activities	Performed satisfactorily in her academic subject with good English
Pamela/F/PE	HD in Nursing (Year 1)	Hospital	Looked after clients and practiced various nursing skills	Learning log sheet and reflective writing	Very passionate about being a nurse and wished to continue to study a degree in nursing upon graduation
Zoe/F/ZL		Hospital	Information not available	Information not available	Information not available
Vincy/F/VL	BSc in Occupational Therapy (Year 2)	Ward visit	Information not available	Information not available	Good English and interested in the field

*BA – Bachelor of Arts; BSc – Bachelor of Science; HD –Higher Diploma

Table 1. Demographics of informants in this study.

3.3. Nature of the five disciplines

Four disciplines (physiotherapy, occupational therapy, radiography and nursing) out of the five in question can be grouped under the category of 'health sciences'. The nature and epistemological basis of these health sciences disciplines contrast starkly with those of social work. Yet the current research by no means intends just to single out the disciplinary differences in enculturation; on the contrary, it was hoped that the analysis of placement work in different fields would also reveal similar patterns and commonalities. The following section provides a description of the two fields and the curriculum details relevant to the later discussion.

3.3.1. Social work

According to the International Federation of Social Workers (2005), social work "promotes social change, problem solving in human relationships and the empowerment and liberation of people to enhance well-being. Utilising theories of human behaviour and social systems, social work intervenes at the points where people interact with their environments. Principles of human rights and social justice are fundamental to social work". To put this definition in a nutshell, social work is a discipline which involves the application of social theories and research methods to assess and improve the well-being of people and societies. From this perspective, social work is both an art and science. From the artistic point of view, social workers are trained to interact skilfully with clients through feeling, empathising and appreciating (HKPolyU 2003). On the other hand, social workers appear to work like scientists by following a set of well-defined protocols to reach out and provide relevant needs and advice to clients (see for example Flexner 2001).

The social work curriculum provides a strong foundation of social science and communication training. The foundation curriculum has the stated aim of inducting students into the necessary attitudes, knowledge, values, beliefs and competence (HKPolyU 2003) of the discipline. Courses are conducted predominantly in English. English is used mainly because of the ideological concern with respect to its seemingly superior role as a medium of instruction in the academic context of Hong Kong (Poon 2004) and as a university requirement. Cantonese is also allowed exceptionally in some courses (particularly those related to practice) taking into account the fact that it is the main vernacular form in Hong Kong and local social workers mainly serve Cantonese-speaking clients in practice.

During the first year, social work students are taught basic social work theories and made aware of the social problems. Values to be upheld in rendering human services are also introduced. Table 2 lists the courses Wayne and Candy took prior to their placement and the respective course assignments:

Courses taken by Wayne and Candy	*Assignments*
Theory & Practice in Human Service	Problem assessment report and integrated intervention plan
Human Behaviour & Social Environment	Group project presentation
Introduction to Social Welfare in Hong Kong	Term Paper
Hong Kong Society	Term Paper
Art of Reasoning	Paper written in class

Table 2. Courses and assignments in first year social work curriculum.

3.3.2. Health Sciences (Physiotherapy, Occupational Therapy, Radiography and Nursing)

Health science, as the name suggests, is the application of science to health-related issues and involves the understanding of human body. Based on the positivist tradition, the work of health science disciplines foregrounds logic and reasoning. In many health disciplines, a generic sequence of work steps is strictly adhered to through which practitioners establish their professional identity and credibility. For instance, in physiotherapy, there are usually five generic stages in a consultation session, namely Subjective Examination, Objective Examination,

Treatment Goal, Reassessment and Home Rehabilitation Program. A more detailed description of each step is laid out in Figure 1.

Generic stage	*Description*
1. Subjective Assessment	The physiotherapist interviews the client thoroughly about their condition.
2. Objective Assessment	The physiotherapist performs special tests with the client (such as range of motion, palpation, muscle strength tests etc) to obtain an objective measure. To ensure correct movement by the client specific communication skills are required.
3. Treatment	The physiotherapist treats the client's condition; this includes educating the client about their condition.
4. Reassessment	The physiotherapist reassesses the client using objective tests.
5. Home Management Programme	The physiotherapist gives the client a home programme to follow (this includes advice and exercises)

Figure 1. Description of generic stages in a Physiotherapy session (Forey 2003).

Quantitative methodologies are preferred over qualitative ones in the sense that health researchers always work with numbers such as temperature or blood pressure readings. Another focus is placed on skills-based training; this does not only include the use of relevant equipment but also the contact with clients both physically and verbally. Laboratory work is frequent in which visual literacy and numeracy are emphasised and required. For instance, in the laboratory session of Pathology, Paul and Joyce were required to use the 40x microscope to view and then draw an alveolar cell with the identification of its different parts (See Figure 2). As for Simon, one of his practical assignments investigated the influence of laser and acupuncture on pain threshold. He made use of statistical software to generate numerical information for analysis. Table 3 shows the courses and the respective assignments taken by Simon and Carl in their second year before they took part in the placement:

Courses taken by Simon and Carl	*Assignments*
Critical Inquiry II	Presentation
Professional Seminar IV	Portfolio
Fundamentals of Electrophysical Therapy II	Laboratory Report
PT Diagnosis & Management in Adult Neurological Dysfunction	Term paper
PT Diagnosis & Management in Paediatric Dysfunction	Term paper
Psychology of Disability	Presentation

Table 3. Courses and assignments in second year Physiotherapy curriculum.

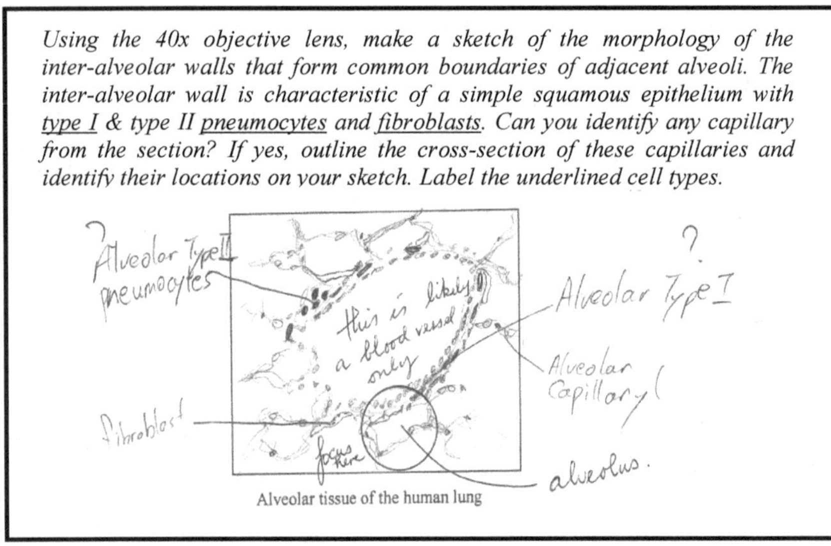

Figure 2. An excerpt from Paul's laboratory report.

3.3.3. Problem-based learning (PBL) curriculum

One of the main instructional strategies adopted by both social work and health sciences at PolyU and other universities in Hong Kong alike is problem-based learning (PBL). PBL has gained popularity recently (Rogal/Snider 2007; Legg 2007) in training professionals by simultaneously developing their problem-solving skills and placing students as active problem-solvers presented with real-world problems (Poon/Reed/Tang 1997). Such a pedagogical approach is seen as a bridge between the academic world and the professional one, with an emphasis on student-centeredness and the teacher taking the role as a facilitator only. The problems presented are always situational, open-ended and often modified in such a way that relevant teaching points are incorporated. Students are expected to define the problems, reflect upon what they know and what they do not know, and critically evaluate the solutions that have come up during the discussion. At times, the outcome will be presented in the form of a written report. For example, Pamela, a nursing student, was required to write a report in response to the following question (See Appendix A for excerpts from Pamela's report):

> *Ah Ling is a 15-year-old girl who had a seizure at school and lost consciousness during her Physical Education lesson. She was sent to a nearby hospital.*

Pamela has divided her report into six sections including 'introduction', 'learning issues', 'basic knowledge', 'education', 'conclusion' and 'reference'. The major parts consolidate what she learnt about the causes and symptoms of epilepsy and most importantly, recognised her role as a prospective nurse in the treatment process.

This section has provided information about the informants' exposure to the kind of discourse practices at the university and the prior knowledge they could 'transfer' to the workplace in their placement. It is crucial to know all this background information because it provides contextual clues about the potential problems arising from the transition from the academic world to the professional workplace. Another important piece of information to note is that the only linguistic exposure these STWs had was limited to academic English. This limited input may also pose obstacles to their enculturation and how they grappled with the linguistic demand in the workplace is thus central to this study.

In the coming sections, I will review the search for epistemological sites, data generation from various sources, and an overview of the research design and schedule.

3.4. Searching for epistemological sites

With the objectives of the study in mind, three major components – discourse practices, placement and professional world – form connections mediated by texts as shown in Figure 3.

To understand discourse practices, naturally the primary source of data is from texts produced in contexts. In the workplace, two contexts are realised, i.e., placement and professional world. Two types of texts are therefore generated from these two sites. These texts were collected and analysed to reveal the linguistic aspects of enculturation reflected in the negotiation of meanings between supervisors and the novices via written feedback, the establishment of novices' identities and roles, and the role played by genre in drawing novices into professional practices. Reflective writing, a genre typically found in professional disciplines, brings all the different perspectives together and switches from an objective engagement in the social world to subjective thoughts. This will be discussed in greater detail in Section 3.5.

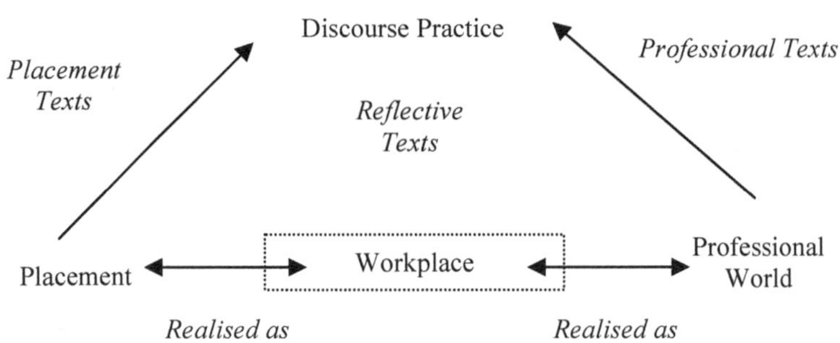

Figure 3. Connections among discourse practice, placement and professional world.

Wenger (1998) collected his data from an insurance company, observing how workers processed various claims collaboratively. His fieldwork included direct involvement (such as attending training courses, processing claims, engaged in conversation and social events with other colleagues), observation and interviews. This gave me a hint on how to go about generating the data for analysis. The potentially fruitful epistemological sites identified would be those organisations/institutions where my informants undertook their placements and I took up the role of participant-observer (Glesne 1999). However, this preliminary plan was rejected because consent had not been granted by the respective authorities. In addition, it was impossible to visit all the sites where my informants undertook their placement because even within the same discipline, the two informants had their placement in different organisations during the same period. I thus had to make a concession by asking the informants to keep a journal so that they could jot down any critical incidents relevant to placement learning. The reflective journals, as distinguished from the reflective texts required by the University, at times also formed the basis of the interviews during which the informants recounted their learning experience in placement, even though these journals did not constitute the main textual analysis in this study. Table 4 shows the relationship between data, data generation methods and the questions this study tries to answer.

Research Questions	Elicited data	Best possible data generation method	Adopted or rejected? If rejected, what are the constraints?	Alternative data generation method possible
1. How do novices learn to adapt to the discourse practices during their placement?				
a. What kinds of texts are produced in placements?	Text types	Text analysis completed with interviews	Adopted	/
b. What are the roles of text-mediated and non-textual-mediated activities that the informants engaged in placement in the process of enculturation?	Informants' participation in a CoP	Participant observation	Rejected because of the cumbersome procedures in gaining consent from various bureaucratic levels	Interviews
c. What social forces are imposed and how do they influence novices' discourse practices??	Social forces imposed	Text analysis complemented with interviews	Adopted	/
d. How do novice writers revise their texts produced and how are they drawn into disciplinary practices via making use of feedback from expert members?	Negotiation of meaning via feedback	Text analysis complemented with interviews	Adopted	/
2. How do informants' roles influence their discourse practices in relation to their identities?				
a. How are roles operationalised in placement?	Organisational roles	Interviews Literature search	Adopted	/
b. What linguistic devices are found and how are they manipulated in constructing and reflecting the roles of the informants in texts?	Writers' roles	Text analysis complemented with interviews	Adopted	/

Table 4. Overview of relationship between research questions, elicited data and data generation methods.

3.5. Data generation from texts

Placement texts served as the primary data of this study. Two main types of texts were analysed: work-related documentation (WR_TXT) and reflective writing (RF_TXT). Work-related documentation points to those which are tied to professional activities, for example, a consultation report written based on a physiotherapy session or a social work proposal to design a program for clients. Reflective writing refers to texts STWs wrote to reflect upon their professional service to clients. It is noteworthy that although two informants in the same discipline undertook the placement at the same time, they had placement at different organisations and were given different tasks to complete, subject to the needs at the time. For example, Wayne undertook his placement in mainland China while Candy had hers in Hong Kong. Table 5 summarises the texts collected from the four main informants and the quantities.

Both types of writing were analysed in terms of the discourse structure and lexico-grammar. Not only do reflective writings provide a medium for the STWs' to share their own thoughts about placement work, they are an important source of information regarding the social context of placement and placement writing. The STWs' choices of participants, processes, circumstances, etc. in their reflection provide linguistic traces of expert-novice interactions as well as roles and identities. This is a way to make up for the participant observation which was not feasible in this study and to cross-check the information provided by the informants during the interview to enhance the reliability of data.

	Physiotherapy				Social Work			
	Carl		Simon		Wayne		Candy	
<u>Main Textual Data</u>	*Quantity*	*No. of words*	*Quantity*	*No. of words*	*Quantity*	*No. of words*	*Quantity*	*No. of words*
1. Work-Related Documentation (WR_TXT)								
Clinical Science Teaching Report	2	310	2	342	N/A	N/A	N/A	N/A
Worksheet	3	674	3	712	N/A	N/A	N/A	N/A
Consultation Report	3	408	3	420	N/A	N/A	N/A	N/A
Proposal	N/A	N/A	N/A	N/A	2	4,253	N/A	N/A
Assessment Report	N/A	N/A	N/A	N/A	N/A	N/A	2	1,126
Session Report	N/A	N/A	N/A	N/A	3	4,957	3	2,221
2.Reflective Writing (RF_TXT)								
Self-Reflection required by the University	7	2,087	7	1,807	5	4,599	5	4,374
Total	**15**	**3,479**	**15**	**3,281**	**10**	**11,510#**	**10**	**5,421#**
Supporting Contextual Data								
1. Reflective Journal required by the researcher	1	*	1	*	1	*	1	*
2. Academic Assignment	3	*	3	*	5	*	4	*

 # These numbers do not add up because self-reflection is also embedded in the session reports

** Word count was not done for the supporting contextual data*

Table 5. Texts collected for main data analysis.

3.5.1. Corpus analysis

Although this research is very much qualitative in nature, the assistance of the corpus tool *WordSmith 5.0* (Scott 2007) to generate quantitative data about the texts has provided a useful point of departure to justify the focus of the later qualitative analyses. Corpus analyses are mainly used in Chapter 7 where quantitative information regarding the choices of processes is needed to filter those processes which are considered insignificant in number. This also makes the qualitative explanation for those significant processes more manageable.

3.6. Data generation from interviews

The adopting of interviewing in the research reflects an ontological position that there is no direct access to the objective reality 'out there' in the world whereas "people's knowledge, views, understanding, interpretation, experiences and interactions are meaningful properties of social reality" (Mason 2002: 63). Through talking interactively with the informants, for example, interviewing, their subjective and unique understandings and experiences will be able to be *reconstructed* (Mason 2002: 63). The dialogic nature inherent in interview enables a researcher to generate rich, contextual, socially situated (Cohen/Manion/Morrison 2001) and often serendipitous data in order to unravel the mystery of the topic in question.

Glesne (1998) reminds novice researchers that it is common to confuse the research questions with the interview questions. She quotes Maxwell (1996: 74) to explain the differences between the two: "your research questions formulate what you want to understand; your interview questions are what you ask people in order to gain that understanding". As compared to research questions, interview questions will be more specific and contextualised (Glesne 1998). Since most of my interviews were based on informants' writing, the interview questions were developed specifically for my preliminary analysis. Interview questions were also sequenced in such a way that rapport with the informants could gradually be established by means such as asking non-directive questions before prompting those centred on the research interests (Taylor/Bogdan 1984).

Even though I had questions on my agenda, they were not blindly followed without regard to the answers given by the informants. A successful interview is based on the negotiation between the researcher and the researched. It has been emphasised that unlike a robot-like data collector, the interviewer, instead of an interview schedule or protocol, is the research tool. The role of the interviewer is not merely to obtain answers from the interviewee but "[to learn] what questions to ask and how to ask them" (Taylor/Bogdan 1984: 77). Semi-structured rather than structured interviews were therefore employed in my study as the former approach would be able to generate a greater breadth of data (Fontana/Frey 2000) through probing, following-up themes and clarifications (Arksey/Knight 1999). In order to get the most out of the interviews, different strategies were employed to elicit informants' responses. Some of the strategies include[4]:

(a) *Probing questions for clarification*

Candy:	Actually we learnt how to engage in an individual in family and groups also we have to learn some some skills that written and such as engagement assessment
Researcher:	Okay engagement *what do you mean by engagement? (INT-CD-01)*

(b) *Probing questions for confirmation of prediction*

Researcher:	Yeah I can see here you say structural and ideological. Can you explain a little more about structural and ideological?
Candy:	As I remember, structural is mean the society structure. Different person in the society has different role
Researcher:	Ideological is beliefs, values and *usually it refers to power, right? (INT-CD-02)*

4 All the interview excerpts cited here and in other chapters are verbatim, unless the STW's response was incomprehensible in the original form, for which modification to citation would be needed. Unless otherwise specified, English was the language of interview and so the translation of such verbal data was not needed.

(c) *Formulating hypothetical questions*

Carl:	Yes, because we need to communication with the patient what what he or she wants to do within a short period of time, then we decide it is realistic or not. Then if it is realistic, then we try to use our treatment to help the patient to achieve the goal
Researcher:	*Just imagine you are a professional, you are given a blank sheet. So, would you think that you will jot down the short term goal so for example, functions (INT-CL-01)*

(d) *Reformulating questions*

Carl:	No, the approach is opposite in my individual report. We just find out if there is any depression. We use the disorder to find out the region of haemorrhage
Researcher:	Okay, quite interesting. How do you feel about working with medical team for rehabilitation of the stroke patient. You mentioned that as in a medical team that involves other people physician nurses. *I mean I mean in actual professional context in the hospital. Would you encounter similar things? I mean you have to work with a lot of other medical teams. I mean professional, do you work as a group? (INT-CL-02)*

Although the strategies mentioned above are those used by me as a researcher, the informants made use of them quite frequently as well. In addition, informants' 'collaborative strategies' are also indispensable in ensuring the smooth running of the interviewing process. This is particularly relevant to the current study which deals with disciplinary knowledge and therefore the informants needed to pitch their responses at the right level. Some strategies are:

(a) *Providing contextualised example*

Carl:	But I think the clinical psychologist is the person who treat this kind most of the time OT deal with the psychiatric patient. So, I think they will be more relevant in this topic than us. But I don't think they are the
Researcher:	the most important
Carl:	yes not the most important
Researcher:	But would the psychological part or aspects of a patient affect the physical
Carl:	Yes
Researcher:	To what extent? I don't know I'm just assuming there will be

Carl: *Let's say a patient with a severe depression. When we need him he or she to do some exercise, may be sometime they would give up easily, but it is not due to their physical function but is their psychological problem (INT-CL-02)*

(b) Rephrasing, reinforced with translation

Simon: for the outpatient center, we mainly will treat the case which referral by the doctors and outpatient center is actually like the physio-clinic, but not the hospital's ward

Researcher: oh physio-clinic, okay

Simon: *that means outpatient, for Chinese is called* **門診部** *(INT-SN-04)*

(c) Elaboration as a form of clarification

Researcher: No. So have you … have you conducted any discussion with your classmates? I mean for problem based learning, you have to is it does it involve group discussion? I mean during course session or conduct seminar?

Pamela: The PBL session, we need to have a group interaction and have a presentation Researcher: But not on this topic?

Pamela: Yes. *Let me explain more. Ah, the problem based learning, we have three scenario this time. And for each scenario tutor will ah explain or help us to to discuss the content. And to find out what area that we should study. And then, we will choose some area for some for ah each group to find information and have the presentation next week (INT-PE-01̂)*

3.7. Research design and schedule

After understanding the inseparable relationship among data, epistemological sites and data generation methods, in this section, an overview of the research design and schedule of the current study is presented. A sound and carefully-designed research enhances the validity of the study.

3.7.1. Pilot study

Before launching the main study, a pilot study was conducted with three participants from the Rehabilitation Engineering (RE) discipline (as part of a discipline-specific research project in collaboration with the Rehabilitation Engineering Centre to help RE students learn to write medical documents during placement). The main aims of the pilot study were twofold: to understand the genre of medical records and to test the practicality of the methodologies originally planned. Through the analysis of medical records provided, I came to be aware of the discourse structure and some of the medical terminologies used. Think-aloud protocols were initially used as a way to tap the cognitive process of revision when completing a writing task. However, it was later concluded that this method was far too difficult and stressful for the participants, despite having a training session offered to them beforehand (Ericsson/Simon 1993). Another reason why this method was not adopted is for practicality's sake: STWs were always required to complete a task in a relatively short period of time during the placement period; at times documentation was done while they were seeing their clients, in which case verbalisation of their thoughts was not possible. This method was therefore replaced by conducting interviews scheduled shortly after they completed the writing task when their memory was still fresh.

3.7.2. Main study – preparation stage

The main study began with the recruitment of informants. After identifying suitable informants, preparation of data generation was underway. To be engaged in a discipline-specific study, grasping some basic disciplinary knowledge is conducive to my understanding and adds credibility to the interpretation of findings. Before collecting the data, I attended a seminar series organised by the social work department on social workers' practice in Hong Kong. One of the seminars titled 'Orality and Literacy of Social Work Practice' was particularly relevant to my study. Also, I volunteered to work with a professor to put together a proposal to bid for a departmental research grant investigating the interpersonal meaning construed in physiotherapy consultation sessions using the APPRAISAL framework. Interviews and the actual consultation sessions between the physiotherapist and the client (who was in fact the principal investigator of that project) were audio-taped and I was given access to the data. These involvements, which I call 'ancillary engagement', provide a means of understanding the discourse of social work and physiotherapy practices and broaden my knowledge base of the two fields.

Informants were also interviewed before the placement. These background interviews were conducted around their academic assignments in order to discern the concerns arising from the transition from academia to workplace. These interviews also allowed me to keep constant contact with the informants so that their motivation of participating in my study could be maintained as far as possible.

3.7.3. Main study – data collection stage

Since I had nine informants from five disciplines, the times they had placement were staggered. Their writings were collected as soon as they had finished their placement. Preliminary analysis was done on the texts before the interviews. Since site visits were impossible, I asked each of the informants to keep a journal to document any incidents they found relevant to placement learning, particularly in terms of written communication, on the site. Guidelines as to what they could document were provided; yet they were free to decide what to go into the journal. Some did include drawings in the journal which added an interesting dimension to the data analysis (see later section on crystallization). As the work assigned to the STWs during placement was often ad hoc, I had to keep close contact with the informants and be prepared to make adjustments to the research plan in order to collect the most useful data possible. For instance, once I was informed by Wayne that a lot of comments were given to his proposal drafts, both linguistic and content ones, and that multiple drafts were required before the final submission to the centre's supervisor for approval, I asked him to send me his work and we discussed his revision in response to the comments over the phone and instant messenger.

When he came back from his placement in mainland China, I conducted in-depth interviews with him to double check with him the rationale behind his revision. Preliminary analyses of texts were necessary as most of the interviews were based around them.

3.7.4. Main study – post-data collection stage

After collecting relevant data, transcription of interviews began. Since there were altogether 36 interviews amounting to around 20 hours of verbal data, I had to make decisions on how many interviews I needed to transcribe and how detailed the transcription should be. Since I focused mainly on four informants' data, I transcribed all the interviews with them completely, totalling 17 interviews lasting approximately ten hours. As for other informants' data, I only transcribed parts which had direct relevance to placement learning.

An important characteristic of qualitative research is that the data undergoes an iterative, cyclical process before the findings can be claimed credible. Fretchling and Sharp (1997: 1) suggest that qualitative analysis consists of:

> a loop-like pattern of multiple rounds of revisiting the data as additional questions emerge, new connections are unearthed, and more complex formulations develop along with a deepening understanding of the material

Apart from the prescribed ones, new themes emerged under the scrutiny of various texts from informants and they were cross-referenced with data generated from the interviews as far as possible increasing the reliability of the claims.

3.8. Relevance to my study

After reviewing the various sources that generate data, the section intends to explain how the methods adopted lead to the study that follows. In the first place, this study is concerned with a critical stage of STWs' academic and professional life. At the level of conceptualisation, the objectives of this study can be reconsidered as (1) STWs' perceptions and experiences of placement work, (2) resources (e.g. texts) in drawing STWs' into a CoP and (3) STWs engagement with these resources.

3.8.1. Use of interviews

Interviews conducted before the placement helped me understand STWs' perception and expectations of placement work. Interviews conducted after the placement provided STWs' accounts of learning approaches (e.g., observation), interactions with different parties (e.g., clients, expert members), challenges faced (e.g., performing tasks that had yet to be learnt) and concerns based on their own work experience in the placement.

3.8.2. Use of textual analysis

Textual analyses in this study have two purposes. The first purpose is to investigate how texts can draw STWs from the disciplinary practices. In connection with this, worksheets and reports with pre-existing headings/questions are analysed with respect to the lexico-grammatical construction, vocabulary items chosen, multimodal resources and the rhetorical organisation. In other words, this is the analysis of text construction from the perspective of expert members. The second purpose is to understand how STWs interact with texts. This is analysed with respect to STWs' adherence to the genre requirement, revision processes, choices of vocabulary items and grammatical structures. This is thus the analysis of text completion from the perspective of novice members.

After understanding the relevance of methods to the current study, the following section aims at putting the nuts and bolts of this research into a sound methodological framework.

3.9. Positivistic triangulation vs postmodernist crystallization

Triangulation as a way to demonstrate concurrent validity by the use of a multi-method of data collection has been widely accepted in literature, particularly in qualitative research methodology (Cohen/ Manion/Morrison 2001). Yet triangulation carries so much a positivist implication, through which a researcher looks for a relatively "definitive truth" (Ellingson 2009: 22). This is based on the assumption that there is an object which can be triangulated using different methods. For example, to understand how a novice writer revises a piece of written work, a researcher may gather useful data from conducting think-aloud protocol and follow-up interviews around the texts being revised (see Figure 4).

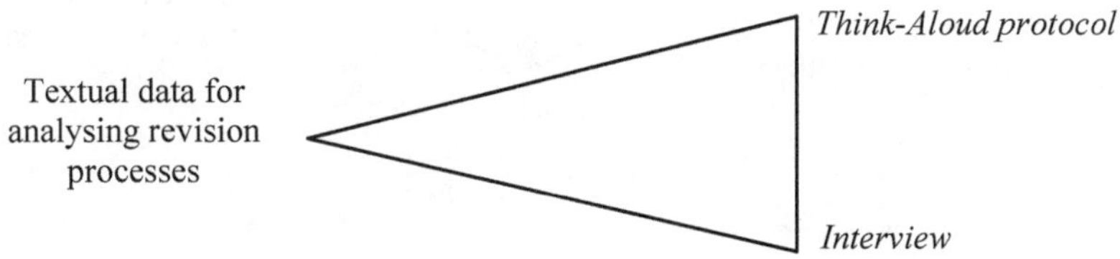

Figure 4. An example of methodological triangulation.

However, with the increasing complexities of social phenomena and popularity of postmodernism, doubts have been raised as to whether there is a truth out there that can be discovered completely. Richardson (2005, 2000) therefore proposes a move from a two-dimensional triangle to a multidimensional, dynamic and crystal-like shaped model to capture such complexities, which is crystallization, as quoted as the epigraph at the very beginning of this chapter.

Crystallization can be conceived as a metaphorical representation of a combination of inquiry methods and perspectives. The research object of this study 'enculturation' is multifaceted in its own right and multiple perspectives are needed to understand it more fully. In this respect, the different ways of knowing and producing knowledge are emphasised. Figure 5 presents a representation of the current research by means of a crystal. It is important to be borne in the mind that the adoption of crystallization in this study is mainly to provide me with a 'thinking object' used to conceptualise the whole research approach.

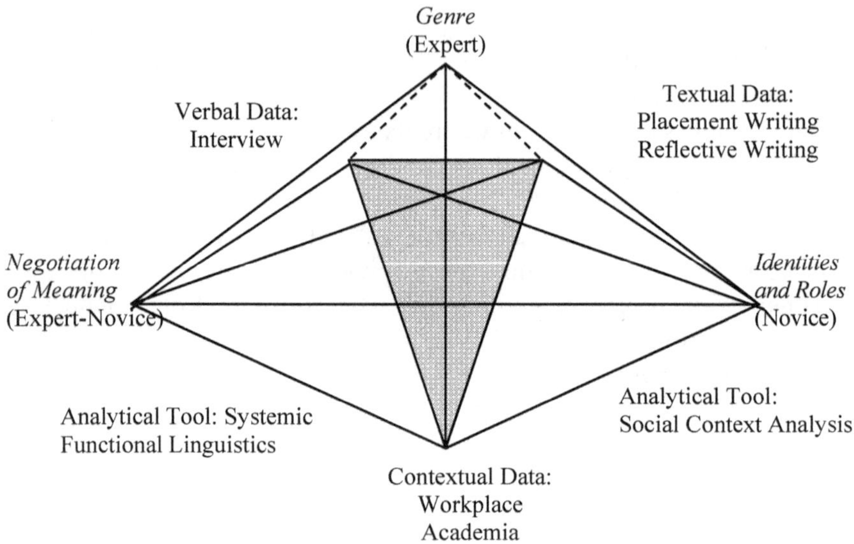

Figure 5. Diagrammatic description of crystallization: A metaphorical representation.

3.9.1. Multiple ways of knowing and producing knowledge

Similar to triangulation, crystallization emphasises the different forms of generating knowledge. In this project, textual analysis was supported by in-depth qualitative semi-structured interviews. Coding textual data lends itself to a more realist, positivist pursuit whereas semi-structured interviews a social constructivist, emergent one along the qualitative/quantitative continuum (Ellington 2009; Guba/Lincoln 2005). Owing to a unique nature of the project, knowledge of the disciplinary knowledge would be helpful when engaging with the data. My participatory role as a researcher of a project regarding placement learning of the health disciplines enhanced my knowledge of the genre of medical documentation. In other words, I participated in related activities peripheral to my research study. Such peripheral engagement nonetheless placed myself in a more first-person, interpretive perspective.

Crystallization appreciates the multiple perspectives yielded. The 'multiplicity' described here, I argue, foregrounds the perspectives that come about as a result of the researcher's conscious choices of data sources which legitimate multiple dimensions of analysis. In this project, genre analysis places professional/placement texts and their 'producers' in the centre of attention, providing insight into their roles by helping 'text consumers' (i.e., novices) acquire generic and professional competence. Another perspective comes from the novices by virtue of textual representation to shape and construct their identities and roles. Investigating the novice and expert member's exchanges in the feedback-revision processes further adds an interactive dimension to the analysis. Supporting materials such as informants' academic assignments, researcher's field notes taken during relevant seminars and involvement in research projects offer an ancillary perspective.

3.9.2. Reflexivity in action

One of the ethical arguments of the postmodern philosophical thinking is the relationship between discourse and power (Butler 2002). Discourse here goes beyond the general understanding as 'stretches of language' to mean "a historically evolved set of interlocking and mutually supporting statements, which are used to define and describe a subject matter" (Butler 2002: 44). Discourse in this sense is ideological; the form of presentation and what to present to the readers about the social reality are very much researcher's choice. The narrative presented is merely a re-construction rather than simply a 're-production' by the researcher who is subject to the various discourses available to him/her (Richardson/St. Pierre 2005) which in turn influences the way he/she perceives the social world. This is also pointed out by Tusting and Barton (2006: 38):

> the postmodern approach […] seeing the attainment of a single narrative explaining any phenomenon as a way of imposing power that aims to silence dissenting voices, rather than as a representation of truth

Postmodernists also query the existence of 'absolute truth' because language, as a form of representation, is an inherently unreliable construct of culture. This is therefore important for a qualitative researcher to be reflexive about his/her practice (Glesne 1998). To Cohen, Manion and Morrison (2001: 141), a highly reflexive researcher needs to be "acutely aware of the ways in which their selectivity, perception, background and inductive processes and paradigms shape the research". Reflexivity thus was taken into serious consideration during the whole research design and process manifested in various ways such as:

- Since I was not the teacher of any of the informants, they would not feel coerced to take part in the research or be afraid of their participation in any way having an impact on their academic study.
- As an outsider of the disciplines investigated in this research, I was aware of the fact that I was taking an etic (outsider's) perspective to see things and my understanding depended a lot on informants' recount of experience. I therefore had to find ways to make my claims and findings more credible.

3.10. Trustworthiness checks: reliability and validity concerns

While in the first instance it appears that concepts of reliability and validity have been underscored mainly in quantitative studies, Mason (2002) reiterates that they are also of relevance to qualitative research. In this study, steps have been taken to guard against threats to them. As researcher's interpretation can be subjective, the analysis was once sent to the informants for checking to see if there were misrepresentation of their 'voices'. Having two informants in a single discipline allows the possibility of cross-checking with data to a certain extent which also enhances reliability. Careful control by means of avoiding leading questions and minimising power differences between the researcher and the researched was taken into serious account in interviews.

Each research method, according to Denzin (1989), can only lead to "different features of empirical reality" and cannot "completely capture all the relevant features of that reality" (1989: 13). Therefore, multiple methods are needed to analyse the same empirical event, i.e., triangulation or crystallization emphasised in this study. Validity was ensured in the research design namely, (1) choosing the appropriate time scale to carry out the data collection for this research, which is the period shortly after the informants completed their placements when their memory was still fresh, (2) adopting the most effective possible data generation methods (see Table 4), (3) maintaining the motivations of the informants by offering them help with their English, and (4) using an appropriate sample, which is formed by those whose studies involve placement learning.

A specific type of validity, namely the construct validity (Brown 1995), was seriously considered in the research design and data analysis. The underlying construct of this text-driven study is 'practice'; it is therefore important to establish a link between the textual analysis undertaken and the actual work STWs engaged in placement. In Chapter 6, for example, it is shown that the choice of a lexical item is tied to one of the values STWs need to uphold in rendering human services.

3.11. Transferability

Apart from validity and reliability, another relevant concern in qualitative study is transferability of findings. Transferability deals with "descriptive clarity" (Harris n.d.) that involves the detailed account of the participants involved, the context of research (setting) and the phenomenon so that other researchers can draw inferences from and/or apply the findings to their own context. To enhance transferability, this study covers a wide range of disciplines and two distinct fields (social work and physiotherapy) are highlighted to show similarities as well as differences about the early stage of enculturation into the professional world. Acknowledging research limitations is also crucial to transferability, which will be addressed in Chapter 8.

3.12. Concluding remarks

In this chapter, I have detailed the decisions made from designing the research, piloting the research instruments to generating data from the informants for the main study. This shows a reflexive, gradual approach to making a credible research study. Most important of all, I have also justified the use of crystallization to conceptualise the research design, emphasising the multiple perspectives inherent in the research object.

In the next chapter, I will problematise the term ‘placement’ in order to justify the setting up of the subsequent analysis chapters.

4 Legitimate Peripheral Participation in a Community of Practice: A Conceptual Overview of Placement

> Learning viewed as situated activity has as its central defining characteristic a process that we call *legitimate peripheral participation.* By this we mean to draw attention to the point that learners inevitably participate in communities of practitioners and that the master of knowledge and skill requires newcomers to move toward full participation in the sociocultural practices of a community. (Lave/Wenger 1991: 29)

After outlining the research design, methodologies adopted and data generated for this study, the main theme of this chapter is to provide a conceptual overview of placement, upon which the subsequent analysis chapters are grounded. Despite its growing popularity as a site of investigation in various research studies (e.g., Kell/Jones 2007; Lee/Fitzgerald 2008; Ethridge/Branscomb 2009), problematising 'placement' is necessary because a critical engagement with such a concept seems to have been lacking. The term is used so widely that it may have slid into one's common sense, resulting in ignoring its theoretical constructs.

Although a text-focused approach is adopted in the process of conceptualisation in this study, only two placement texts are constantly referred to because a more comprehensive treatment in terms of the quantity of texts analysed and the level of textual analysis is dealt with in the next three chapters. As a point of departure, consider the following excerpt from a report[5]:

---

5 The grammatical errors appearing in the original report have been corrected.

Organization:
Session Report

Group name: XXX | Worker name: W Wong
Venue: teaching room | Date: 28/7 | Time: 10:30-11:15

Group Member: 10 people | Attendance: 4+1 non-member people
Group members who attend class:
AA, BB, CC, DD, EE (non- member)

Objectives/goals:
In this session, the objective is to help the student learn some knowledge about electricity, lighting, different batteries, static, and some daily, common knowledge. It is hoped that the children can learn some basic skills for themselves.

If one is asked to guess within what context the above text is constructed and who produces it, it seems logical to deduce from the textual clues available that this is an excerpt from a report describing a lesson-like scene. Based on our socio-cultural experiences (Gee 2001), lexical terms used such as *teaching room, attendance, student, learn, knowledge* and *objectives/goals* altogether conjure up typical images of a school lesson. *Electricity, lighting, batteries* and *static* are common terms introduced in a science class. Even the duration of time *10:30-11:15* is a common feature of the genre of schooling. Following this line of thought, the writer of this text appears to be a teacher.

Although on the surface the text appears to be constructed around an academic context, in reality, this text is written in the workplace. It will be shown later that this text is a report written by a STW after a session conducted for his teenage clients in a social work agency in mainland China. This example highlights the fact that genres we interact with nowadays are more complex than we used to think (Coe/Lingard/Teslenko 2002), and that a wider interpretation that goes beyond the textual level is needed. To understand more fully the construction of the text above, it is therefore essential to consider (1) the social activities around which this text is shaped, i.e., how a lesson description is linked to the intervention activities acceptable in the social work professional context, (2) negotiation of meaning via strategic lexical-grammatical choices, i.e., how the meaning of general lexical items is re-contextualised in a placement context and (3) writer's identities and roles, i.e., how the student informant has his identity re-contextualised to a *worker* and the role shaped as a *teacher* are realised in the text.

In this chapter, placement is therefore conceptualised as a form of "legitimate peripheral participation" (LPP henceforth) (Lave/Wenger 1991: 29; Wenger 1998) in relation to the three defining characteristics mentioned above. A working definition of placement is first presented as a frame of reference and to form the basis for conceptualisation. Attention is drawn to the fact that placement is socially and discursively structured. Viewing placement from these perspectives makes apparent the institutional roles of texts and uncovers the institutional factors that impinge upon the construction of texts.

The last part identifies the key contributing factors to the acquisition of knowledge within a placement CoP. This serves as an extension to Bhatia's work on interaction between generic competence and professional expertise (2005: 148); the main difference between the two lies in the fact that the revised model is specific to the learning experience of my informants in placement whereas Bhatia's model is a more general one which can be applied to any professional training context.

4.1. A working definition of placement

Placement has been considered an important intersection between academic experience and professional engagement. Yet the term itself embraces aspects that go beyond the traditional conceptualisation of a learning scene. A working definition for the purpose of this study is thus necessary. Based on the interviews with informants and the literature on the social context of placement learning (e.g., May/Veitch 1998; Dias/Pare 2000; Thames 2002; Andrews *et al.* 2006; Davis 2006), placement is defined in this study as follows:

> Placement is a transitional stage where novices learn gradually to become professionals and enculturate into professional communities. It is also considered as a site in which various forms of re-contextualisation take place: academic knowledge is re-contextualised in the form of various applications in professional practices whereas professional knowledge and techniques undergo re-contextualisation and are often attenuated in ways that are accessible and manageable to novices. Novices' identities and roles are re-contextualised in relation to their level of legitimate participation granted.

The adoption of the key concept 're-contextualisation' in the above definition over 'transformation' or 'transfer' is because the latter terms are too positivistic in nature and imply a divorce from the circumstances whereas 're-contextualisation' highlights the process of change with respect to the contextual variance and participants' involvement/experience.

4.1.1. Problematising placement from a discursive perspective

Taking on a discursive perspective implies that institutions are constructed and sustained through the production of texts of various types and in various forms. In this study, all my informants undertake placement in various organisations. All their teachers, prior to their production of texts, have given them samples (e.g., clinical records, proposals) which are drawn from previous practices to read making them aware of the genre requirements. The informants then need to produce their own texts following those requirements; deviation from those may incur costly consequences (e.g., failing the placement component, preventing them from moving into fuller participation). Although the texts that I analysed in my study are confined to written outputs, texts in spoken form are fundamentally important to the work of my informants. For example, social work novices need to learn from their expert counterparts the way they communicate with clients without upholding judgmental attitudes. The appropriation of institutional talk is important because it provides a legitimate basis for the ensuing interactions and negotiations.

If we accept the notion that text production is a crucial part of the establishment of institutions, then the next step is to investigate how those texts constitute various discourses and their inter-relationship. There is a wide range of texts produced by the university in a material form: policy documents, syllabus, students' transcripts, etc. These texts ensure the smooth running of the university by formulating institutional rules and regulations. A more specific and relevant example is the University Prospectus (of the university where my data was collected) which states that placements are integral to the curriculum (as cited in Section 3.1 of Chapter 3). For example, it is spelt out clearly under Program Structure of Physiotherapy (HK PolyU 2006) that:

> clinical education is in the form of clinical placements.

However, the boundary between academia and workplace where placements take place is not always clear-cut. Ashforth (2001: 5) suggests that:

> The boundaries are real in the sense that the individual perceives them as such [...] Although a given social domain may be more or less institutionalized [...] the boundaries around domains are somewhat idiosyncratically constructed.

Within the workplace institutional discourse, there are gatekeeping mechanisms to regulate whether a person can be granted an entry and remain as a legitimate member with reference to a set of institutional rules, chiefly reified in textual forms as professional/employees' code of practice, scope of practice, organisational regulations in order to offer objective guidelines of appraisals. Under such a rule-governed body, professionals articulate their roles on the basis of the institutions. Having to provide expert opinions to clients, professionals are accountable to their practices, which are usually documented in various textual formats such as written records or audio/video recordings. Professional statuses are not permanent; they are constantly being reviewed and at times contested and challenged. For example, his/her professional status can be at stake when a medical professional is accused of malpractice.

Novices learn to adapt to professional discourse by producing texts professionally or in a reduced form in placement which are often subject to credibility checks by the experts. Such an apprenticeship discourse is a core element in the emergence of placement structure, without which novices will have difficulties gaining access to available resources and feedback that draws them into institutional practices. Therefore, its position in the centre not only suggests a fundamental role in sustaining the structure but also implies the fact that such a discourse is under the influence of multiple discourses surrounding it. Figure 1 is a Venn diagram illustrating the relationship among academic, workplace, placement and apprenticeship discourses.

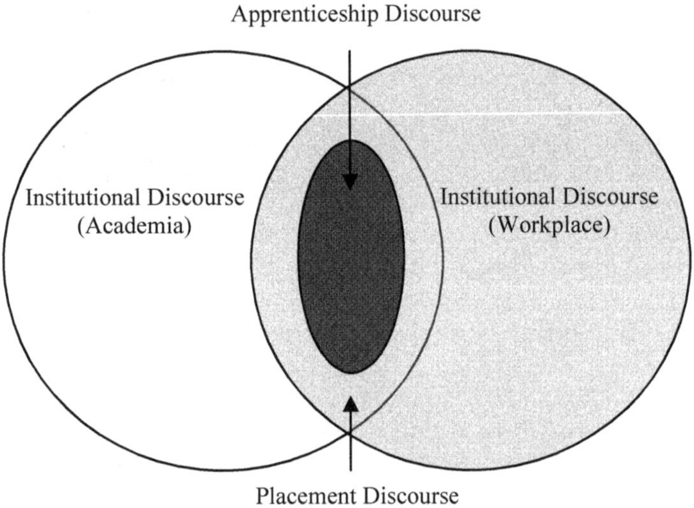

Figure 1. Discursive relationships among four discourses.

4.2. Placement as Legitimate Peripheral Participation (LPP)

4.2.1. Placement texts: a hybrid genre

The previous section highlights the critical role of texts in sustaining the existence of placement. In this section, excerpts from two placement texts are considered, one from social work (Example 1) and one from physiotherapy (Example 2), in order to reveal their pedagogical-professional hybrid nature and suggest the social actions this kind of genre is associated with. The analysis will be used to illuminate the understanding of three main perspectives on placement as LPP, namely, the socio-cognitive nature of activities, negotiated character of meaning and relational perspectives of knowledge co-construction.

4.2.2. Socio-cognitive nature of activities

Wenger (1998) foregrounds the fact that learning *per se* is not the primary goal of a CoP; rather it is constituted naturally through the members' participation in shared, purposeful, patterned activities in response to a particular social need. My preference for using 'activities' over 'tasks' not only captures the sense of active involvement, it also implies the use of concerted efforts, shared resources, tools and artefacts to achieve an aim, which are critical elements within an 'activity system' (Engeström 1999) under the activity theoretical perspective.

In Example 1, in addition to describing the activities in a social work program, the emphasis is placed on prompting STW$_{sw}$s[6] to reflect upon the procedures of conducting experiential programs to clients through a checklist with the heading *facilitating group process* and a list of criterion-referenced items (e.g. *involving group members, attending to others, expressing self).* As for Example 2, STW$_{p}$s document clients' problems via a well-structured form with pre-existing subheadings such as *DOA, ROM, Upper limb strength* whereas their professional counterparts often work with only blank sheets of paper (except perhaps those working at the hospitals). The two examples suggest that to produce legitimate knowledge within a placement CoP then, one needs to take part in various activities shaped by the practices and communal resources developed over time (Johns 1997) as the professional counterparts, although the activities are often reshaped in ways which have their goals oriented towards a

6 The subscript indicates the discipline a STW belongs to: SW = Social Work; P = Physiotherapy.

pedagogical end. These 'pedagogicalised' professional activities are principally textually-mediated (Barton/Hamilton 2005), through which institutional goals and requirements are achieved. The role of discursive practices is understood by the student worker:

> Candy: They *(placement writings)* are very important. They can affect my grade because I mean if I can be a good social worker in my placement but I cannot write it down clearly so I cannot let my professor know what I have done. *(INT-CD-01)*

Apparently, the STW is aware of the broader social implications of her discourse practices which are ultimately used to judge her level of professional competence. Her emphasis on grades rather than professional development may be attributed to her being at the very early stage of academic study and major gatekeepers appear to be university professors. An integral component that showcases professional competence is "generic competence", a term used by Bhatia (1994; 2005: 145) to mean

> the ability to identify, construct, interpret and successfully exploit a specific repertoire of professional, disciplinary or workplace genres to participate in the daily activities and to achieve the goals of a specific professional community or what Lave and Wenger (1991) call 'community of practice' [...].

Example 1 Excerpt from a Social Work Placement Text: Session Report*

Session Report

Session:
Student Name:
Group Name:

Organization:
(Chinese translation)

Group name: ________ Worker name: ________________
Venue: __________ Date: __________ Time: __________

Group Member: ________ Attendance: _______
Group members who attend class:
____
____

Objectives/goals:
____

Status of the Group (including procedural content, arrangement and organization; description and assessment of responses of group members and difficulties encountered)
____
____

Group Development
____
____

Roles of Members
____
____

Group Involvement

Name	Performance				
	Excellent	Satisfactory	Fair	Dissatisfactory	Remark

Suggestion
____
____

Follow up
____
____

Facilitating group processes **促進技巧**		
Skills	**Grading**	**Self-reflection**
5/. Involving group members 協助組員投入 verbal invitation, minimal encouragement		
6/. Attending to others 專注技巧 non-verbal such as eye contact, body position and verbal behavior that convey empathy, respect, warmth , trust…		
7/. Expressing self 表達和自我披露 helping members to express their views and feelings, worker's self-disclosure in suitable moments		
8/. Focusing and clarifying skills 聚焦和澄清 focusing the group processes in a particular directions. This can be done by clarifying, asking a member to elaborate, repeating a particular communication, redirect the group if the interaction has been side-tracked by irrelevant issues, etc		
9/. Requesting information, questioning and probing skills 發問和探查、搜集		
10/. Analyzing skills 分析技巧 pointing out patterns, identifying gaps in the data, and establishing mechanisms or plan		

*Note *Only the form is shown here. STWsw's entry has not been included.*

Example 2 Excerpt from a Physiotherapy placement text: Sci Clinical teaching report (WR_TXT-CL-03).

SCI CLINICAL TEACHING REPORT

Name of patient: XXXX
Name of physiotherapy student: YYYY

S/E:
DOA: 24/6/04
HPI: Preterm – B5 week, admitted for corrective osteotomy
Dx: L tibia deformity (varus)
PMH: - BPD not on Rx
- ROD, R eye blindness, L eye poor vision
- TB°, HT°

O/E:
- v.s. stable

Chest: - no pain
- pin tract wound on L leg
- external fixation
- skin T° normal
- calf soft
- ~~no~~ DVT sign -ve
- No swelling

ROM:

AROM		**R**	**L**
Knee	**F**	√	95°
	E	√	0°
Ankle DF		√	limited
	PF	√	limited
	IV	√	√
	EV	√	√

MMT:

		R	L
Knee	**F**	√	4/5
Ankle DF		5/5	4/5
	PF	5/5	4/5
	IV	5/5	4/5
	EV	5/5	4/5

Upper limbs strength √ √

**Texts circled denote teacher's feedback/revision*

Bhatia's interest in the generic competence of professionals also sheds light on the current project concerning newcomers. In other words, genre acquisition is fundamental to the success of novices' enculturation. In the first instance, newcomers need to be inducted into the selection of the most appropriate form of representation (e.g., lexical vs numerical vs visual), register of language and discipline-specific lexis to construe the reality. These are considered 'social facts' that are attributed to only human groups instead of to the individuals making up those groups in a social structure (Porpora 1987). For instance, before undertaking placement, student physiotherapists have to learn the bednote writing which involves knowing what information is needed and terminologies used in documentation in the field. Figure 2 is an excerpt of the handout on bednote writing.

Bednote writing in Physiotherapy (in-patient)

...

CONTENT

- Date of record
- S/E: DOA: 1/1/96 (MUST include *year*)
  HPI: S & F, land on left side, can't walk.
  Δ: # [L] TOF
  Mx: eg. OT: AMA, DHS
  PMH: - previous conditions & OT done.
  - DM^+, HT°, IHD°, PTB°
  - HT^+ (Rx^+, regular FU^+)

...

(Other investigation (X-ray, MRI, lab. sheet), OT sheet, Nurses vital sign chart)

...

Figure 2. An excerpt from handout on bednote writing.

The STWp's documentation in Example 2 apparently is in line with the bednote writing conventions handout. Apart from using the discipline-specific abbreviations (e.g. *TB*, *HT*), a full form of representation of date with day, month and year (i.e., *24/6/04*) is adhered to. The seemingly trivial information such as the year of the date of admission is significant in the context of physiotherapy documentation, as seen from the very strong modal *MUST* being used in the handout and in the uppercase. The value of this temporal information goes beyond record-keeping; it provides a structure to a client's medical history by establishing logical intertextual links between records. This dimension of genre acquisition is concerned with the newcomers' awareness of the discoursal resources available and the ways these resources are exploited to make "meaning potential" (Gee 2001: 55). Genre knowledge has also been conceptualised as a form of "situated cognition embedded in disciplinary activities" (Berkenkotter/Huckin 1995: 3). Newcomers build on the existing genre knowledge (e.g., the experience of completing a problem-based learning assignment in social work or physiotherapy) adhering to conventions, institutional requirements, readership and disciplinary methodologies, all of which being socially constructed, to reconstruct the genre appropriate to the context of professional communication. Figure 3 summarises the perspectives of genre acquisition taken on board in this study.

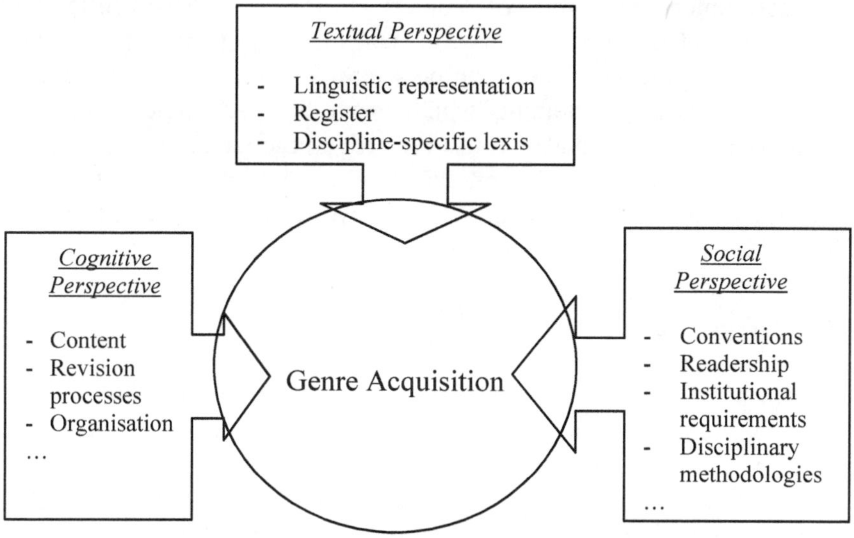

Figure 3. Perspectives of genre acquisition.

While it appears that being able to appropriate genre is an important determining factor of newcomers' placement success, disciplinary practices enacted by various placement genres in a CoP is equally crucial to novices' enculturation. Consider the following excerpt from the social work session report in Example 1:

Skills	Grading	Self-reflection
5/. Involving group members 協助組員投入 verbal invitation, minimal encouragement	2	The worker invited the student to join the game and sharing, however, the skills were not very well.

(WR_TXT-WW-04)

Although this genre is accomplished in the workplace, it is also at the same time pedagogically and reflectively-oriented. The finer descriptors *verbal invitation, minimal encouragement* provide novices with clearer instructional guidance as to what is expected within the realm of *involving group members*, which is more abstract in nature. The self-assessment in terms of numerical scores and self-reflection obviously put the novices into a critical mind to evaluate one's own professional practice. It thus can be seen that placement genres are in fact 'hybridised' by default, which enact the pedagogical practice, professional practice and at times reflective practice (especially in the case of social work) in the context of placement to project a learning trajectory for novices. Chapter 5 will give a detailed account of the interaction among these genre-based practices.

4.2.3. Negotiated character of meaning

Within a CoP, meaning is always negotiated instead of being fixed, static or "locked up in dictionaries" (Wenger 1998: 51). To say that meaning is negotiated suggests its fluidity in nature and readiness for contestation. Although genre-based practices may provide some regularities and consistent patterns to novices' enculturation process, no two discourse events are exactly the same. Consider Example 2 again. Based on the subjective examination, the STWp conducted tests on the client in order to obtain results about such as vital signs (*v.s.*

stable), chest pain (*chest – no pain*) and skin temperature (*skin T° – normal*). Yet the combination of these tests is specific to this particular client only. In other words, there may be a fixed number of objective tests to be deployed in a physiotherapy session; yet which tests to choose and how they are sequenced and conducted may vary from one client to another.

Similarly in social work, theories are broader generalisations but how they are realised in the professional social work practice is subject to ambient contextual factors such as a client's psychological needs and geographical resources available. The social work session report example at the very beginning of this chapter reveals that the STWsw chose to adopt a group teaching mode as a way to help those clients. However, an individualised approach may be more appropriate in another situation.

With the change of work approaches, the concomitant discourse practices in turn are subject to change. This means that although all practices have their roots in and emerge from historical development, it is as the result of re-contextualisation of old practices that new meaning is produced. Re-contextualisation of practices is characteristic of placement which involves knowledge transfer from academia to workplace:

> Carl: I think most of time. I think for learning physiotherapy studying physiotherapy. I think practical is very important because every time we learn just in our university and practice with our classmate. It's not a real patient and when in reality, I think face to face to the patient is very different because the situation will change a lot it's not so ideal and we try to perform our test on patient and besides our technique is not very good and not so sophisticated and I think it's a quite good experience for us. *(INT-CL-01)*

Carl is aware of the gap between educational experience, being very 'ideal', and real world which is a lot more complex (Paretti/McNair 2008). The meaning of having 'good' diagnostic techniques Carl experiences in an academic setting may be contested when facing real clients. In addition, what it means by 'good' is not internally validated but externally by the client as well as the clinical educator through their responses and reactions during the course of consultation. What they feel and perceive, which is also based on their own socio-cultural experiences, enter into the negotiation of the meaning of 'good'. In this respect, meaning is always situated and negotiated.

Compared with the professional world, validation of practices in placement is usually conducted in a more localised and immediate manner in the form of verbal and/or written feedback from the fieldwork supervisor/clinical educator. For newcomers, feedback is not only seen as a prompt for revisions; it is at the same time an imposition, as these apprentices are very unlikely to be resistant or act against the feedback in this social structure where legitimate knowledge is chiefly validated by the feedback giver, based on which academic progression is granted. For instance, in Example 2, the STWp writes *no DVT sign* under O/E; and yet the teacher corrects this to *DVT sign -ve*. The inappropriate form of representation may be due to STWp's over-generalisation from *no pain* and *no swelling*. Although the change may seem very negligible, it exerts an impact on the STWp's future documentation practice that when a sign of something is considered, '+ve' or '-ve' should be used in the representation.

Although multiple drafting provides very rich data for the analysis of negotiation of meaning via feedback, this is often not a common practice at work taking into account the pressing timeframe of placement work. One-off comments that prompt acceptance and later reflection are more typical and so a full picture of the roles of feedback cannot be attained without them. Chapter 6 will take a close look at the revision processes of Wayne, as he is the only informant who was engaged in multiple drafting.

4.2.4. Relational perspectives of knowledge co-construction

A person's existence is particularly dependent on others in a learning CoP. More specifically, for the placement contexts investigated in this project within which STWs find their way in to the professional world, clinical educators, supervisors, co-workers represent the history of respective practices of the expected standard (Davies 2006). In order to become a fuller participant, a novice needs to learn and sustain the practice. It is thus as the result of the co-participation of newcomers and expert members that a CoP continues its existence. Such a reflexive nature of discourse can be traced through the lexico-grammatical resources used to talk about placement work, for example, transitivity which describes the configuration of participants associated with different process types. The following is a description of the procedural content in a social work session:

> Every participant was encouraged to join the activities. During the outing, the student worker gave chances to the participants to express the feeling and gave freedom for them to prepare for a party.

In the above description, there are two main participants (*student worker* and *participants*). The student worker takes up the role of a *provider*, offering opportunities to participants to talk and make preparation for the party realised by the material process *gave* and *encouraged.*

In addition, the ways the STWs represent and address themselves in placement work (e.g., in the above example, the use of third person *student-worker* in social work reflective writing instead of the usual first person *I*) provides important information about the shaping of the hybrid identities, i.e., student-professional, in placement. During the participation in the process of negotiation of meaning, STWs realise their specific scope of work and level of competence through the linguistic choices they deploy, i.e. reification. In other words, participation makes apparent the identity of the STWs and their identities influence how they 'reify' their experiences linguistically. This dualistic relation forms the basis of my proposition of having a separate term, *role*, in addition to *identity*. Sarangi (2007, 2010) also criticises the fact that identities and roles were used indistinguishably "by scholars within and across different analytical domains with overlapping ontological and epistemological trajectories" (2010: 33). However, these two terms have different meanings in this project which merits a further discussion. My use of the term 'roles' is similar to role-expectations or identity-at-work (Sarangi/Roberts 1999) and Goffman's (1971) dramaturgical metaphor 'performer' in the sense that we both treat roles as a functional and 'performing' entity with reference to the context presented. The term *identities* is used in this study as simply a separate category to mean the socially-determined identities of these STWs, i.e. as student-professionals. This distinction is in line with the perspectives of the role theory (Biddle 1986: 68):

> [R]ole theory concerns one of the most important characteristics of social behaviour – the fact that human beings behave in ways that are different and predictable depending on their respective social identities and the situation.

In the first place, the separate use of the two terms can avoid confusion in the forthcoming discussion chapters. For example, when I write 'the role of STWs…', I am referring to the work and responsibilities at the workplace rather than their actual writing processes. More importantly, the separation further makes an important theoretical point as to how identities influence the STWs' roles and in turn how roles influence text generation which reflects the STWs' identities, as illustrated in Figure 4.

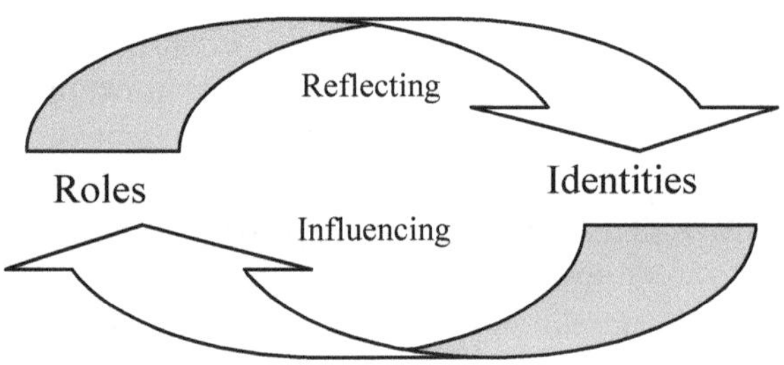

Figure 4. Roles and identities relationship in this study.

Following from these lines of argument, these STWs embrace three identities in placements: *student*, *student-professional* and *professional*. Concomitantly, they are *learners* acquiring relevant professional knowledge and take up the role of *practitioners* offering consultations to clients. In other words, they have the hybrid roles of *learners-practitioners*. These intertwining properties constitute a triadic role-identity relationship (see Figure 5). The distribution of these roles-identities is not always even but depends on the degree of legitimate participation granted. For example, towards the early stage of their academic study, it is expected that the role of 'student' will be more prominent than that of 'professional' in the placement, while it is the other way round when the students are approaching the end of their degree courses.

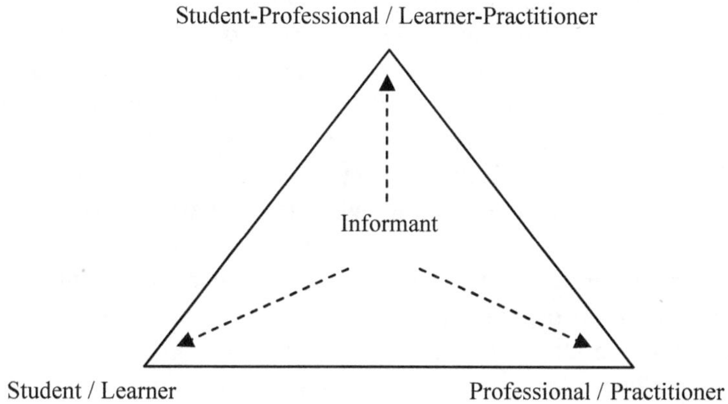

Figure 5. Triadic role-identity relationships of informants in placement.

4.3. Key contributing factors to knowledge acquisition in placement

The sections above have conceptualised placement as a form of LPP, highlighting the dynamic construction of such a social structure. This section identifies relevant contributing factors that play a role in knowledge acquisition in placement from the perspective of student workers. The immediate goal of STWs in placement is to perform satisfactorily in order to progress to the next stage of academic and professional life; to achieve this, STWs need to demonstrate acquisition of knowledge. Bhatia (2005) has identified eight key contributing factors to the acquisition of professional expertise, namely, *education knowledge, training experience, discursive competence, discursive practices, apprenticeship, legitimate peripheral participation, language for specific purposes* and *communication skills training,* subsumed under two broader categories of discursive knowledge and disciplinary knowledge. While all these factors are readily transferrable to the context of placement, two new factors are needed in order to fully understand the pursuit of such enterprise which centres around learning. They are *reflective practice* and *boundary objects*, which will become the focal areas in this section. Both *apprenticeship* and *legitimate peripheral participation* have been discussed in the previous sections and so they will not be dealt with again here.

These STWs are in their different stages in their academic studies, meaning that they bring with them various degrees of *education knowledge* to the professional context. For example, the two physiotherapy informants are in their second year of study while the two social work informants are in their first year of study. The different academic stages to which the STWs belong also shape the training experience, for example, the degree of autonomy in offering professional advice and the tasks required to handle. It is no doubt that *discursive competence* and *discursive practices* are crucial to the success of placement learning, with the former focusing on the ability to dovetail disciplinary content and discipline-specific language to effect actions and the latter focusing on the choices of appropriate genre to satisfy institutional goals.

The two interrelated contributors proposed by Bhatia – *language for specific purposes* and *communication skills* – deserve a lot more discussion, taking into account the rather complicated diglossic situation in Hong Kong (Poon 2004), in spite of the fact that this issue was touched upon briefly in Chapter 2. The different statuses and functions ascribed to English and Cantonese Chinese in the city have implications for the placement training program. While English is adopted as the medium of instruction and documentation, Cantonese Chinese is a primary vernacular form used to communicate with the majority of clients and other professionals. This disparity poses another dimension of challenge to second language (L2) novices as a translation process is involved from "orality" (Tsang 2007: 51) (being the L1 of the informants) to literacy (L2) as suggested by Tsang (2007: 53-54),

> Couched in the form of conventional university courses, social work education requires students to do a lot of reading and writing. Even in the practicum, or fieldwork placement, that forms an integral part of a social work course, students are accountable for their work mainly through written proposals, reports, reflective journals, evaluation reports and other similar devices… Social work students with Afro-Caribbean or Asian ethnic origin may be bilingual, speaking in their mother tongue and writing in the English language. They may think in terms of, and feel at ease with speaking, their mother tongue. Yet they have to write and account for their practice and learning in written English. The spoken and written languages represent the two sides of self-identity (Rai 2004: 156); the former is to be denied and suppressed in the study of a social work course.

The above line of argument suggests that the provision of university English enhancement courses offered by language instructors contributes to the novices' success in placement. Disciplinary experts/ academics, as pointed out in Carl's reflective journal, play a crucial role in the enhancement of communication skills. One kind of communication skills Carl learnt from the placement was that he needed to be assertive when expressing opinions:

> Before the placement, I have no concept on these *(assertiveness)* skills. I found it quite useful for me. I think it is very important to all of the professions, especially physiotherapist…. If I show certain assertive behaviour such as saying no, making request to change our decision and expressing my protocol more detail and with reasons. May be our answer to our CE will be protocol B. *(RF_TXT-CL-02)*

The value of *reflection* in the learning process has been highlighted by many researchers (Kember 2001; McClure 2008). Reflection goes beyond problematising solutions or performance; it serves as a bridge between theory and practice, between pedagogical and professional practices, turning it into "learning situations, and so the practitioners can continue to learn, grow and develop in and through practice" (Jarvis 1992: 180). Reflective practice (see Chapters 5 and 7 for details) therefore is emphasised in all the placement contexts investigated in this study, with such practice being reified in a discursive form through STWs' engagement in reflective writing.

Another important contributor to the acquisition is the presence of "boundary object", a term used by Star & Griesemer (1989: 393) to represent an object having different meanings when situated in different social worlds with the significance of maintaining intersecting coherence:

> This (*Boundary object*) is an analytic concept of those scientific objects which both inhabit several intersecting social worlds… and satisfy informational requirement of them. Boundary objects are objects which are both plastic enough to adapt to local needs, and the constraints of the several parties employing them, yet robust enough to maintain a common identity across sites… They have different meanings in different social worlds but their structure is common enough to more than one world to make them recognizable, a means of translation.

In the context of placement, texts produced are essentially boundary objects as they coordinate perspectives along the overlapping zone of the two CoPs, academic and professional, as suggested by Ketter and Hunter (2003). Such boundary objects play a crucial role in helping STWs see knowledge transfer of the two CoPs as being coherent rather than disjointed. Some of the texts in placement are sent back to the academic department to which the STWs belong as a proof of work done and occasionally as a validation of knowledge acquired. For the professional world, the major concern of these texts produced lies in the justification of ensuing actions through assessments. The texts will then be kept in filing cabinet for future record. What connect the two worlds are shared terminologies, assessment methods and procedures, values and interpretation. In physiotherapy placement, a STWp keeps a record of clients' self-reported health conditions, results of objective tests, proposed treatment plan and goals according to the documentation practice comprehensible to the physiotherapist community. For instance, regarding the representation of ROM in Example 2,

<u>ROM:</u>

AROM			R	L
	Knee	F	√	95°
		E	√	0°
	Ankle	DF	√	limited
		PF	√	limited
		IV	√	√
		EV	√	√

The cross-sectional arrangement between parameters (e.g., *Knee F vs R*, *Ankle PF vs L*), and the combination of paralinguistic signs (*√*), degree of motion (*95°*) and linguistic form (*limited*) are standardised ways of representation in physiotherapy documentation, which are recognised in both the academic and professional contexts. The record goes into the file of the client's health history to be read by other health professionals who follow up the case, and at the same time it is treated as an academic assignment assessed by the clinical educator and approved by the academics at the university. In this respect, texts produced in placement, being the boundary objects, "help in the constitution of spaces where discussion and debate can begin and relevant information exchanged" (Gibbon 2005).

These contributing factors play a significant role in novices' enculturation to the professional world. Based on the multidimensional model presented by Bhatia (2005), an extended version with reference to the discussion above is illustrated graphically in Figure 6.

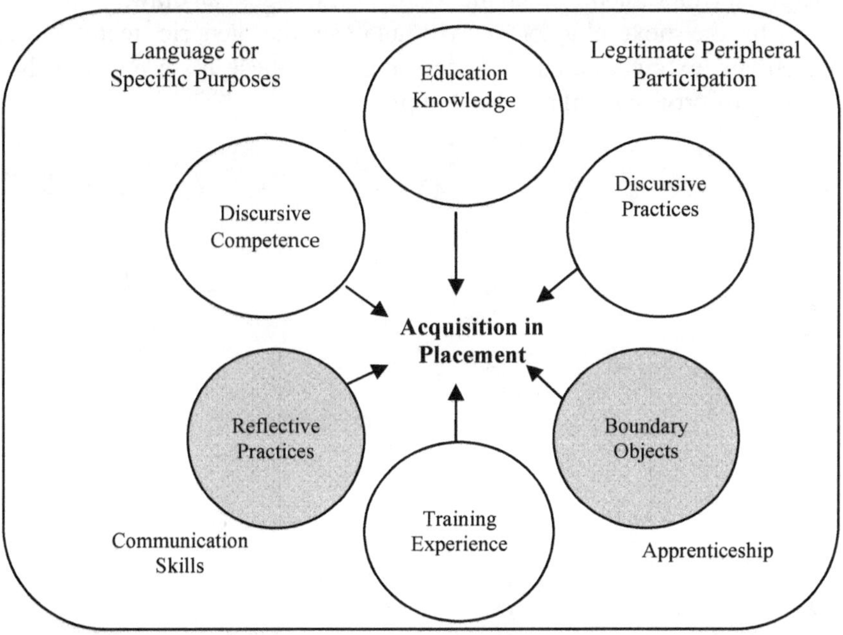

Figure 6. Key contributors to acquisition in placement (an extended version based on Bhatia (2005)).

4.4. Concluding remarks

In this chapter, I have justified the setting up of the following three analysis chapters with respect to the conceptualisation of placement as a form of legitimate peripheral participation, and as a social and discursive structure: Chapter 5 on interactions between genre-based practices, Chapter 6 on the roles of feedback in drawing novices towards disciplinary practices and Chapter 7 on identities and roles in placement practices. Each chapter therefore contributes to a critical dimension of placement viewed from three angles, i.e. task-designers (expert-members), task-consumers (student workers) and the interaction between these two.

I have also identified two new contributors, *reflective practice* and *boundary objects*, which facilitate the enculturation of novices in addition to the eight contributors identified by Bhatia. They provide a frame of referential entities upon which the following analyses can draw.

In the next chapter, I will analyse the generic features of placement texts collected to understand how these texts mediate the learning of professional actions and practices.

5 Genre and Practice: Interactions of Genre-Based Practices in Placement

> Genres are intimately linked to a discipline's methodology, and they package information in ways that conform to a discipline's norms, values, and ideology. Understanding the genres of written communication in one's field is, therefore, essential to professional success. (Berkenkotter/Huckin 1995: 1)

The traditional notion of genre aligns communicative purpose and discourse structure of texts through identifying "a set of formally definable text features that certain texts have in common across various contexts" (Russell 1997a: 513). The major purpose of undertaking genre analysis, following this view, then was oriented to pedagogy and sought 'stability' and "routine operation" (Russell 1997a: 516). For example, the Create a Research Space (CARS) model posited by Swales (1990) helps writers structure the introductory section of a research article. Bhatia (1994, 2005), nevertheless, contested this simplistic view of genre, criticising the fact that this only takes into account text-internal factors. Having realised that professional texts are often embedded within more than one genre, i.e., genre mixing or interdiscursivity, Bhatia raised the question of genre integrity, arguing that genres can only be fully understood by considering both text-internal and text-external factors. His work on genre integrity has practical relevance to this study because placement texts, accomplished by STWs who assume hybrid identities as student-professionals, exhibit the characteristics of both academic and professional genres as mentioned in the last chapter. In Chapter 4, I used two texts, the social work session report and physiotherapy Sci Clinical Teaching Report, to argue for the need to have a wider interpretation of placement genres. In this chapter, using the same type of texts together with other placement work-related documentation (WR_TXT), I take a step further to look at how texts, from the perspective of design and consumption, draw novices into the disciplinary practices, with the assumption that learning takes place with the use of these placement texts. Texts constructed by expert members reflect the genre expectations and thus provide tangible linguistic evidence as to how texts mediate and facilitate STWs' learning. By comparing the genres and the engagement in genre construction, i.e., discourse practice, of the two main disciplines in question, this chapter aims to answer the following research question:

1b. What are the roles of genres and practices in placement?

The analysis will centre around three main areas, namely, the lexico-grammatical and multimodal resources deployed, the organisation of texts and the context of writing, which are in line with the three perspectives of genre acquisition, i.e., textual, cognitive and social, which were mentioned in the previous chapter.

5.1. Textualisation

Placement writing is a complex act which is situated in two very different socio-cultural contexts, i.e., academic and professional worlds, bringing different sets of assumptions, values and identities into the use and interpretation of lexico-grammatical and multimodal resources.

5.1.1. Lexico-grammatical choices

Both physiotherapy and social work exhibit the characteristics of having discipline-specific academic terms in their placement texts. These terms become 'professionalised' phrases as shown in the manipulation of the grammatical structure. Complex nominal groups are commonly found in physiotherapy texts while phrases of high lexical density (Stubb 2001; Glave 1998) are found in the social work placement texts.

5.1.1.1. Physiotherapy

5.1.1.1.1. Use of discipline-specific lexical terms

In the first instance, lexical choices in the placement work documentation play a fundamental role in directing STWps to the appropriate disciplinary methodologies:

Example 1*(WR_TXT-CL-01)*

a) Sci Clinical Teaching Report *(the name of a documentation)*
b) Objective Examination / Tests
c) … initial hypothesis to the source (s) and the cause(s) of the symptoms
d) Comparable sign

Example 2 *(WR_TXT-SN-07)*

a) Outline the systematic way you would read an orthopaedic patient's X-ray
b) Remember the five stages of fracture healing, at what stage during the healing process would you consider commencing active movement of a joint adjacent to a fracture site?

Example 3 *(WR_TXT-CL-01)*

a) Suggest any possible predisposing factors to the patient's conditions
b) Describe three different types of internal fixation that may be used to manage fractures of the proximal femur. Include the type of fracture that would indicate the use of each IF device and how the physiotherapy management would be influenced.

Example 4 *(WR_TXT-CL-01)*

a) Rate the irritability of the disorder
b) List six safety consideration prior to mobilising an orthopaedic patient for the first time
c) List the structure to be considered as possible sources for each area of symptom

The above underlined phrases and expressions found from the work-related documentation share the commonalities in that they signify the epistemology of the field which is one of scientific (*Sci*), emphasising observation (comparable *sign*), testing (*examination/test*), retesting (*initial, hypothesis)* and experimental data (*objective test*). Examples 2 (a) and (b) highlight the importance of correct sequences in treating a client during the course of physiotherapy consultations (*systematic, stages*). In addition, the availability of multiple sources of complaints or treatment options (*possible, three different types)* together with the use of modals of possibility (*may be used*) in Example 3 indicate the need to make decision on selections based on the various tests conducted. Modals also imply tentative conclusions/outcomes as a result of the decisions made (*would be influenced*). The imperative structures headed by the verbs *list* and *rate* in Example 4 imply a mathematical and systematic representation of information respectively. These also tie in with the fundamental practice of physiotherapists who always work around numerical data and undertake systematic analyses before offering treatment options.

5.1.1.1.2. Use of complex nominal groups for case construction

As mentioned in Chapter 3, problem-based learning is a popular teaching method in Hong Kong. Problem question/case writing is therefore a critical component in professional training (Naumes/Naumes 2006). Analysing the grammatical structure reveals how cases are constructed and framed within the context of targeted learning. Example 4(b), which is taken from a worksheet STWps needs to complete during placement, presents a complex grammatical structure with the presence of three nominal groups:

> List [six safety consideration][prior to mobilising an orthopaedic patient][for the first time]

The head noun *consideration* in the first nominal group is pre-modified by the numerative *six* followed by the classifier *safety*. In the prepositional phrase that follows, a gerundive noun phrase with *orthopaedic* classifying *patient* headed by the gerund *mobilising* is preceded by the preposition *prior to*. The prepositional phrase at the end further refines the description by specifying the number of occurrence *the first time*. A combination of these complex nominal groups in a clause succinctly presents all the relevant conditions needed to be taken into account. In this case, the conditions foregrounded are the sequential and temporal dimensions expressed by *prior to* and *the first time* respectively. Two important rhetorical functions of such a construction can be identified. In terms of professional practice, STWs need to be alerted to the interactions of all these seemingly trivial yet critical conditions in treating a client; failing to respond to these conditions may incur serious consequences on the client and/or their professional standing. In terms of pedagogical practice, such a condensed and focused description of conditions offers virtually no leeway for interpretation other than the intended one. The STWp's answer to this case therefore must be within a very limited scope, through which targeted learning is achieved. A similar grammatical construction is exhibited in Example 4 (c):

List [the structure to be considered][as possible source][for each area of symptom]

The complex nominal group is formed by two noun phrases and one prepositional phrase. The first noun phrase is headed by the noun *the structure* followed by the verbal group *to be considered*, specifying the main information required. Together with the second noun phrase with the conjunction *as* and the noun *source* modified by the classifier *possible,* the prepositional phrase featuring the preposition *for* and the noun phrase with pre-modification *each area of symptom* further refines the information to be provided by the STWps. It is also noteworthy that the generality of the nouns used in this example such as *structure, source* and *symptom* in fact necessitate the presence of pre-/post-modifications in order to confine the meaning construed and the description of relevant parameters.

5.1.1.1.3. Use of questions for case construction

In addition to imperative statements, another common pedagogical practice adopted to elicit information is the use of questions. The following are some examples extracted from the worksheets STWps need to complete:

Example 5 *(WR_TXT-CL-01)*

a) Where would you position yourself (w.r.t. the patient) when mobilising a Day 1 TKR patient on a rollator? Why?
b) What factors would you consider with care for the objective examination (e.g. pain, irritability of the symptoms, stiffness, recent fracture, latency of the onset of symptoms, possibility of cord involvement, etc.)?

c) What would you expect the weight bearing status for the following orthopaedic patients to be? You may use the abbreviations NWB, PWB, FWB or WBAT (weight bearing as tolerated).
   - Day 2 Total Knee Replacement (cemented)……… _________
   - Day 1 fracture ankle in Backslab ………………… _________

The above examples share the commonality that the information required of STWps is phrased in an interrogative form. The use of the personal pronoun *you* (*would you position, would you consider, would you expect*), which appears to go against the impersonal nature of scientific language (e.g. the use of passives), emphasises a more personal and unique experience in a consultation session. In addition, all the processes are pre-modified by the modal *would*, suggesting hypothetical situations which are subject to changes in real situations.

Similar to using imperative forms, questions must be set as specifically as possible to make learning effective. Such specification is indeed necessary for pedagogical processes so that knowledge can be assessed. Consider the lexico-grammar of Example 5(a) again:

> Where would you position yourself (w.r.t. the patient) when mobilising a Day 1 TKR patient on a rollator? Why?

The WH-interrogative begins typically with a WH-element, which in this case is *where*, followed by the mood structure with the finite *would* and subject *you*. The residue provides more substantial information about the topic, including the prompt about orientations presented by the predicator *position* and complement *yourself* as well as the circumstantial adjunct of time with the following structure:

[when]	[mobilising a Day 1 TKR patient]	[on a rollator]
WH-element	*verb phrase*	*prepositional phrase*

The adjunct contains a WH-element, a verb phrase and a prepositional phrase. The verb phrase is headed by the verb in a non-finite form *mobilising* and the classifier *a Day 1 TKR* to pre-modify *patient*, followed by a prepositional phrase formed by a preposition *on* and the noun phrase *a rollator*. All these elements provide a very specific and well-defined context to the question. Most importantly, this specification involves STWps' knowing discipline-specific categorisation in terms of temporality (*Day 1*), the type of client (*TKR patient*) and the rehabilitation equipment (*on a rollator).*

Apart from contributing to the grammatical structure of the sentence, all the extracts under Example 5 provide the specific information requested in the form of an 'add-on' component. This information is put either in parenthesis (e.g., *w.r.t the patient, pain, irritability of the symptoms ... possibility of cord involvement, etc., cemented*) or presented as a stand-alone sentence as in Example 5(c):

> You may use the abbreviations NWB, PWB, FWB or WBAT (weight bearing as tolerated).

The use of the root modal *may* in the above sentence seems to suggest that permission is granted to STWps to use the simplified form of representation. In fact, it may be considered the preferred representation given the limited space available. In addition, the provision of suggested answers as *NWB, PWB, FWB or WBAT* has reformulated the question expecting an open-ended answer to one that requires a selection from choices. Apparently, the STWps learn and/or consolidate the use of discipline-specific abbreviations, with the full form provided for those expressions which may be new to novices (*weight bearing as tolerated* in this case).

5.1.1.2. Social work

5.1.1.2.1. Use of narrowly defined descriptors

As compared with physiotherapy texts, social work texts produced in placement are characteristically qualitative, highly evaluative and self-reflective. While the former two characteristics are applicable broadly to most practitioners in the social work field, training self-reflective social workers is one of the main pedagogical aims in placement.

In addition to having a form for filling in the details about the session conducted with clients, STWsws are also presented with a checklist to evaluate groupwork skills (see Figure 1 for an excerpt from the form and Appendix B for the full version). The checklist contains three columns including a list of evaluative items, STWsws' self-rating of skills discharged against the evaluative items and self-reflection. The pedagogical nature of the task is realised in and construed through the list of evaluative items, most of which contains a broader category constructed by a gerund phrase (e.g. *linking members' communication*) followed by a more narrowly defined descriptor (e.g. *searching for a feeling link or an information link*). By working through this checklist, STWsws are directed to the appropriate disciplinary methodologies, practices, expectations, and roles within the context of professional social work. However, the work done which is expressed by the conceptual subheadings (e.g. *Analysing skills*) in the checklist may pose difficulties to novices as these academic terms are being re-contextualised in a workplace setting, and yet these STWsws lack the exposure to a variety of real-life professional scenarios. Detailed and well-defined descriptors construed by appropriate lexico-grammatical choices are therefore necessary in drawing their attention to the relevant experience in placements.

In terms of reflection, the checklist prompts STWsws to think what is lacking (e.g. those items without a score) and what needs improvement (e.g. those items with a low score), which are the mental activities that reflective social work practitioners always engage in in their professional work.

Facilitating group processes **促進技巧**		
Skills	**Grading**	**Self-reflection**
5/. Involving group members **協助組員投入** verbal invitation, minimal encouragement		
6/. Attending to others **專注技巧** non-verbal such as eye contact, body position and verbal behavior that convey empathy, respect, warmth, trust…		
7/. Expressing self **表達和自我披露** helping members to express their views and feelings, worker's self-disclosure in suitable moments		

Figure 1. An excerpt from the group skills evaluation form.

5.1.1.2.2. Use of phrasal forms for 'readers' economy'

Taking a closer look at the processes used to construct the categories and descriptors can give an idea of how knowledge is packaged and how knowledge transfer is promoted in this text. Table 1 shows that the work of a social worker involves various kinds of actions (e.g. *providing feedback to members, establishing positive group norms*) and encourages active involvement (e.g. *helping members to participate an activity*) with clients and yet maintains a professional-client power relationship (e.g. *coaching, disciplining*).

Material		**Verbal**		**Mental**	
Involve	Provide	Express	Describe	Attend (to)	Validate
Help	Model	Clarify	Summarize	Focus	Break down
Establish	Rehearse	Request	Convey	Identify	Reframe
Conduct	Coach	Question	Elaborate	Synthesize	Redefine
Link	Discipline	Probe	Repeat	Cultivate	View
Search	Design	Point out	Present	Support	Assert
Resolve	Participate	Respond	Invite	Develop	
Share	Find	Encourage		Redirect	
Interact	Accomplish	Suggest		Reflect	
Fulfil		Affirm		Lead	

Table 1. Processes used in the social work checklist.

A range of grammatical structures can be found from the checklist, with the commonality that they are all in phrasal forms. Such a reduced form has a crucial pedagogic function, which is to make the phrases dense with informational content. This can be expressed by "Lexical Density" to indicate the percentage of lexical words in a text following the formula: 100 x L/T where L stands for the number of lexical words and T represents the total number of words of a text (Gilmore 2004). The high lexical density (72.85) of the checklist indicates a very high informational content construed through content-related words with concrete meaning. This focuses STWsws' attention on key attributes and in terms of work efficiency, contributes to 'readers' economy' given the tight working schedule these

STWsws have in placement. Such an economy of phrasal forms is realised grammatically as follows:

Example 6
(a) [PROCESS: MATERIAL] providing [GOAL] feedback [CIRCUMSTANCE] to members

(b) [PROCESS: VERBAL] describing [VERBIAGE] patterns of the group's interaction

(c) [PROCESS: MENTAL] cultivate [PHENOMENON] a supportive culture in the group

(d) [PROCESS: MATERIAL] helping [GOAL] members to participate an activity…
→ [PROCESS: MATERIAL] to participate [GOAL] an activity…

(e) [PROCESS: MATERIAL] disciplining

The most common grammatical structure deployed in the construction of the checklist is a *process* followed by the recipient of the action which can be animate or inanimate (*GOAL/ VERBIAGE/PHENOMENON)* as in Example 6(a) to (c). This is obviously tied to the placement work, in which how something is done is as important as what is achieved. In some cases, to further elaborate the context of situation, a circumstantial adjunct (e.g., *to members*) is added as in Example 6(a). In Example 6(d), the additional information is construed through the second process (*participate*). On the contrary, Example 6(e) indicates the simplest grammatical form possible, with the process (*disciplining*) realised in the gerundive form. This is possibly because of the semantic richness of this process which does not require other grammatical properties to define its context of use.

5.1.1.2.3. A guided reflection

The detailed descriptors under each subcategory shown in Figure 2 build up a frame of reference for STWsws as regards what aspects of professional work are critical and worth deeper thoughts. Not only do these descriptors provide a structure of thinking, they supply lexical resources to frame reflection. Such resources seem to be particularly useful for Wayne who is weak in the use of English and has a very limited range of vocabulary.

Data collection and assessment 資料整理和評估		
Skills	**Grading**	**Self-reflection**
9/. Requesting information, questioning and probing skills 發問和探查、搜集	*3*	*The worker clearly know what thing need to do, and before the group, he do some information and try the possible for the game, unfortunately , the worker misunderstand and calculation for group member and each task's time. Therefore, each part are overtime,*
10/. Analyzing skills 分析技巧 pointing out patterns, identifying gaps in the data, and establishing mechanisms or plan	*2-3*	
11/. Synthesizing skills 綜合技巧 providing feedback to members, describing patterns of the group's interaction	*2-3*	*The group interaction in the group mate however, the interaction with worker, is not too strong, it will make use of the who actively member to let the focus on the worker.*
12/. Summarizing skill 撮要 to present the core of what has been said and provide members an opportunity to reflect on the problem.	*3*	*The group member have an opportunity to self-reflection, and thing about the unfair problem, however, the worker can't join the discussion and the leading was changed to the student. In the next time, the worker show the strength*

Figure 2. Guided reflection (WR_TXT-WW-04).

Example 7

11/. Synthesizing skills 綜合技巧 providing feedback to members, describing patterns of the <u>group's interaction</u>	*The <u>group interaction</u> in the <u>group mate</u> however, the <u>interaction</u> with worker, is not [too strong], it will make use of the who actively member to let the focus on the worker.*
12/. Summarizing skill 撮要 to present the core of what has been said and <u>provide members an opportunity to reflect on the problem</u>.	*<u>The group member</u> [<u>have an opportunity</u>] <u>to self-reflection</u>, and thing about the [<u>unfair</u>] <u>problem</u>, however, the worker can't join the discussion and the leading was changed to the student. In the next time, the worker show the strength*

Although Wayne's self-reflection contains many grammatical errors which at times impede comprehension, he manages to highlight all the relevant issues such as *group interactions*, *opportunity to self-reflection* and *problem* required in the checklist by providing simple responses in terms of degree (*not too strong*), presence (*have an opportunity*) and categorisation (*unfair*). Such a rudimentary form of "guided reflection" (Williams 2002; Sutton/Dalley 2008), I argue, acts as a springboard to the later more elaborate and dyadic intervention from the expert members by means of written feedback and face-to-face conferencing.

5.1.2. Multimodal resources

In addition to textual representations, the use of other multimodal forms in fields such as physiotherapy is crucial and is considered a valid genre resource. Social work, on the other hand, does not rely much on multimodal resources to make meaning.

5.1.2.1. Physiotherapy

The use of visuals such as diagrams, in the case of physiotherapy, is more or less taken-for-granted. As mentioned in Chapter 3 (see Section 3.5.3.2), health sciences' students are constantly exposed to visual data in their academic work. In placement, STWps are always presented with human-body diagrams. Sometimes they are required to indicate on the diagram which part of a client's body is the area of concern so that other practitioners who follow up the case can immediately focus the attention on that body part. STWps also need to rely on diagrams to aid assessment. For example, in one of the cases, a group of STWps is required to calculate the impairment level of the client. STWps are given a chart labelled 'standard neurological classification of spinal cord injury' (Figure 3) containing a diagram of a human body divided into many regions; each region is represented by a code. Based on the diagram on the chart, STWps then perform various tests on patient's key muscle and sensory points and record the results in numerical forms (e.g., 2 represents 'active movement, gravity eliminated' for key muscle and 'normal' for key sensory point). Adding up all the numbers generates three scores, namely, *motor score, pin prick score* and *light touch score*. In virtue of these scores and other necessary information, the STWps are able to determine the 'ASIA impairment scale', in lay terms, the class/ seriousness of a patient's neurological injury. The task makes the STWps aware of the importance of multimodal literacy to the work of a professional physiotherapist.

5.1.2.2. Social work

The use of multimodal resources in discursive practices of social work appears to be of a lower priority of concern than physiotherapy. This is not surprising because of the soft, multifaceted nature of the discipline which deals with many different areas of social issues. These issues are often very complex, which can rarely be represented in forms other than textual.

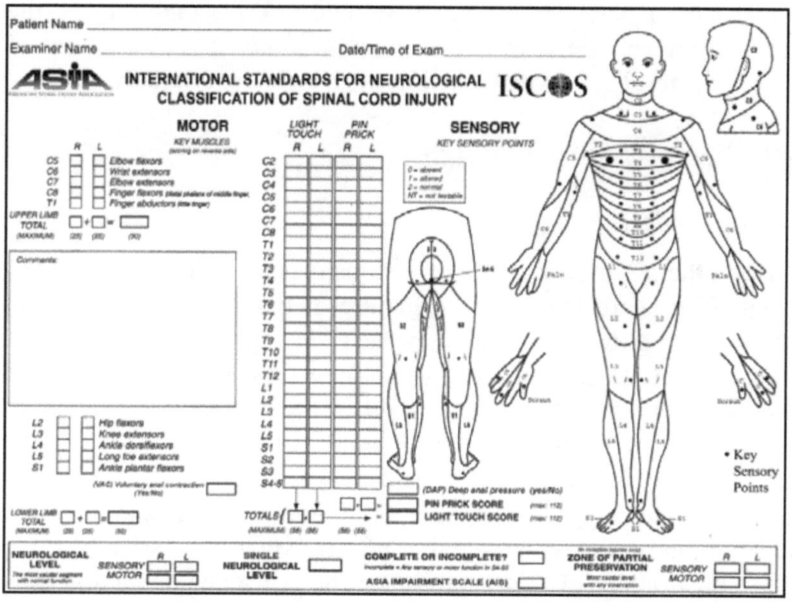

Figure 3. A chart STWps use to assess a patient's neurological injury (American Spinal Injury Association (ASIA), revised and reprinted 2011).

5.2. Organisation

Simply put, organisation addresses the cognitive patterning of a text. Although it seems that placement texts may not show strict move-step generic structure as other well-defined genres such as research articles, they are 'stabilised as they are' in their schematic structures which enact and facilitate learning emerging from the historical development of work practices.

5.2.1. Rhetorical organisation

The organisation of placement texts is not arbitrary but is intended to achieve certain rhetorical functions, i.e., rhetorical organisation. In the physiotherapy text analysed, the moves embedded in the organisation intends to scaffold STWps with situated cognition and facilitates the demonstration of knowledge. As for social work placement texts, the focus appears to show the stakeholders a coherent structure of STWsws' professional work over time with reflection built in.

5.2.1.1. Physiotherapy

5.2.1.1.1. Problem-oriented organisation

In a physiotherapy placement, the various discursive forms presented to the STWps share the common feature of being problem-oriented, which is "a highly organised approach that encourages a precise method of documenting the logical thought processes of health care professionals" (Willis 1996: 47). In other words, the organisation of reifications is not random; instead it guides the STWps through the examination of clients in a logical way. Take the *Sci Clinical Teaching Report* (Figure 4) written by Simon as an example; the documentation begins with the basic information of the patient and the name of the student physiotherapist. In the real documentation, it is much more formalised with patient's demographic details to be read by the professional physiotherapist. The subjective examination (S/E) documents patient's self-reporting details of injury or complaints:

Example 8 *(WR_TXT-SN-01)*
S/E
History of injury: On 11/9/02, he fell down from height when repairing lift #C6-7
Medical/surgical management: 23/9/02 operation was done (ant. spinal fusion knocking plate gt) C5-7
Rehabilitation: 10/02 admitted to KH PT Dept.
Social history: take care by family members, applying for public housing
Present complaints: can't control LL, UL weakness

Example 8 shows the information gathered from the subjective examination of a client. The arrangement of the subheadings presents a logical flow of information across a timeline, from the patient's medical history to current situation. This interaction between past and present seems to make sense to the STWp, reflected in his use of past and present verb tenses respectively:

He fell down from height (past tense)
Operation was done (past tense)
can't control LL (present tense)

The objective examination (O/E) is more complex and involves a combination of STWps' visual, mathematical and ultimately textual representation. In this stage of the consultation, STWps will conduct various tests on the client and observe client's responses. The data are mainly quantified in the form of X/5, supplemented with qualitative description when necessary. An example of O/E has been described in the previous section with reference to Figure 3 and information is required to be presented in a tabulated form as shown in Figure 5.

	Passive	Active
Lower limbs		
Upper limbs		
Other body parts		

Figure 5. O/E in tabulated format in Sci Clinical teaching report.

SCI CLINICAL TEACHING REPORT

Name of patient: XXXX
Name of physiotherapy student: YYYY

S/E:
History of injury: On 11/9/02, he fell down from height when repairing lift #C6-7
Medical/surgical management: 23/9/02 operation was done (ant. spinal fusion, knocking plate gt) C5-7
Rehabilitation: 10/02 admitted to KH PT Dept.
Social history: take care by family members, applying for public housing
Present complaints: can't control LL, UL weakness

O/E:
Muscle power – chart
Sensation – body chart
ROM (passive/active)

ROM:

	Passive	**Active**
Lower Limbs	N/A	N/A
Upper Limbs	N/A	N/A
Other body parts	N/A	N/A

Functions:
oral care: independent
feeding: independent
dressing: dependent
sitting: needs assistance (poor stability)
transfer (bed to chair): needs assistance
wheelchair movement: independent
toileting: urination – catheterization
defecation – needs drugs
coughing without use of abdominal and intercostals muscles

Neurological level (ASIA): A

Short term goals:
decrease LL spasticity
increase UL muscle strength
train sitting balance
increase muscle length of hamstrings
prevent pressure sore
improve bed mobility
reduce depression

Figure 4. Sci Clinical Teaching Report (WR_TXT-SN-01).

At a later stage of the placement, STWps are not given any form to complete but a blank sheet. Such a cross-sectional presentation of information is still adhered to. Another example of O/E is illustrated below in Figure 6 *(WR_TXT-SN-02)*.

O/E: - Vital signs stable
- On rediav drain
- Homan sign -ve

ROM:

	R	L
AROM ankle DF	+10°	√
PF	30°	√

SMMT:

	R	L
Quad	√	√
Bicep	5/5	5/5

Figure 6. An excerpt from a STWp's Clinical Report without subheadings provided.

Under the subheading of Functions as shown in Figure 4, the STWp put down the level of ability in performing various daily activities such as sitting and toileting. The rhetorical function of this is to further build up the evidence to justify the treatment goal. The presentation is therefore straightforward, with the daily activities (e.g., *feeding*) followed immediately by the assessment of the level of dependence expressed mainly by an adjective (e.g., *independent*) or a verb phrase (e.g., *needs assistance*).

On the basis of the above information, the STWp devises the short term goals. Although this subheading is put under the O/E, I consider that this constitutes part of the treatment; stating and explaining to patients realistic goals to achieve in a short period of time is of paramount importance. The language used in this section is clearly reader-oriented, aiming at demonstrating knowledge to the expert members (e.g., clinical educator): it is highly specialised with the use of discipline-specific abbreviations (e.g., *UL*, *LL*) and terminologies/phrases (e.g. *spasticity*, *pressure sore*).

If we compare the organisation of the report and the generic stages of a professional physiotherapy session outlined in Figure 2 in Chapter 3, it can be seen that they more or less map on each other (Figure 7). In this respect, by constantly participating in the discursive practice STWps will be able to scaffold the cognitive skills required of professional physiotherapists, i.e. sequencing. This has been made explicit to the STWps:

Simon:	yes because we we al-also learn the way of the sequence of how to recording down the information and the rate… because this form, the sequence is very logical and the part put on the first is the things we will performed first. If we we haven't the chance to using this form we may do the task in a sequence that which is not so good
Researcher:	ah ah good you mean the sequence is very important for your as a physiotherapist
Simon:	because the sequencing, if use a appropriate sequencing, we can save more time and and some task is quite demanding will put to the later stage because we want to do some simple task. Don't make the patient feel too tired.
Researcher:	okay ah so actually this form is carefully designed
Simon:	yes
Researcher:	okay so, you told me that you learn how to document patient in similar way. Right? I mean, the sequencing, did you learn, I mean, during your course, I mean, you are second year students, did you learn how to document patient's record?
Simon:	they haven't any formal class to teach us
Researcher:	but this kind of training actually helps, I mean, you to understand. Okay this sequence is all is quite important
Simon:	hmm[7] *(INT-SN-02)*

7 Simon's response *hmm* signifies agreement.

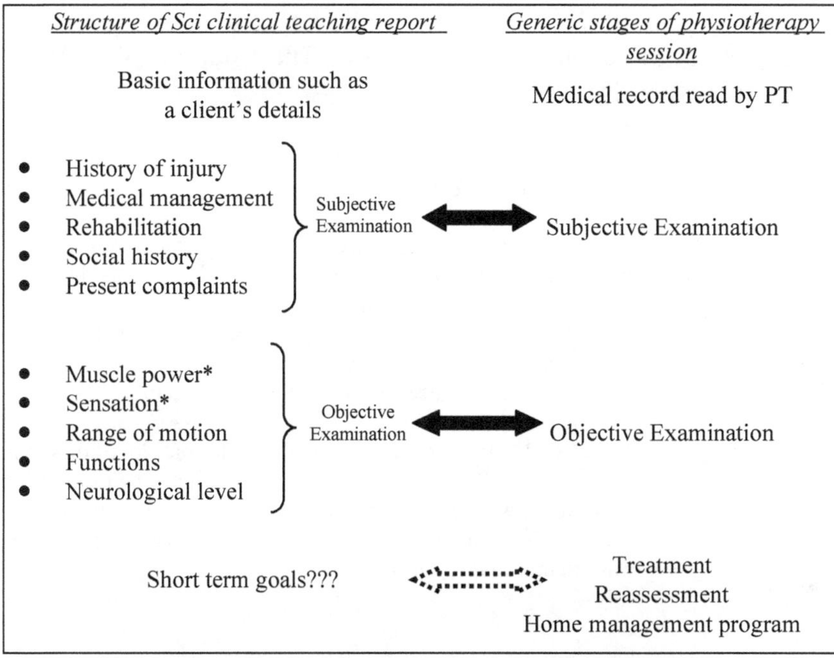

Note. * The results of these two examinations are recorded in a chart
** Stages more or less mapping on each other
*** The placement does not contain the whole treatment process

Figure 7. A comparison between structure of the Sci Clinical Teaching Report and generic stages of a physiotherapy session.

The analysis and interview excerpts above together suggest that there is an interaction among discourse, pedagogical and professional practices. Simon seems to realise the assumptions, values and ideology invested in the construction and interpretation of the text presented; and yet at the same time he immediately associates text production with professional work done on clients; for example, the appropriate sequence of assigning tests to clients. Another important point to note is the lack of this kind of task in the academia and therefore engaging in this written task repeatedly in the workplace gives rise to the situated cognition which is very essential to health professionals. This exemplifies that the acquisition of genre knowledge goes beyond shaping a written text to learning how to perform a social action (Bazerman 1994). The value of this kind of placement text is also recognised by Carl:

Researcher:	You told me that when you become a professional, you actually have similar kind of report, but you don't need to record the history of injury
Carl:	No. I mean the progress sheet is some line paper, some paper have lines but didn't have the title, just let us to standardise how to write down all the information
Researcher:	ah just a blank sheet you mean, Okay I see. But does this help, I mean now that you learn what kind of things you need in a document when you see a patient. So, does it help, I mean when you become a professional, you only have a blank sheet
Carl:	I have said before, in reality, I think is a lot of a lot of different situations. So, I think it is just a standardised rough outline. I think when we are not quite sure about the documentations. We always miss some points. Then we need to went back home and refer to this kind of sheets

(INT-CL-01)

Apparently, Carl is aware of the pedagogic value of such a re-contextualised textual activity in the sense that, on the one hand, it frames and standardises across the board what needs to be included in the documentation of a physiotherapy session; on the other hand, novices can treat such a progress sheet as a source of reference and reminder about the textual organisation in future practice.

5.2.1.1.2. Spatial organisation

The work of healthcare professionals is very much three-dimensional; observation, movement, physical touch on various muscle and bones. In other words, these professionals always work with more than one variable at a time. In connection with this, the use of tabulated form under ROM of O/E has made the textual organisation cross-sectional as shown in Figure 3. This kind of tabulation of information also appears in the form used by professional physiotherapists in one of the hospitals in Hong Kong (see Figure 8). Such a textual arrangement may make it easier to visualise relationship between variables under investigation. Not only is this able to speed up the documentation process, it facilitates interpretation and validation of data.

Objective Examination

Movement Lt/Rt	Active ROM	Passive ROM	Strength
Forward Flexion	/	/	/
Abduction	/	/	/
Extension	/	/	/
Int. Rotation	/	/	/
Ext. Rotation	/	/	/
Horizontal Add.	/	/	/
Horizontal Abd.	/	/	/

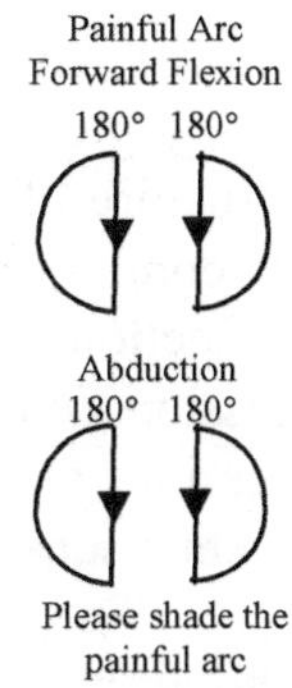

Figure 8 O/E in tabulated format in professional documentation.

Another important feature of textual organisation is spatial arrangement. The design of the space given reflects the assumptions and expectations of the person who constructs the form. It also imposes limitations and constraints over the consumption of the text by users. This can be exemplified by the fact that less space is given to less important information such as demographics, social history, etc. Each piece of information under demographics and Subjective Examination is provided with only a single line for the STWps to fill out details whereas a larger space without lines is provided for more important details such as O/E, Functions and Short Term Goals. Although it sounds trivial, such a semiotic feature has an important discourse and symbolic value in relation to grammar of visual literacy (Chandler 2006; Kress/van Leeuwen 1996). Such a spatial arrangement also implicitly directs the novices' attention to the sections where detailed descriptions are needed.

5.2.1.2. Social work

5.2.1.2.1. Presenting a structure of practice across timeline

Unlike physiotherapy texts where the organisation is geared towards the logical progression of a consultation session, the rhetorical structure of social work placement texts points to linking a recount of a combination of events across timeline and working towards reflection. I will take a closer look at the discourse organisation of the session report (Figure 9) a STWsw completes after a consultation session, making the analysis more in line with that of physiotherapy texts discussed in the previous section.

The analysis of the rhetorical organisation reveals that STWsws should be concerned about how the evaluation of the present situation (i.e., what happens during the program) and previous experience (i.e., objectives set and the sessions before) have an impact on future practice. The text above brings all these temporal elements together so that STWsws can see the coherence of knowledge construction and the meaning-making process that goes beyond the immediate context of discourse practices. This has been enforced through the pre-existing headings appearing in the form, from the *objectives/goals* set before the session to the assessment (e.g. *group involvement*) conducted during the session to the *follow-up* actions to be taken in the future. The focus of this section is placed on two linguistic resources which mark temporality: processes and circumstantial adjuncts of time.

Structure of Session Report

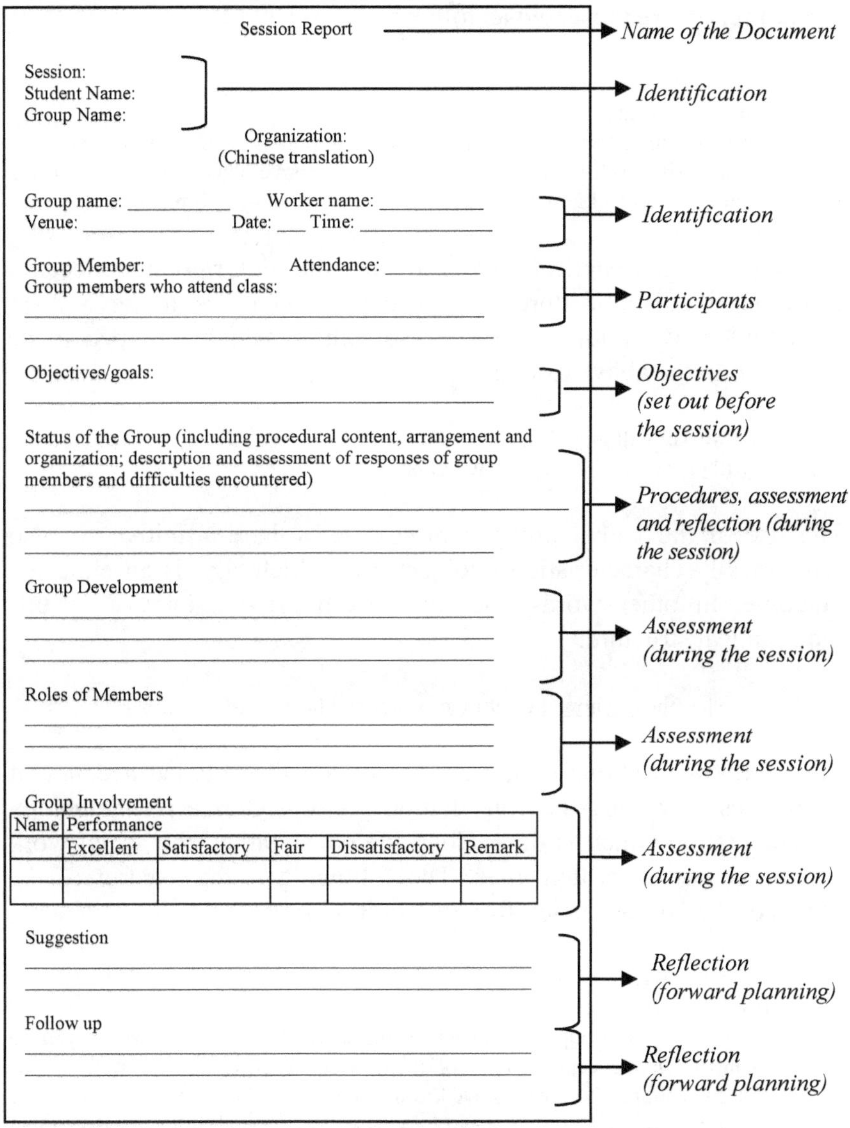

Figure 9. Rhetorical structure of a session report in social work placement.

The main part of the report starts off with the objectives, stating the goal to be achieved in the session. The objectives in Wayne's first session report are presented as follows:

> Example 9 *(WR_TXT-WW-02)*
> Objectives/goals:
> Introduction of the of group members, group purpose and group content. The worker will give the group mate to guess the above object, then it will take a small game to let know the nature of water and heat transformation.

Despite the grammatical errors made, the description reflects a common linguistic feature of 'objectives' which is to have them presented in the future tense, i.e., something which is hoped to be achieved. In the above example,

> The worker will give the group mate…
> It will take (we will use) a small game…

The use of the verbal group complex 'let + bare-infinitive' is also semantically characteristic of 'objectives' which signals an expected outcome. In other words, the sense of futurity is implied in this grammatical structure:

> … to let (them) know the nature of water and heat transformation

The next two sections of the report contain the detailed account of what goes on during the consultation session. Unlike physiotherapy documentation which is done along the consultation, the social work session report is written after. The following is the excerpt of the Status of the Group section from the first session report:

> Example 10 *(WR_TXT-WW-02)*
> It was a terrible group gathering. Firstly, when the time was at nearly 10:15, I want to let the group mate to attend the conference room, however, only 5 members in the centre, some of them were absence, another went to the church. The members who stayed in the centre that did not want to attend the class, because of playing a new radio. The worker was hardly to invisit them to classroom. However, when every members sit down on the chair, the breakfasts were brought to the centre by the other child. It is because that the

children have the right to eat the breakfast, therefore, it waste 20 minute to them, at the moment, some of them have eaten the breakfast, but some of them haven't eaten. Therefore, some member feel boring in the Conference room.

In the beginning of the group, the group members was noted at the coke, they said that they want to drink coke, and always compare with the my partner group, it is because he always gave the member candy and food. Afterwards, I introduced my name, the group name and the class time table to member, then I gave them two pieces of puzzles to them in order to introduce the group objectives and some norms. At the beginning the members did not know co-operation together, at the middle phase, the members award them need to co-operation. [...] After the breakthrough of some pieces, the motivation increasing. The member were a little bit happy. After then, I gave them a blank contact to sitting group norms...

In Example 10, there are linguistic traces reflecting the writer's adherence to the genre expectation in spite of the STWsw's very low English proficiency. In the first instance, the verbs used are generally put in a past timeframe. Some examples are:

...they did not want to attend the class, another went to the church
The breakfasts were brought to the centre...
I introduced my name, the group name and the class time table...
I gave them two pieces of puzzles to them...

The main focus of this section is on procedures; procedural elements are made explicit through the use of circumstantial adjuncts:

Firstly, when the time was at nearly 10:15
when every members sit (sat)down on the chair
In the beginning of the group
Afterwards
Then
At the beginning
at the middle phase
After the breakthrough of some pieces
After then

The adjuncts show that the writer makes an attempt to develop a temporal framework as the text unfolds, revealing the sequential development of the session.

While the above section of the report deals with what happens during the session, the last two sections 'Suggestion' and 'Follow-up' aim to exert impacts on future practice. For instance:

> Example 11 *(WR_TXT-WW-02)*
> Suggestion:
> The worker should control the member drop in and drop out problem, it need to confirm that who is the member and other can not attend the group. And the time control need to be done better, try to let to put more care about the not-active member, let them more involve in the group it may be change the data or time of gathering. It is because that some of the member will go to the church in the Sunday.
>
> Follow-up:
> In the next lesson, I will review the knowledge of the water and let them to think about what did they write on the group contact in order to let them think about this behaviour

Example 11 shows intertextual links established beyond the current piece of writing. The Suggestion section is realised as a form of reflection, construed mainly through modality:

> The worker <u>should control</u> the member…
> It <u>need (is needed)</u> to confirm that…
> … time control <u>needs</u> to be done (kept) better….

The use of the modals *should* and *need* convey the sense of obligation, which points to something that seeks improvement in the next attempt (see Section 7.2.6 of Chapter 7 for further explanation on the reflective practitioner role). As for 'follow-up', the link to the future practice is made explicit through the use of future tense and the circumstantial adjunct:

> <u>In the next lesson</u>, I <u>will review</u> the knowledge……

This description under 'follow-up' will be recycled and reproduced as the objectives/goals in the next session report.

It can be seen that the session report connects the past, present and future events mainly through processes (i.e., verbs) and circumstantial adjuncts of time. Other linguistic resources such as the use of modals also assist in shaping such continuity of practice. Temporality thus provides a rhetorical structure to the discursive practice and at the same time brings with it linguistic forms appropriate to the genre.

5.3. Contextualisation

Contextualisation covers items that point to the immediate context of writing as well as the broader context in relation to the social world. The awareness of the context within which the text is produced is crucial to the understanding of the integrity of a genre. The production of the text may appear to start from the text design by expert members (who can be academics, professionals or collaborative work by both) and end in a closure when STWs complete the task. However, such a product-view overlooks some of the key constructs in the actual production of a placement text: participants' roles and "participatory mechanism" (Bhatia 2005: 127), and institutional requirements. Participants' roles and "participatory mechanism" refer to the critical participants involved in the production, interpretation and use of texts. In addition, the engagement of these social beings, the STWs' discourse practice, is very much subject to the institutional requirements of both worlds, as pointed out in Chapter 4.

5.3.1. Participant's roles and participatory mechanism

Textual construction is never a solitary act. A piece of written work can be completed by a person but the process of shaping it requires the participation of 'others'. In placement, at least two major participants can be identified: the clients who are the source of data collection, and expert members who give feedback on STWs' work. Co-construction of texts involving more than one writer is found to be quite frequent at very beginning of the physiotherapy placement.

5.3.1.1. Physiotherapy

At the initial stage of placement, texts are often constructed in the context of collaborative learning, involving more than one participant. Parks (2000: 104) considers this type of sharing of responsibilities in writing "traditional collaboration":

> This refers to two or more writers working on the same text who assume equal responsibility for the text produced; actual involvement in terms of contributions to the finished product may vary or be more equally shared.

In physiotherapy placement, it is common to have a clinical educator supervising four STWps working on a case. Each of the four STW_ps was given a different role in a physiotherapy consultation session:

> Carl: objective is just we carry out some assessment by ourselves and for example range of motion and the muscle tone and the sensation test and skin skin skin sensation test some assess their functional skill for example side lying, sitting, see whether they can perform it
>
> …
>
> Researcher: so you had to do this final version based on your notes
>
> Carl: <u>our</u> notes[8]. It's a group- *(INT-CL-01)*

The emphatic remark *<u>our</u> notes* made by Carl foregrounds the collaborative nature of the task with someone testing the range of motion, sensation and functional skills as well as taking notes of the results of the respective part. This kind of shared responsibilities and distributed cognition lowers the anxiety of a STWp about handling clients alone and at the same time has the individual exposure to real world tasks. This also exemplifies the negotiated character of the enterprise, with a professional task turning to a pedagogical activity.

8 Carl emphasised the possessive pronoun *our*.

Such degree of dependence on others will be reduced when a STWp progresses from one stage to another.

Another critical participant involved in the genre acquisition in placement is the expert members, in this case, the professional physiotherapist and the teacher at the university. The expert member contributes to the writing activity through his/her intervention in the data collection procedures of STWps:

Researcher:	Oh okay good, did the PT in the hospital demonstrate how to do the assessment?
Carl:	He let us try first and then he correct us *(INT-CL-01)*

Performing correct assessment procedures is fundamental and a prelude to accurate documentation. This may ensure that the client responds accordingly who will in turn supply relevant data within the expected range in addition to having the STWps' assessment techniques trained.

The role repertoire the expert members play in the pedagogic aspect of the genre cannot be neglected. The main role they play is to give feedback to what STWs perform, as reflected from the previous interview excerpt, and write in the placement texts. In terms of feedback to written tasks accomplished in physiotherapy placement, it is found that the effects it takes are for future writing. This suggests the participatory mechanism is effectively enacted across the timeline. Figure 10 *(WR_TXT_CL-04)* illustrates the feedback given by the teacher.

	Passive	Active
Lower limbs	N/A *Describe the toness status of the L.L.*	N/A *No active movement*
Upper limbs	N/A *Full*	N/A *Full active sh. elb. movt* *Some active wr. & fing movt L > R*
Other body parts	N/A	N/A *Huff but not able to cough no intercostal movement* *minimal abdominals*

Figure 10. Teacher's feedback[9] on physiotherapy documentation.

9 Italicised words denote teacher's feedback.

It can be seen that the feedback draws the novices to the unambiguous discourse practice which is narrowly defined, evaluative (e.g. *full*) and makes reference to areas of concern by a physiotherapist (e.g. *inter-costal movement*). However these comments have no immediate effects on the current writing activity since teacher's feedback is seen as a closure to the writing cycle, i.e., the STWps cannot take it back and change anything to the documentation. Yet the comments are useful for future reference in physiotherapy documentation. The role of teacher feedback is recognised by the STWps:

Researcher: Okay, I see that your teacher have put some notes about you have put down not applicable, but what about this kind of notes written by your teacher?

Carl: I think it's not clear enough for documentation, our lecturer guides us to write more clear *(INT-CL-01)*

5.3.1.2. Social work

Unlike the student physiotherapists, STWsws in their placement usually work alone with an expert member (the fieldwork supervisor) monitoring their discourse and professional practices. The focus of the feedback is on raising STWsws' awareness of the importance of being reflective on practices. The following is an example of teacher's feedback to Wayne's session report:

> You are too focused on the failure experience. Did you see the positive and constructive effect of this experience?
> Actually, understanding on the children is the priority need in the group process, we are not serving ourselves but THEM!!
> We have explored a lot of alternatives after the group but you did not put this into your reflection.

The feedback given has an immediate relevance to Wayne as he had the chance to revise his proposal based on the suggestions before the final submission. The question posed *'Did you see the positive and constructive effect of this experience?'* prompts Wayne's reflection on his way of thinking and practice which in turn influences how he goes about articulating it in his next draft. Since expert members' feedback plays a fundamental role in novices' enculturation to a CoP, Chapter 6 will be devoted entirely to the investigation of Wayne's revision processes in response to the feedback given during his placement period.

5.3.2. Institutional requirements

In order to have the placement work documentation accepted by expert members, STWs need to satisfy the genre expectations defined by the community members. The institutional requirements impinging upon the STWs are not confined to those set by the professional world; those defined by the academia also constantly influence the way STWs' shaping of the written work.

5.3.2.1. Physiotherapy

Discourse practices of healthcare disciplines such as physiotherapy are often rather rigidly set with well-defined descriptive categories, appropriate choice of disciplinary methodological approaches, allowing less or even no leeway for private intention. The format of the documentation in placement is usually fixed and stabilised drawing STW_Ps' attention to standard procedures and logical progression from one step to another. The range of terminologies available is relatively narrow and the vocabulary chosen must be unambiguous in interpretation and appropriate to the context of physiotherapy. Take an excerpt from a physiotherapy consultation report as an example:

Example 12 *(WR_TXT-CL-02)*
DOA: 24/7/04
HPI: R knee pain
Δ: R OA knee
PMH: - DM°, HT°
- good general health
SH: - live with husband
- walks with frame
- NSND

Example 12 shows the information at the beginning of a clinical report. The items included and the use of discipline-specific abbreviations (e.g. *HPI* (History of Previous Injury), *DOA* (Date of Admission)) and symbols (e.g. '*Δ*') are important reifications to meet the genre expectations (see Figure 2 in Chapter 4 on the requirements in bednote writing). The information selected to be included under SH (social history) should be relevant to the treatment goals.

5.3.2.2. Social work

As mentioned before, the major goal of social work placement is to have the STWsws trained to become reflective on practice. This includes various levels of operation at work, from the choice of lexis to the choice of appropriate theoretical references. However, at times institutional requirements may seem to be at odds with novices' perception:

> Candy: Hm in fact not really because there's a certain kind of format. Basically what they need is terminology. You simply need to show off the terminologies. This is helpful in terms of recalling your memory of what you have done. A lot was done in the summer, some 20 programs, memory of what the program was. I think this is more important. *Values, theories are not that important.*
>
> *(INT-CD-04)*

Example 13 *(RF_TXT-CD-01)*

<u>Non-judgmental attitude</u>

During the placement, the student worker experienced the professional value of non-judgmental attitude. When approaching the participants, using the non-judgmental attitude would help to understand clearer about the situation and the needs of the participants

[...]

<u>Practice of theories</u>

During the fieldwork of the student worker, social learning theory and experiential learning had been used. Moreover, community integration was needed for the service target in this community. As student worker's assessed in the beginning of the fieldwork, it was better for the age of the service target to learn by experiencing.

In social learning theory, it is believed that children can learn from others. They can learn through imitation and copying other's behavior. In the group hold by the student worker, some positive behavior and speaking were encouraged. The other group members will then try to follow that behavior and speaking.

Apparently for Candy, engaging in work-related reflective writing is not primarily a means to trigger reflection but to show off what terminologies, values and theories she learnt at the university. It is interesting to note such a different perception of textual requirements between Candy and the university, even though Candy's writing complies with the writing requirements set out by the University to include things such as values and theories. In her reflection, Candy does not consider values and theories important in her actual work, and yet she decides not to 'go against the flow' as she realises these are what the gatekeepers look for and her success of placement partly depends on her own account in this report. In Example 13, Candy includes one of the most important values in rendering human services, i.e., upholding a non-judgmental attitude. The use of the modifier *professional* reinforces the re-contextualisation of an academic concept as a workplace-related one. Candy also highlights the application of theories by stating the names of the two theories explicitly as '*social learning theory and experiential learning had been used*' followed by exemplification. The pedagogical value of this institutional requirement is thus made obvious. Norton (1997) recognises that assessment of reflective writing very often turns out to be an assessment of subject knowledge rather than writer's reflective abilities.

5.4. Concluding remarks

In this chapter, I have linked the placement genres to the associated practices. By analysing and comparing the textualisation, organisation and contextualisation of placement texts of the two distinct disciplines, different means and approaches are revealed in terms of drawing STWs into the disciplinary practices. A summary of the differences is presented in Table 2.

		Physiotherapy Texts	*Social Work Texts*
Main pedagogical & professional goal		Directed towards disciplinary methodologies	Reflective
Textualisation	*Features of lexico-grammatical choices*	Use of complex nominal to specify unique contexts Use of questions	Use of a wide range of processes Use of reduced forms for 'reader's economy'
	Features of multi-modal resources other than linguistic ones	Visual literacy integral to textual practice	Not as important as linguistic representation
Organisation	*Features of rhetorical organisation*	Logical sequences in parallel with the consultation session	Bridging the past, present and future practice
Contextualisation	*Feature of participant's role and participatory mechanism*	Collaborative Expert members giving comments and feedback	Collaborative Expert members giving comments and feedback
	Institutional requirements	Within a very defined set of categories and terms	Reflective-cum-epistemological

Table 2. A comparison between Physiotherapy and Social Work placement texts.

From the above discussion, it can be seen that two genre-based practices, i.e., pedagogical and professional practices, are interacting with the discourse practice in the context of placement learning as shown in Figure 11. The findings in this chapter also suggest that an additional genre-based practice, reflective practice, is *embedded* in the social work practice.

Figure.11. Interactions of genre-based practices in placement.

Through discourse practices, pedagogical practice and professional practice are able to merge, re-contextualise, re-define and re-produce new forms of texts or tasks, which are very much interdiscursive (Bhatia 2005; Fairclough 1992), showing the presence or traces of more than one discourse in a text. These new texts are on the one hand 'pedagogicalised' professionally in nature, and on the other hand they are also 'professionalised' pedagogically, on the other. They are thus inter-dependent on each other and self reflexive in nature. This kind of hybrid discourses, as suggested by Lewis and Ketter (2004: 120), has a "transformative potential" which links language to learning. This is done by providing STWs with opportunities to appreciate the shared and reconcile the conflicting discourse practices along the boundary of two overlapping CoPs (Ketter/Hunter 2003).

In the next chapter, I will trace the writing journey of Wayne in order to understand how he responded to the feedback of his fieldwork supervisor.

6 Moving towards Disciplinary Practices: Roles of Feedback and Revision in Placement Learning

> Providing marker feedback is an opportunity for the experienced members of the discourse community to frame the discipline's discursive practices for novice participants. (Woodward-Kron 2004: 142)

An important aspect in second language writing research is novice writers' use of feedback to revise the texts produced. The above quote from Woodward-Kron (2004) implies that feedback is crucial to novices' appropriation of genres and specific repertoires in attaining the generic competence that allows them to participate meaningfully in the various activities and achieve the goals of a specific community. In other words, novices, at the early stage of enculturation in particular, need to be guided upon their choices of appropriate content, vocabulary, register, tone and be directed attention to the accepted norms, values, practices and culture-specific sensitivity in the context where the writing is produced. Feedback from experienced members is one of the effective means of drawing novices towards respective disciplinary practices; therefore, it is worth noting that feedback has an indispensable value in pedagogy and learning.

The texts under scrutiny in most feedback research are academic writing; the feedback given is mostly language-related and the ultimate agent being influenced is confined to texts or within the level of textual space. However, the point of departure of my study is 'learning in a professional context' and so my research into feedback concerns how feedback can facilitate novices' learning to write workplace documents like their professional counterparts; and more importantly, to show a novel relationship between revising texts and refining professional practices.

Another important issue raised is that feedback often ties in with teachers' practices and beliefs, the usual outcome of which is to inform pedagogies and ultimately, to help students improve their accuracy and quality of writing *over time* (Ferris/Roberts 2001). These studies can broadly be classified into two types: synchronic and diachronic. Synchronic feedback research mainly concerns aspects as identification of various *types* of error (e.g., treatable vs untreatable errors) (Ferris 1995; Hyland/Anan 2006), effectiveness of different *forms* of feedback (e.g., code-marking; direct vs indirect feedback), *modalities* (Abbuhl 2005) of feedback (written vs oral vs electronic) (see for example Tuzi, 2004 for a comparison of the three modalities), *scales* of feedback (comprehensive vs selective) (Lee 2003) and teachers' *choices* of corrective feedback (e.g., grammar correction vs discourse error correction) (Hyland/Anan 2006). On the other hand, diachronic studies on feedback are relatively scarce and yet these studies provide rich information regarding the socio-political dimension of feedback (Li 2006), i.e., why a writer accepts or rejects feedback and how the text is revised in response to the feedback given if accepted. In order to get the most out of the revision processes, a diachronic analysis was undertaken to investigate how a novice (Wayne) has revised texts based on an expert member's (his fieldwork instructor) written feedback during the context of placement. A single case study approach was adopted because (i) Wayne was the only participant that engaged in multiple drafting and more importantly, (ii) his supervisor provided elaborate feedback, relating both to content and, surprisingly, language, which makes the data rich enough to better illuminate our understanding of Wayne's learning trajectory. On this basis, this chapter aims to answer the following research question set out in Chapter 1:

1d. *How do novice writers revise their texts produced and how are they drawn into disciplinary practices via making use of feedback from expert members?*

In the following section, I will first explain the coding system and the rationales behind the categorisations. Then the main analysis is presented with reference to two modes of teacher's comments[10] (TCs henceforth): overt correction (OC henceforth) and feedback prompt (FP henceforth), with the former having the teacher provide the correct forms while the latter requiring the novice to do the revision, usually involving a much larger scale of rewriting. Much emphasis is on the feedback and revision for evaluative language because of its being ubiquitous in texts which involve assessment. Providing a fair assessment while presenting a situation that deserves critical attention can be a struggle for novices. It is therefore important to understand how the novice wrestles with the evaluative language with the help of teacher's comments.

6.1. Coding scheme of teacher's comments (TCs)

Before launching into the detailed analysis of Wayne's interaction with the TCs, an overview of the coding scheme and categories is needed. One of the challenges qualitative researchers face is to devise a meaningful coding scheme which is on the one hand broad enough to capture all relevant phenomena while on the other hand, specific enough to limit the codes to a manageable number (Mason 2002). The codes adopted in this study reflect the specific nature of the project and the text analysed: since the text is a discipline-specific one and the feedback is given by a content teacher who is a social work fieldwork instructor, one of the two main categories in my scheme is *discipline-specific comments*. Subsumed under this broad category are codes including *categorisation, meaning of content expressed, link to actual practice, representation,* and *structuring and organisation of thoughts/claims/ideas*. In addition to content-related comments, Wayne's teacher, unlike most other content teachers, provides numerous *language-specific comments* which are worth looking into.

10 Wayne's teacher was in fact his fieldwork instructor who followed him through the whole placement. For the sake of convenience, 'teacher's comments' will be used to represent the feedback given by the instructor.

They can be classified into *grammar* and *spelling error/typo*. Table 1 summarises the codes used in the analysis illustrated by relevant examples taken from Wayne's placement texts.

6.1.1. Defining codes

When defining the codes, I first visited the data a couple of times to come up with a list of preliminary codes. The preliminary codes, especially those under *discipline-specific comments*, were generated based on the readings done on language practices in the field of social work. For example, *categorisation (CA)* is a daily activity of a social worker which "involves a set of processes which result in facts, opinions or circumstances being established as one type or category rather than another" (Hall/Slembrouck/Sarangi 2006: 15). The preliminary codes were then applied to indexing the data, yet eventually it was found that recoding was necessary because some of them were 'loaded' in meaning. For example, I regrouped "clarification for content/meaning' into a more general code *meaning of content expressed* because the former inherently underlies the mode of TCs, which in this study includes OCs and FPs. Failure to differentiate the 'purpose' from 'mode' makes it difficult to understand the interaction between OCs and FPs and their respective roles in genre acquisition.

Type of Comments	*Codes*	*Examples*
Discipline-specific Comments	Categorisation (CA)	They will steal money or robbery the bank → They may involve in anti-social and criminal activities such as robbery and stealing.
	Link to the actual practice (P)	What are the selection criteria?
	Meaning of content expressed (M)	encourage favourable behaviour → encourage and reinforce favourable behaviour
	Representation (REP)	Please use a balance sheet
	Structuring and organisation of thought/ claim/idea (SQ)	It will be more logical for you to link up this crisis with your group design
Discipline/Language-Specific Comments	Word Choice/Terminology (WC)	The theory back up → Theoretical Framework
Language-Specific Comments	Grammar (G)	Will be hold → will be held
	Spelling error / typo (SP)	analysis date → analysis data
Other Comments	Choice of Content (C)	In this column, you need to analyse your observa-tion and intervention in the process.
	For further discussion (D)	Will be further discussed in supervision
	Intertextuality (INT)	References?
	Redundant information (RE)	and less aggressive behaviour → (deleted)

Table 1. Overview of the coding system of TCs.

6.2. Wayne's placement texts: an epistemological site

During his placement period, Wayne worked in a social service agency in mainland China, which pledges to rescue street-children by putting them back onto the right track. To make the street-children better use their time, Wayne's main duties were to design and co-ordinate various activities for them so that they could learn something useful related to their daily lives. For each of the activities Wayne initiated, he had to write a proposal detailing the rationales of the programme with respect to the needs assessments, relevant social work theories, expected outcomes, etc. After drafting the proposal, Wayne would pass it to his fieldwork instructor who supervised his work throughout the placement period for comments and discussions. Wayne then revised his proposal based on the TCs and handed it in again to the instructor for further comments until the proposal was considered ready to be sent off to the agency for ultimate approval. Upon approval of his proposal, he conducted five sessions with his group of clients (ten clients in total), each lasting from 45 minutes to 1.5 hours. After conducting each session, he had to complete a document labelled 'Session Report' detailing the information of the session such as programme objectives, clients' participation and most importantly Wayne's self-reflection and evaluation. The instructor would read this document and give feedback on Wayne's description and reflection as well as her observation of Wayne's performance in conducting a session. In this case, two contexts of feedback can be identified, i.e., feedback used for revision of the same piece of written work (proposal drafts) and feedback that has an impact on his professional actions (conducting the session with clients) and the next piece of written work ('Session Report'). Table 2 summarises Wayne's data used for this chapter.

Types of Data	*Genre*	*Catalogue No.*	*Length*
Written	Proposal (1st draft)	WFP1	1,733 words
	Proposal (1st draft + TCs)	WFP1-TC	1,878 words
	Proposal (2nd draft)	WFP2	2,520 words
	Proposal (2nd draft + TCs)	WFP2-TC	2,589 words
Spoken	Interview (proposal drafts)	INT-WW-05	52 minutes 58 seconds*
Written	1st Session Report	WSR1	1,247 words
	1st Session Report	WSR1-TC	N/A**
	2nd Session Report	WSR2	1,641 words
	2nd Session Report + TCs	WSR2-TC	2,101 words
	3rd Session Report	WSR3	N/A***
	4th Session Report	WSR4	1,044 words
	4th Session Report + TCs	WSR4-TC	1,213 words
	5th Session Report	WSR5	1,025 words
	5th Session Report + TCs	WSR5-TC	1,384 words
Spoken	Interview (Session reports)	INT-WW-06	31 minutes 17 seconds
		Total amount of written data including TCs	18,375 words
		Total amount of spoken data	84 minutes 15 seconds

* This interview was conducted via msn video conferencing because the STWsw had his placement in mainland China.

** This report is not available because the instructor only gave verbal feedback.

*** This report is not available because the STWsw was not required to write one for this session.

Table 2. Wayne's data used for this chapter.

The written data under scrutiny in this chapter involves eleven texts totalling 18,375 words. They include the first draft of the proposal (1,733 words), the first draft of the proposal with TCs (1,878 words), the revised version (2,520 words) and the revised version with TCs, which is also the final version (2,589 words). As for the session reports, except for the feedback to first session report and third session report which are unavailable, the number of words of the rest of the reports totals 9,655 words. All TCs are indexed with a code in such form as 'WFP1-02-OC'. 'WFP1' represents the version of the draft (1 means the first draft), '02' indicates the sequence of the TC and 'OC' represents overt correction, to be distinguished from 'FP' which is a prompt for changes such as *What good behaviour and how?*. Table 3 provides a total count of each type of TC based on the coding scheme set out in Table 1.

Table 3 provides an overview of the number of occurrence of each type of TCs. It shows that the total number of TCs decreases by half in the second version (68 in total) compared to 133 in total in the first draft of the proposal, both in terms of OCs and FPs. Among all types of TCs, *meaning of content expressed* has the greatest number of occurrence in the two proposal drafts (42 and 20 in WFP1 and WFP2 respectively), implying that the teacher's main priority is getting the message across to facilitate the operations of the workplace. In this respect, it is expected that *discipline-specific comments* outnumber other types; it is nonetheless surprising to note that 'language-specific comments' also shares a rather significant proportion of the TCs, accounting for about 40% in total.

After a quantitative analysis of TCs, the following sections will explain the rationale behind the TCs and more importantly, Wayne's responses to these comments. Section 6.3 will focus on OCs for which changes at the lexico-grammatical level are dominant. Section 6.4 will show how linguistic representations construed mainly through transitivity are able to show the effects FPs have on Wayne's actions.

Types of comments		Categories	WFP1-TC		WFP2-TC		WSR2-TC		WSR4-TC		WSR5-TC	
			OC	*FP*	*OC*	*FP*	*OC*	*FP*	*OC*	*FP*	*OC*	*FP*
	Discipline-Specific Comments	Categorisation (CA)	6	1	1	-	-	-	-	-	-	-
		Meaning of content expressed (M)	22	11	15	3	-	1	-	4	-	-
		Link to actual practice (P)	-	10	-	4	-	14	-	7	-	21
		Representation (REP)	-	1	-	1	-	-	-	-	-	-
		Structuring and organisation of thought/claim/idea (SQ)	-	-	-	4	-	-	-	-	-	-
Language-Specific Comments												
		Word Choice/Terminology (WC)	29	-	8	-	-	-	-	-	-	-
		Grammar (G)	33	-	21	-	-	-	-	-	-	-
		Spelling errors/typos (SP)	5	-	5	-	-	-	-	-	2	
Other Comments		Choice of content (C)	-	-	-	-	-	2	-	-	-	-
		For further discussion (D)	-	1	-	-	-	-	-	-	-	-
		Intertextuality (INT)	-	2	-	1	-	-	-	-	-	-
		Redundant information (RE)	12	-	5	-	-	-	-	-	-	-
		TOTAL	107	26	55	13	0	17	0	11	2	21

Table 3. Total counts of each type of TCs.

6.3. Teacher's overt corrections (OCs)

6.3.1. Revising discipline-specific word choices and terminology (WC)

One of the most important yet demanding skills novices need to grapple with in a professional workplace is to be able to make use of appropriate vocabulary items/terminologies/phrases to communicate with other discourse members. This, however, goes beyond the level of merely the correct choices of discipline-specific vocabulary but more challengingly, asks students to use them in correct forms and register and to recognise disciplinary uses of apparently ordinary terms. Teachers or workplace professionals share the role of helping novices initiate into the respective CoP by introducing linguistic resources required of them. Out of the total 201 feedback points given to the two proposal drafts, about one-fifth involves a certain level of 'boundary action' (Wenger 1998) to bring the informant into the CoP of social work via vocabulary and collocation refinements (27.1% in WFP1). For example,

[WFP1-44-O][11] It will be the society unstable factor in China
[WFP1-44-OC] They are the potential threat to the stability of the society

Some of these refinements prompt the use of grammatical metaphors (Halliday/Matthiessen 2004; Thompson 1996) (e.g. the change from the inanimate pronoun *it* to animate pronoun *they* in the above example), usually in the form of nominalising material processes (e.g. *stability* from *(un)stable*) (Schleppegrell 2001; Galve 1998). Others prompt terminology constructions, which characterises the dynamism of the discipline in question.

Each discipline has its own knowledge and 'way of saying things', i.e. in-group jargon. For example, in social science there are terms like *postmodernism, positivism, behaviorism*, etc. Discipline specific vocabulary also includes processes which are not often shared across various disciplines, e.g. *titration* in chemistry, *prefabrication* in

11 *O* denotes the novice's wordings and *OC* the teacher's correction.

civil engineering and *redeeming* in accounting. In addition, some ordinary laymen terms take on special meanings when they are used in a specific discipline. For instance, *damages* in legal contexts would mean compensation. Further, as far as collocation and set expressions are concerned, some of them may seem odd and are not encountered in other fields of study, e.g. *reasonable/reasonably prudent*[12] in tort law, and *participant observation* in the social sciences.

As mentioned in Chapter 3, social work, broadly speaking, is a discipline which deals with human beings and society, subsuming various subfields such as psychology, social sciences, education, etc (Jordon 2003). The intricacies of social work *per se* therefore present challenges to novices when it comes to describing its on-going activities, e.g. assessing human behaviour. Social work, similar to other disciplines, has its own terminologies. However, unlike medical or engineering terms, social work terms are less 'technical' and seem more 'approachable' in the sense that they appear quite often in general contexts in our daily lives. The wide range of vocabulary at the writers' disposal nevertheless may make it even harder for one to choose the most accurate description for the reality and phenomenon being presented.

6.3.1.1. From general to a more 'technical' vocabulary items/phrases

Part of the reasons why one can easily classify a term as a medical or scientific one is because these so-called technical terms are often coined conforming to some morphological rules. 'Technical terms' in social work, as mentioned before, are not easily recognised as shown in the following two examples:

Example 1

[WFP1-40-O]	… it is because the children that <u>have been label</u> as a street children, the lower social status in the society
[WFP1-40-OC]	It is due to the <u>labeling effect</u> and they are trained to 'accept' themselves being in a lower social status in the society

12 Both *reasonable* and *reasonably prudent* are commonly used in tort law when discussing cases of negligence.

Example 2

[WFP1-47-O]	The academic is the most influence their ability of sense of successful
[WFP1-47-OC]	The academic achievement is the most influential factors in building their ability

In Example 1, Wayne analyses the reasons why the clients lack motivation in doing anything. It appears that he wants to engage his discussions with reference to social work concepts reflected from his use of the classifier *social*, objectifying what can be considered writer's subjective interpretation: *lower status*. It can be seen from WFP1-40-OC that the teacher takes the discipline-specific concept and process *labeling* as a modifier to confine *effect*, a noun which is often associated with scientific processes, for example, greenhouse effect. This nominalisation not only intensifies the disciplinary nature of the phrase but also enhances the lexical density of the clause. In addition, the existential clause is foregrounded by the new information *the labeling effect*, which has presented itself as a cause of problem framed within the context of the discipline. As for Wayne, *label* is downplayed as a material process in the dependent *that*-clause. Wayne shows that he realises the preference of nominalisation over his lexico-grammatical construction:

Wayne:	comparatively my paragraph my first draft of the proposal we should have a lot of social work concepts in our writing
Researcher:	yes?
Wayne:	okay labeling effect just say label labeling effect behind labeling effect children there may be a long term influence I just used the word label I can communicate the message but not the exact wordings
Researcher:	It seems to me the term is rather technical
Wayne:	in fact the term she used is more precise and the meaning is stronger now that I read it again I discover that her use of wordings are more accurate *(INT-WW-05)*

Wayne is aware of the lack of precision of his lexical choices and the stronger semantic contents embedded in the nominalisation. Not only is he directed toward a more technical description, the associated implication of the use of *effect* (i.e. having a long term influence) which goes beyond the current situation of *labeling* also makes sense to him.

Similarly, in Example 2, the original material process *influence* is transformed into a modifier (*influential*), collocating with *factors*. Again, the noun *factors* can be very commonly found in discipline-specific writing because it belongs to a register which is more formal than lexis with similar meanings such as *reasons*. *Factors* here also confines the context of *influence*, pointing to the source rather than the effect. On the other hand, the use of the pre-modifier *influential,* also typical of a formal register, forms a complex nominal which further exemplifies the characteristic of technical English. The following example shows a similar inclination towards refining the scope within the social work context with the use of *facilitating factors*:

Example 3

[WFP1-18-O]	It is the advantage for the running the group
[WFP1-18-OC]	These are the facilitating factors and foundation for running the group

6.3.1.2. Moving from local to problematising 'social' issue

Learners' engagement in school-based writing is always confined to interacting with 'simulated' real-world problems to display academic knowledge in textual forms: analysing the rubrics in question, synthesising related references and finally writing up the answers according to academic conventions. As for workplace-based writing, the emphasis is on action taking "rather than on a leisurely reflection on thought processes or on creative expression" (Beaufort 1998: 180). The most fundamental difference between academic and workplace-based writing is that the latter is strategically shaped to reflect the institutional points of view instead of individual ones. All this accounts for why workplace-based learning is an important site for testing against "myth of transcendence", the assumption that despite the difference in domains, writers can comfortably "transport and translate what they have learned as writers from one domain to another" (Dias *et al.* 1999: 223). In the case of Wayne, the question lies in how he learns to situate his writing within a broader social world and its connection with his professional writing. Consider the following example:

Example 4

[WFP1-06-O]	...will be provided in basic subject such as reading, writing, math for them
[WFP1-06-OC]	... provides also non-formal education such as basic reading and writing skill and math for them

In Example 4, when discussing the content of the courses provided by the centre, Wayne 'packages' reading and writing as basic *subject*s while his teacher revises it to a kind of *skill* – something that is valued in society, especially in the rural area of mainland China where Wayne conducted his placement. I consider such a revision crucial to novices not only in terms of making them more aware of terminologies used but more importantly, teaching them to problematise issues with reference to the real world. This is in fact particularly relevant to Wayne, who is learning to categorise 'social' problems as an everyday activity at the juncture of professional and discourse practices in social work. The word *skill*, in this case, is contextualised within a "social space" (Prince 1996: 98) which underpins ideologies and cultural values of a society. The addition of *non-formal education* also intensifies the social nature of the problem.

The following example also accentuates the social problem involved:

Example 5

[WFP2-34-O]	... they may be the potential to be "Mang liu" who easily to believe to other
[WFP2-34-OC]	They have the potential to become "Mang liu" who involve in gang behavior

In Example 5, the phrase *gang behavior* signals a very negative and serious problem as a result of being unable to make wise decisions. Apparently the extent to which this phenomenon deserves attention is much greater than what is described by Wayne as *easily to believe to other*.

6.3.2. Revising nominal groups

6.3.2.1. Inclination towards nominalisation

Another prevalent disciplinary discourse practice is the inclination towards nominalised processes. Nominalisation is a grammatical resource for the construction of noun phrase subjects, and for the re-presentation of information as given. From the perspective of 'process' put forward by Chafe (1985: 108), nominalisation is activated "by which verbs like *tend, prefer, speak, refer*, and use or adjectives like *abstract* become noun phrases that can then be the arguments of other verbs or the objects of prepositions." The following examples illustrate nominalising processes:

Example 6

[WFP1-74-O]	… the stress children can positively express their comment, and learn to co-operate with other
[WFP1-74-OC]	To encourage self-expression and cooperation in the group

Example 7

[WFP2-45-O]	…And let the street children a opportunity to create or applied some useful material for themselves
[WFP2-45-OC]	Eventually, the group activities provide opportunity for them to experience creation and application of knowledge.

In Example 6, when describing the tangible aim of the group programme, Wayne makes use of the material processes *express* and *learn to co-operate*. The OC, however, reflects an inclination towards a more condensed and succinct expression via the use of the nominalisations *self-expression* and *co-operation*. In other words, nominalisation is a kind of grammatical metaphor which saves a lengthy explanation of ideas. Also, nominalisation is often used to conceptualise statements to produce terminologies/professional jargon used in a particular CoP to ease communication. Similarly, in Example 7, the original material processes *create* and *applied* are nominalised as *creation* and *application*; the difference between these two nominalisations lies in the fact that the former is pre-modified by a verb while the latter is followed by a post-modification, forming a relatively complex nominal group.

6.3.2.2. Towards categorisation (CA): complex nominal groups

One of the main functions of nominalisation, as identified by Lock (2005: 61), is a reflection of "science's concern with categorizing, labeling, and describing phenomena". It has already been pointed out in Chapter 3 that social work can be considered both an art and a science. The categorisation process involves a systematic enquiry into differentiating what something is from what it is not. For example, a social worker needs to categorise whether the behaviour of a client is socially acceptable or not. Categorisation is essentially a social and institutional process which underlies legitimacy and shared understanding of authoritative power (Jerkins 2000).

Table 3 indicates that categorisation is one of the major error types in Wayne's texts (5.26% in WFP1). TCs reveal that rather than using simple nominalisation, categorisation is represented by a complex nominal group with pre-modification. Consider the following examples:

Example 8

[WFP2-86-O] ... It is the important to use the group to teach them a subject, it can be use the group norms to let them regularly to do the group

[WFP2-86-OC] ... Besides, constructive group norms will help them to behave themselves in the group and to learn <u>desirable pattern of behavior</u>.

Example 9

[WFP1-42-O] ...in the long run, if the street children have not sense of successfulness and the confident, they will not have the motivation to improve their quality of life.

[WFP1-42-OC] ... if they do not change this perception, they will not have the motivation to improve their quality of life in the long run. They will continue to adopt a <u>passive and non-productive role</u>.

Example 10

[WFP1-43-O] ... They will still to do the street children or street man, if they can not find enough money to buy food or live, they will steal money or robbery the bank.

[WFP1-43-OC] In some worst cases, they may involve in anti-social and criminal activities such as robbery and stealing.

In the first instance, the grammatical construction of the nominal group is the same for all the three examples, i.e., pre-modification of nouns. The modifiers intensify the complexity of the nouns and confine the expressions so that the description can be more accurate. A closer look at these pre-modifiers shows the way in which the OCs subtly draw the informants towards fuller participation in the CoP. Pre-modifiers are commonly considered abstractions of major concepts/ideas addressed. The above three examples show a preferred and consistent professional practice where generalisations are made based on evidence. In writing, these generalisations are realised through narrowly-defined categories, which are often formed by the deployment of pre-modifications.

Another commonality among these examples is the alignment of two attitudinal meanings in the categorisation. There is an overtone of judgment about the behaviour of the clients, and yet this judgmental attitude has been weakened through the use of impersonal entities such as *pattern, role* and *activities*.

Examples 9 and 10 show a common linguistic feature found in the revisions made by Wayne's teacher: two adjectives used together as pre-modifiers. One of the possible reasons is the inherent fluid nature of adjectives and the fact that their meanings are often context-dependent. Putting two adjectives together can further refine the scope of meaning of the object being modified and has a stronger GRADUATION of meaning in terms of FORCE (intensity):

... They will continue to adopt a passive and non-productive [+FORCE (INTENSITY)] role

... they may involve in anti-social and criminal [+FORCE (INTENSITY)] activities

6.3.3. Revising evaluative language

EVALUATION provides analytical categories to make systematic comparisons between Wayne's wordings and the TCs possible in terms of ATTITUDE (what is being evaluated) and GRADUATION (how meaning is scaled). Further, EVALUATION as lexis is the building blocks of several error types as *categorisation, meaning of content expressed* and *word choices* in Wayne's texts which are predominantly evaluative in nature.

Understanding what entities are being evaluated in Wayne's placement texts allows the comparison of the typical kind of attitudinal resources expected in a text and the writer's choice of EVALUATION. This has an implication for socialising the STW into the institution and learning disciplinary practices. Martin (2003: 161) accounts for such importance:

> Every institution is loaded with couplings of this kind *(appraisal)*, and socialization into a discipline involves both an alignment with the institutional practices involved and an affinity with the attitudes one is expected to have towards those practices.

There are four main areas that are evaluated in Wayne's proposal drafts and session reports including:

a) Current provisions in the social work agency and social background; for example[13],

> Kunming Jiaxin Children assistance center is an organisation that provide the *basic* [+APPRECIATION (COMP)] needs such as clothing, food, *clean* [+APPRECIATION (COMP)] water and medicine…

b) Clients' individual background and behavioural development; for example,

13 The examples used to exemplify the things being evaluated are taken from the version revised by the teacher.

About 80% centre users *have not completed their primary school education* [t-JUDGMENT (CAPACITY)]... a lot of them just *know some basic knowledge* [t-JUDGMENT (CAPACITY)].

... the street children are *lacking of confidence* [-JUDGMENT (CAPACITY)] and *motivation* [-JUDGMENT (TENACITY)].

c) Effectiveness of the programs; for example,

To engage the street kids in some *meaningful* [+APPRECIATION (VALUE)] and *productive* [+APPRECIATION (VALUE)] learning activities

d) The STW himself; for example,

If the social workers (teacher) exhibit *genuineness* [+JUDGMENT (VERACITY)], *warmth* [+JUDGMENT (NORMAL)] and *friendliness* [+JUDGMENT (NORMAL)] in their encounter and communication with children ...

While in the first instance epithets (e.g. *meaningful*) are by default evaluative in nature, the above examples show that other grammatical forms/structures are also able to reflect the evaluative meaning such as nominalised attributes (e.g. *genuineness*), nominalised attributive relational processes (e.g., *the street children are lacking of confidence*), mental processes (e.g., *a lot of them just know some basic knowledge*), etc. On the other hand, EVALUATION can be expressed either explicitly (inscribed) and implicitly (evoked); the code of the latter form of EVALUATION is preceded by 't-' to signal there is a token of attitudinal meaning. The grammatical resources in EVALUATION, as shown here, are so rich that writers have to appropriate them strategically to make the assessment sound just and fair.

6.3.3.1. Toning down of attitudes

The core element of social work, as mentioned above, is assessment. Regardless of the object of assessment, it involves a social worker's judgment. However, social workers, like many practitioners in other professional fields, have to suppress if not totally avoid upholding a judgmental attitude (Baldock/Prior 1981). This is why a real challenge is presented to novices when they have to tone down their judgmental attitude in a piece of writing which is virtually entirely judgmental. The following examples aim to show how the teacher's OCs suppress the judgmental attitude. The interview transcript that comes with each example reflects Wayne's awareness of the need to tone down the negative judgment.

Example 11

[WFP1-65-O]	The intervention point of the problem [-JUDGMENT (NORMALITY)]
[WFP1-65-OC]	The intervention focus

Researcher:	so what about the intervention point of the problem the intervention focus
Wayne:	actually it has the same meaning in Chinese but where is the focus in this moment she hopes me don't think it's a problem problem means negative
Researcher:	negative
Wayne:	okay the focus is neutral, objective wording

(INT-WW-05)

Example 12

[WFP1-72-O]	It hope that the street children will join the group and don't waste time [t-JUDGMENT (TENACITY)] in the street
[WFP1-72-OC]	To engage the street kids in some meaningful and productive learning activities [+APPRECIATION (VALUE)]

Wayne:	the first sentence don't waste time is judgment
Researcher:	negative
Wayne:	negative very negative okay the meaning productive is positive more positive I realise that my classmates like to use positive and objective words to describe things people's values are different you may think that it does not work but they will try to use very positive words to say something
Researcher:	that's right
Wayne:	you may say that they are just cheating themselves but they hope that twist on the level of words to twist the message this is ok
Researcher:	so you think it's a standard practice in social work to use positive instead of negative
Wayne:	now that I thought about it why my classmates get a good grade because they use very positive I am not sure if it's objective even minor things will be praised and teachers

may think that they have found something. Perhaps our job is to raise the minor things and praise them

(INT-WW-05)

Example 13

[WFP1-30-O] therefore, they will leave the centre and go to the street for playing, stealing, and other misbehavior [-JUDGMENT (VERACITY)] etc

[WFP1-30-OC] They will leave the centre and prefer wandering and playing in the street. They will adopt undesirable [-APPRECIATION (QUALITY)] pattern of behaviour [-JUDGMENT (VERACITY)] such as stealing.

Wayne: undesirable pattern of behaviour I think she did not want to judge whether the behaviour is right or wrong she did not want to judge it she wants to use a more objective to see it. I mean my understanding is it's not desirable but misbehavior you judge it it's wrong it's very very important the basic principle is non-judgmental attitude you should be objective to see but I use misbehavior I judged it it's misbehaviour it's wrong it's not acceptable. It is very dangerous if you treat that as wrong at the very beginning your direction will be wrong but now you use undesirable it's just not desirable it's just a kind of diversion from what you have expected but you did not judge it's wrong

(INT-WW-05)

Examples 11 and 12 concern the name of the section heading and the objective of the programme respectively. A judgmental attitude has been reflected in Wayne's choices of word. Wayne's use of *point of the problem* has been replaced by *focus* in the OC, which is attributed to the choice of the judgmental lexeme *problem.* The correction implies that social workers should remain neutral even in writing and avoid negative evaluation which is unsupported by facts. Similarly, as pointed out by Wayne himself, the phrase *don't waste time* in Example 12 is judgmental and he realises the preference for positive word choices used to appreciate the program *per se* (*meaningful and productive activities*) than to make judgment about a person. Such a discourse practice, to Wayne, is a way of getting a good grade at school, and yet he doubts the objectiveness, reflected in his use of the hedging device *perhaps* when thinking about their job as a STWsw.

This seems to imply that Wayne is ambivalent about what the real situation is and the preferred representation of reality. This example highlights an important issue that enculturating into a new CoP is by no means an unproblematic process. Novices often have to reconcile the conflict between institutional requirements and personal ideologies, like Wayne in this case.

Example 13 is a more complex example since both Wayne's choices of evaluation and the OC are judgmental in nature and expressed in an explicit way. Wayne's interview data provides a reasonable explanation for the suggested changes. The word *misbehavior* points to a wide range of behaviours which are considered inappropriate, ranging from personal ones to social ones. Such a lexical choice is strongly infused with a negative connotation. As for the OC, the toning down of a judgmental attitude can be viewed from two perspectives: (1) The lexical choice of *undesirabl*e, as suggested by Wayne, has something to do with the expectation of people instead of passing direct judgment on the act of clients, and (2) the adjective *undesirable* in the complex nominal (i.e., *undesirable pattern of behaviour*) functions to modify *pattern* (being a negative APPRECIATION of entity) instead of being an immediate collocate of *behaviour*. Such strategic lexical choices help soften the already very negative evaluation built up in the preceding sentences to a great extent. In addition, the revision from ... *and other misbehavior* to *undesirable pattern of behavior* is a move from purely descriptive to categorisation, as explained in detail in section 6.3.2.2.

6.3.3.2. Objectifying subjectivity

In this section, I take a closer look at a major section of Wayne's proposal which is concerned with the assessment of the clients' background and behavioural development, through which proposing new initiatives at the centre is justified. This is to have a clearer view as to how arguments are built up at the discourse-semantic level. A comparison between Wayne's and his teacher's choices of ATTITUDINAL and GRADUATION resources will be made.

Example 14a: Analysis of ATTITUDE

Wayne's assessment

I have discovered that the street children always play the table tennis, play Chinese chess and watching Television in the centre. At the beginning, the streets children will feel *funny* [+AFFECT (INTEREST)] form the playing and watching, however, the *attractions of these game will be lower* [-APPRECIATION (IMPACT)], it is because that *the centre have just provide these games* [t-APPRECIATION (COMPLEXITY)]. As the results, the street children feel the centre *boring* [-AFFECT (INTEREST)], therefore, they will leave the centre and go to the street for *playing* [t-JUDGMENT (NORMAL)], *stealing* [t-JUDGMENT (PROPRIETY)], and other *misbehavior* [-JUDGMENT (VERACITY)] etc. one of the street children told me that, sometimes, they will go to the computer centre (web bar) to *gambling* [t-JUDGMENT (PROPRIETY] or *smoking* [t-JUDGMENT (VERACITY)] etc. furthermore the children go to the street, they also will learn some *misbehavior* [-JUDGMENT (VERACITY)] by peer influences, or social learning. Therefore, it must make some *interesting* [+APPRECIATION (IMPACT)] game or game for them to play in order to let them still in the centre.

Teacher's Revision

I have discovered that the street children *like* [+AFFECT (AFFECTION)] playing the table tennis, Chinese chess and watching Television in the centre. At the beginning, the street children will have fun [+AFFECT (INTEREST)] from joining these activities, however, they will *lose their interest* [-AFFECT (INTEREST)] *and patience* [-AFFECT (INTEREST)] gradually. The centre do not *provide any further training or organization on these activities* [t-APPRECIATION (COMPLEXITY)]. It is *not surprise* [-AFFECT (SURPRISE)] to find that children soon become *boring* [-AFFECT (INTEREST)]. They will leave the centre and *prefer* [+AFFECT (AFFECTION)] *wandering* [t-JUDGMENT (NORMAL)] and *playing* [t-JUDGMENT (NORMAL)] in the street. They will adopt *undesirable* [-APPRECIATION (QUALITY)] *pattern of behavior* [-JUDGMENT (VERACITY)] such as stealing [t-JUDGMENT (PROPRIETY)]. One member told me that, sometimes they will go to the computer centre (web bar) to *gamble* [t-JUDGMENT (PROPRIETY)] or *smoke* [t-JUDGMENT (VERACITY)] etc.

Example 14a compares the way Wayne assesses his clients with that of the teacher's revision. In Wayne's assessment, the dominant attitudinal resource deployed is, as expected, JUDGMENT encoded mainly through nominalisation such as *stealing*, *smoking* and *misbehavior*. These judgmental lexical choices are all oriented to what Martin (2003: 156) calls "social sanction" concomitant with legal implications. Affective statements are formulated to express the clients' interest and dislike (*funny* and *boring* respectively) infused in the mental process *feel*. However, there is a leap from an affective statement (i.e. *feel the centre boring*) to judgmental ones, first with implicit evaluation (*playing* and *stealing*) then followed by an explicit one (*misbehavior*). The explicit judgment appears to be an umbrella term that semantically covers the previous two terms; yet the way these attitudinal resources is structured is an instance of INTENSIFICATION. However, these lexical items strung together do not share the common values.

TCs show a different way in building up rhetorical power and linking with the daily activities of social workers, i.e. categorisation. First, unlike Wayne, TCs include a lot more affective statements encoded in various grammatical relations:

> Mental process: …the street children like playing the table tennis….
> …They will leave the centre and prefer wandering…
>
> Material process followed by nominalised attributes:
> …they will lose their interest and patience…
> … street children will have fun…
>
> Attributive relational process: … the children soon become boring (bored)

Since the thematic positions of all these affective statements are all taken up by *the street children*, it appears to show that the writer is very aware of what the clients think. This nevertheless distances the writer's alignment to the claims and makes them sound credible and objective, softening the authoritative ENGAGEMENT (attribution) infused in *I have discovered* at the very beginning of the text and the "thematised comment" (Thompson 2004: 152) '*it is not surprise* (surprising)'. This self-positioning as an expression of the validity of the assessment needs to be appropriated by newcomers.

The text then moves from being affective, which forms the basis of argumentation, to entirely judgmental, through which the writer's alignment becomes more explicit. Similar to Wayne, TCs begin the judgmental resources with the implicit nominalised behaviour as *wandering* and *playing*; yet it is followed by an extended nominal group with pre-modification – *undesirable pattern of behavior* – to abstract the concepts mentioned earlier. The generation of appropriate categories as this one is essential for professional work because it is the basis for framing the ensuing interactions and actions (Hall/Slembrouck/Sarangi 2006). Having come up with the category which is an explicit evaluation, the writer returns to implicit judgments realised through nominalisation *stealing* and infinitives *to gamble* and *to smoke*.

Undertaking the analysis of GRADUATION of the same text shows clearly how TCs can strengthen the rhetorical power.

Example 14b: Analysis of GRADUATION

Wayne's assessment

I have discovered that the street children always [+FORCE (FREQUENCY)] play the table tennis, play Chinese chess and watching Television in the centre. At the beginning [+FOCUS (SPECIFICITY)], the streets children will feel funny form the playing and watching, however, the attractions of these game will be lower, it is because that the centre have just [+FOCUS (AUTHENTICITY)] provide these games. As the results, the street children feel the centre boring, therefore, they will leave the centre and go to the street for playing, stealing, and other misbehavior etc. one of the street children told me that, sometimes, [+FORCE (FREQUENCY)] they will go to the computer centre (web bar) to gambling or smoking [+FORCE (INTENSIFICATION)] etc. furthermore the children go to the street, they also will learn some [-FOCUS (AUTHENTICITY)] misbehavior by peer influences, or social learning. Therefore, it must make some [-FORCE (AMOUNT)] interesting game or game for them to play in order to let them still in the centre.

Teacher's Revision:

I have discovered that the street children like [+FORCE (INTENSITY)] playing the table tennis, Chinese chess and watching Television in the centre. At the beginning [+FOCUS (SPECIFICITY)], the street children will have fun from joining these activities, however, they will lose their interest and patience [+FORCE (INTENSIFICATION)] gradually [+FORCE (TIME)]. The centre do not provide any [+FORCE (AMOUNT)] further [+FORCE (SCOPE)] training or organization [+FORCE (INTENSIFICATION)] on these activities. It is not surprise to find that children soon [+FORCE (TIME)] become boring. They will leave the centre and prefer [+FORCE (INTENSITY)] wandering and playing [+FORCE (INTENSIFICATION)] in the street. They will adopt undesirable [+FORCE (INTENSITY)] pattern of behavior such as stealing. One member told me that, sometimes [+FORCE (FREQUENCY)] they will go to the computer centre (web bar) to gamble or smoke etc.

Example 14b shows the analysis of GRADUATION. The revised version reflects a better use of the GRADUATION resources both in terms of quantity and quality. Wayne uses non-specific pointers (*some*) to pre-modify the evaluative meaning. Nevertheless, not only does this fail to strengthen the tone but also blurs the categorical meaning. OCs show a wider range of instances of GRADUATION to amplify the attitudinal meanings via spatial (*further*), temporal (*soon, gradually*) and quantitative terms (*any*). The teacher's version also illustrates two possibilities of grading attitudinal meaning (Hood 2004): (1) GRADUATION is encoded separately from the attitudinal meaning (e.g., *soon*), (2) some attitudinal terms are semantically infused with GRADUATION (e.g. *prefer* vs *like*).

The interaction between the ATTITUDINAL meaning and GRADUATION, as shown above, plays a critical role in building up rhetorical power. The purely subjective assessment is being 'objectified' through distancing personal alignment to the claims and emphasising the objective parameters of the social world, for example, frequency and temporality.

6.4. Feedback prompts (FPs)

The previous section reveals that Wayne's novice status and weak linguistic repertoires put him in a position where the teacher's overt correction is seen as an imposition embedded with social forces. Acceptance thus seems to be the only option for Wayne. This section shows a more active participation in the revision processes by Wayne who has to act on the feedback which is often a prompt for changes/clarification of meaning.

6.4.1. An overview of FPs

While revisions made by the teacher shown in the previous sections reflect an orientation towards improving Wayne's writing at the linguistic level, FPs draw Wayne's attention to the content, primarily linking the immediate context of his writing to the outside world and his professional practices as a social work student worker. Among the 88 FPs shown in Table 3, *Structuring and organisation of thoughts/claims/ideas (SQ), Choice of content (C), and Representation (REP)* are considered text-internal FPs, whereas *Intertextuality (INT), For further discussion (D)*, and *Link to actual practice (P)* go from text-internal to text-external. *Meaning of content expressed (M) and Categorisation (CA)* can go various ways depending on the context. Consider the following example of FP:

Example 15

[WFP2-14-FP] It is true that they are lacking for formal education. But try to compare the value of formal and non-formal education in their cases. What subject knowledge is important and significant to them besides language, history and geography?

The first FP *it is true that they are lacking for formal education* is a confirmation of Wayne's professional assessment, being external to the text. Then the request for the comparison between the two types of education realised in the second FP *But try to compare the value of formal and non-formal education in their cases* brings the context of writing from external to internal. The last FP, *What subject knowledge is important and significant to them besides language, history and geography?*, prompts Wayne to think about his professional work again. It can be seen from this example that a complex mechanism may be involved in revising contents in response to FPs.

Another interesting point about Example 15 is that the FPs are given to Wayne's second draft of his proposal, which is also the final draft, meaning that Wayne did not get to revise his written work based on the FPs. However, such kinds of comments are very crucial in the context of professional training, in which the instructor extrapolates the potential problems in a STW's actual practice from writing.

Wayne also realises the importance and instrumental value of this practice-related comments along his learning pathway:

> Researcher: Why would she ask question here since this is already the last draft?
>
> Wayne: ok she let me stimulate my thought and thinking about the problem in the actual practice. I have no time to have reflection she tried to use the final chance to let me know to remind to think more and more deeply and we enjoyed this learning pattern. Through questions and discussion, we stimulate thing about what we should do what we really have to do hope me that when have free time ask me questions like this. When you ask more and answer, you will try to know the actual need… *(INT-WW-05)*

Ferris (1995) found from her work that students tended to pay more attention to the teacher's feedback on earlier drafts than the final ones. As for Wayne, although final, he sees the feedback on it as continuity rather than closure.

6.4.2. Analysing FPs

Apparently, what the FPs do in Example 15 does not simply initiate lexical changes or reformulation of ideas; what is emphasised is their effects on Wayne's action which will ultimately be realised in a linguistic form. In this case, Wayne was required to reconsider the wider context of the clients' needs in terms of education, which will help justify his proposal on learning the daily applications of science. To see changes in action (especially over time), transitivity analysis is needed as it focuses on the experiential meaning shaped by both the participants and processes involved in a discourse. This is particularly relevant to Wayne's case as he interacted with the same group of clients over a substantial period of time. Any suggested changes in actions are realised in the FPs and his revisions.

6.4.3. Responses to FPs: Wayne's revision

In this section, Wayne's revision to each type of textual link established by FPs will be examined. More specifically, the error types embedded in the FPs will first be identified and the way Wayne reacted to the changes is explained.

6.4.3.1. Text-internal FPs

This type of FPs mainly prompts clarification of meaning and re-organisation of ideas. For instance,

Example 16

[WFP1-34-O] Some phenomenon from the nature, according his mind that they did not explain, it is a risk that he may be created by someone, it may be created his money form something miracle thing, however, these thing are applied some theory that he did not know. it may cheated by his money or do some stupid things

[WFP1-34-FP] <u>Please rewrite the whole paragraph, I am totally at lost!</u>

[WFP2-34-O] Therefore, they are lack of the critical think ability. It is potential risk that they will be cheated by the strange in future, it is because that they are easily to believe someone. In the future, they may be the potential to be "Mang liu"盲流 who easily to believe to other

[WFP2-34-R][14] Therefore, they are lack of the critical think ability. It is potential risk that they will be cheated by the strange (stranger) in future, it is because that they are easily to believe someone. In the future, they may be (have) the potential to be (become) "Mang liu"盲流 who easily to believe to other (involve in gang behaviour)

Example 6.17

[WFP1-75-O] The tangible aim of the group:

1. It hope that street children will join the group and don't waste time in the street.

---

14 *R* indicates Wayne's revision in response to the feedback prompts.

2. It hope that learn about some science knowledge form the group
3. The stress children can positively express their comment, and learn to co-operate with other

[WFP1-75-FP] The tangible aim of the group:

Teacher's OCs
1. To encourage the street kids in some meaningful and productive learning activities
2. To teach some basic science knowledge through interesting experiment and activities
3. To encourage self-expression and cooperation in the group

Are these objectives in the cognitive, attitudinal and behavioral domain?

[WFP2-75-O][15] It the cognitive domain: it hope the street children will learn some basic science knowledge and some scientist's story.

It the attitude domain: it hopes the street children know if they will to try and change, therefore, it will be possible to success. It teaches them the cause and consequences relationship. It hopes that after the program, they will thought about the consequences before action

In the behavior domain: it hopes the user can learn to co-operation with the others and have more polite in classroom. And learn to sharing with the other.

[WFP2-75-FP] Try to use a chart to represent the different items in cognitive, attitudinal and behavioral domain

[WFP2-91-FP][16] 3. Group objectives are organized in several domains and it lead to a more comprehensive direction of the group activities.

Incidents of FPs which address meaning are scarce as they are predominantly realised by the teacher's overt corrections. The admonition (*please rewrite the whole paragraph, I am totally at lost!*) with the use of exclamation mark and the adverbial (*totally*) in Example 16 culminates a strong illocutionary force, strengthening the

15 This is also the revision to the first draft.
16 This is part of the holistic feedback placed at the end of the second draft.

assertion (Sbisà 2001) of the need to rewrite the whole paragraph for it being virtually incomprehensible. As for Wayne's revision, it seems that he attempts to produce a meaningful discourse through explicating logicality by virtue of explicit connectors as *therefore* and *it is because*. What is even more noteworthy in relation to Wayne's way of getting the message across is his incorporation of the Chinese translation after the transliteration of the Chinese term 'Mang Liu' ('gang' in English literally). This strategy, though unusual, is perfectly acceptable in this context where writing is practicality- and goal-driven. As long as meaning is made clear, it fulfils the purpose and the means to achieve it is not a major concern. This seemingly 'easy way-out' nevertheless reflects Wayne's resourcefulness in making meaning, as he becomes aware of his insufficient lexico-grammatical resources.

Example 17 shows the teacher's concern with categorisation and presentation of information. Although, on the surface, the interrogative form of feedback (i.e., *Are these objectives…?*) asks for the writer's confirmation, such an indirect speech act (Cruse 2004) underlies a request for a categorisation of the objectives into various domains. As in the previous example, Wayne has found a shortcut by flagging the three domains as the subheadings of the objectives. Wayne's revision, although surprisingly not entirely the teacher's rewrite, shows traces of the influence of the TCs: (1) the overall tone of the section is positive, (2) the use of nominalisations such as *co-operation* and *sharing* and (3) bringing in the perspective of the provider with regard to the description of aims (*it teaches them the cause and consequences relationship*) in addition to that of the clients. The teacher's OCs presented in WFP1-75-FP also introduce parallelism and such a subtle aspect of grammatical reformulation seems to have an effect on Wayne as each description of domain begins the same way, with the description of the type of domain (e.g., *in the behavior domain*) followed by a stance marker *it hopes*.

The next two FPs (WFP2-75-FP and WFP2-91-FP) seem to suggest that while Wayne's revision satisfies the requirement of categorising objectives (WFP2-91-FP), the 'shortcut' of arranging them as subheadings does not seem to live up to expectation

(WFP2-75-FP). Another format of representation of information (*chart*) is thus asked for.

6.4.3.2. Text-internal-to-text-external FPs

In the previous example, the end-of-draft holistic feedback (... *it lead to a more comprehensive direction of the group activities*) has gone beyond the immediate context of writing to address the needs of the professional activities, implying a relationship between writing and its broader social goal. Such extension, going from text-internal to text-external, is prevalent in the FPs of Wayne's session reports. This is understandable as each session report is an individual entity, and yet the professional activities mediate the writing and provide the structure and coherence of these individual reports. Consider the following FPs which are the comments given to Wayne's second and fourth session report:

> [WSR2-02-FP] Again, do not look at the result of the program but the PROCESS! What motivated the children to commit in the game? Why did they participate in the game eventually? Any positive characteristics you could identify concerning their learning and ability?
>
> [WSR2-09-FP][17] XX, you are too focused on the failure experience. Did you see the positive and constructive effect of this experience?
>
> [WSR4-03-FP] You have experienced some 'positive' dynamics in this session.

The above FPs together with Wayne's interview transcript under Example 12 highlight the instructor's concern with the focus on positive behaviours (reflected in both WSR2-02-FP and WSR2-09-FP) of the clients during their experience of participation in the program (WSR2-02-FP). In other words, two main issues are raised from the FPs: (1) having more positive evaluation and (2) being attentive to the process. In this respect, a comparison of evaluation and transitivity will be made to see how effective FPs are in making Wayne adjust his working approach which is then realised in his writing.

17 This is part of the holistic feedback placed at the end of the second session report.

The following is a comparison of the ATTITUDINAL meaning realised between the second and fourth session report, with the focus on the description of the session (see Tables 4 and 5).

Inscription/Evocation	*The Appraised*	*Attitude*
Satisfied	atmosphere	+APPRECIATION (QUALITY)
not obey the rules of the game	clients	t- –JUDGMENT (VERACITY)
Serious	cheating problem	– APPRECIATION (QUALITY)
Unfair	clients	– AFFECT (INSECURITY)
can't control the group	Wayne	t- –JUDGMENT (CAPACITY)
Fair	method	+ APPRECIATION (COMPOSITION)
get lost in the group	Wayne	t- –JUDGMENT (CAPACITY)
Easy	some clients	+JUDGMENT (CAPACITY)
not willing	clients	t- –JUDGMENT (VERACITY)
Good	clients' presentation	+APPRECIATION (QUALITY)
give a big hand	clients	t- +JUDGMENT (TENACITY)
did not succeed	task	–APPRECIATION (QUALITY)

Table 4. ATTITUDINAL resources in Wayne's second session report (description of the session).

Inscription/Evocation	*The Appraised*	*Attitude*
Serious	problem [before]	? APPRECIATION (IMPACT)
unhappy, boring, sleepy	clients [before]	– AFFECT (DISSATISFACTION)
Low	clients' spirit	– APPRECIATION (IMPACT)
Good	effect	+APPRECIATION (IMPACT)
Quiet	clients	– JUDGMENT (TENACITY)
pay attention	clients	t- +JUDGMENT (TENACITY)
pay attention	clients	t- +JUDGMENT (TENACITY)
less misbehavior	clients	+JUDGMENT (VERACITY)
Afraid	Wayne	– AFFECT (DISINCLINATION)
not well	client's spirit [before]	– APPRECIATION (IMPACT)
Happier	Wayne	+AFFECT (HAPPINESS)

Table 5. ATTITUDINAL resources in Wayne's fourth session report (description of the session).

Tables 6 and 7 show the transitivity analysis of Wayne's second and fourth reports respectively.

Participant$_1$	*Process (type)*	*Participant$_2$*
group mate	reviewed (material)	*learning contract*
the atmosphere	was (relational)	*[satisfied]*
We	played (material)	*the game*
the group	was divided (material)	*[into 2 subgroups]*
the group	transmit (material)	*a Chinese word*
the game	let (material)	*the children*
the children	know (mental)	*the heat transmission*
the group mate	did not obey (material)	*the rules of the games*
some of them	said (verbal)	*the answer to others*
cheating problem	was (relational)	*[very serious]*
the group mate	felt (mental)	*[unfair]*
the worker	can't control (material)	*the group*
the group mate	wanted (mental) to eat (material)	*the candy*
each group	monitor (material)	*other group*
(the group mate)	have (relational)	*argument*
I	would like (mental) to share (material)	*the original idea*
I	talk (verbal) about	*the fair problem*
the worker	gets (mental)	*[lost]*
the leading	was transformed (material)	*group mate*
the worker	used (material)	*Skills*
the worker	stop (material)	*the discussion*
the final part	was (relational)	*application of knowledge*
one group	was (relational)	*[easy]*
other group	was not willing (mental) to complete (material)	*the game*
the reason	was (relational)	*that...*
They	did not know (mental) how to draw (material)	
one group's presentation	was (relational)	*[very good]*
other group	give (material)	*a big hand*
other group	encourage (verbal)	*Him*
the worker	released (material)	*Tension*
the worker	thought (mental)	*a team spirit game*
the mate	did not join (material)	*[the game]*
some people	want (mental) to join (material)	*[the game]*
group dynamic	was applied (material)	-
the task	did not succeed (material)	-

Table 6. Transitivity analyses of Wayne's second session report (description of the session).

Participant$_1$	*Process (type)*	*Participant$_2$*
the centre	provided (material)	*another interest course*
I	change (material)	*the session*
the worker	had (relational)	*serious problem*
the worker	discussed with (verbal)	*Them*
the main theme	was (relational)	*the discipline*
the children	show (mental)	*[unhappy, boring and sleepy]*
I	suggested (verbal)	*washing their face*
Children	pay (mental)	*more attention*
the spirit of group mate	were (relational)	*[very low]*
I	gave (material)	*them 5 mins*
the children	expressed (verbal)	*their feeling*
the effect	were (relational)	*[good]*
some children	gave (material)	*the self reflection to me*
the content	gave (material)	*them encouragement*
the content	review (material)	*the successful experience*
They	have discussed (verbal)	*this topic*
I	did not give (material)	*them too long*
the children	discussed (verbal)	*This*
the class	started (material)	-
I	introduce (verbal)	*the main theme*
I	gave (material)	*Them*
the children	talked about (verbal)	*what they learnt*
I	teach (material)	*Them*
the children	made (material)	*A compass*
I	discover (mental)	-
They	were (relational)	*[quiet]*
I	feel (mental)	-
the timing of making compass	was (relational)	*[not enough]*
the children	did (material)	*the product*
I	modified (material)	*the plan*
They	try (mental) to speak (verbal)	*common sense*
I	gave (material)	*them example*
I	let (material) them think (mental)	*the principle*
This	is (relational)	*the new thing*
They	have (relational)	*some questions*
I	have (relational)	*the opportunity*
I	explained (verbal)	*More*
I	began (material) to make (material)	*the compass*
I	gave (material)	*them material*

They	paid (mental)	*Attention*
They	did (material)	*this compass*
a child	is (relational)	*my assistant*
a child	help (material) pass (verbal)	*the idea*
some children	chat with (verbal)	*Me*
each children	paid (mental)	*Attention*
They	share (material)	*Material*
some children	was (relational)	*Fast*
some children	finished (material)	*the product*
I	will give (material)	*Them*
the children	help (material) to teach (material)	*other child*
I	did (material)	*the product*
the group mate	did not have (relational)	*misbehavior*
the group mate	do (material)	*this product*
the worker	needs (mental)	*some task*
the worker	face (material)	*a problem*
the worker	would like (mental) to choose (material)	*a game*
the worker	let (material) them feel (mental)	*[happy]*
I	was (mental)	*[afraid]*
the group	would be (relational)	*out of control*
the worker	choose (material) to share (material)	*for them*
the group spirit	was not (relational)	*[well]*
the worker	was (relational)	*[happier]*
They	will speak (verbal)	*some jokes to other*
They	play (material)	*with other*
the member	help (material)	*other group mate*

Table 7. Transitivity analyses of Wayne's fourth session report (description of the session).

6.4.3.2.1. ATTITUDINAL resources

The analysis of ATTITUDINAL resources shows that the descriptions of the two sessions contain more or less the same amount of EVALUATION. The second session begins with a positive evaluation (*satisfied*) and ends with a very negative one (*did not success* [succeed]). A rather negative picture of the session is presented with the negative evaluation reflected insofar as the worker (*can't control/get lost in the group*) and the clients *(not willing*, feeling *unfair*) are concerned. Apparently Wayne makes some adjustment to the focus of his professional practice in response to the FPs and the adjustment is made explicit to the instructor through the fourth session report. The most noticeable outcome of the adjustment is reflected in the process of change, from a negative beginning (*low* spirit) to a very positive closure (*happier*), with clients paying attention and behaving themselves. Such positive group dynamics is pointed out by the instructor in the end-of-report feedback (WSR4-03-FP).

6.4.3.2.2. Transitivity analysis

First and foremost, Wayne obviously has taken on board the FPs by detailing the process of the session (*do not look at the result of the program but the PROCESS!*). The length of the fourth session report is almost double that of the second one in terms of the description of the session details. When it comes to processes, participants are involved and interactions take place. Not only can transitivity analysis show the various process types, it aligns the participants involved in the action. It thus makes apparent the interactional patterns between participants. Table 8 compares the number of each process type and interactional pattern between the two session reports.

		2nd Session Report (309 words)	4th Session Report (597 words)
Process Types	Material	21 (6.8)*	35 (5.9)
	Verbal	3 (1.0)	12 (2.0)
	Mental	8 (2.6)	10 (1.7)
	Relational	7 (2.3)	14 (2.3)
Interactional Pattern	Wayne ⇔ Clients	5 (1.6)	23 (3.9)
	Clients ⇔ Clients	5 (1.6)	6 (1.0)
	Wayne ⇔ Entities	1 (0.3)	4 (0.7)
	Clients ⇔ Entities	8 (2.6)	8 (1.3)

*Number in bracket denotes no. of occurrences per 100 words.

Table 8. A comparison of number of process types and interactional patterns between the two session reports.

Table 8 shows that without surprises, with the increase in the length of the report, the number of all types of processes increases as well. It is noteworthy that the number of verbal process per 100 words in the fourth report (2.0) is double that of the second one (1.0), implying that more discussions/conversations going on in the session were reported. Among the 12 incidents of verbal processes, eight of them have the clients as the sayer. For instance,

Example 18
Some of children [SAYER] chat [PROCESS: VERBAL] with me [RECEIVER] freely.

Wayne is sayer for the remaining four instances with the clients as the target of the conversation. Yet in one instance, the clients are not just a passive receiver but an active discussant:

Example 19
A (The) worker [POSSESSOR] had [PROCESS: REL.] some serious problem(s) (which) need(ed) to (be) discuss(ed) with them [POSSESSED].
→ some serious problems [VERBIAGE] need to be discussed [PROCESS: VERBAL] with them [DISCUSSANT].

Looking from the perspective of interactional patterns, it is not difficult to see the improvement of Wayne in conducting the session realised in his written reports. The fourth session is dominated by the interaction between Wayne and his clients (56.1%) while the clients interact more with entities (42.1%) e.g. *the game*, than with Wayne (26.3%) in the second session. The interaction reported between the clients and the entities decreases by half in the fourth session (1.3 vs 2.6 per 100 words in the second session).

6.5. Concluding remarks

In this chapter, I have analysed two modes of teacher comments and the respective roles in shaping the discourse and professional practices of the novice informant Wayne. Wayne is very receptive and responsive to comments given, which is unsurprising, given his learner role and the fact that discursive competence is indicative of professional competence in this placement setting.

One major conclusion which can be drawn from the analyses of overt correction is that the fieldwork instructor basically rewrites everything for Wayne. This phenomenon is consistent with Lee's (1997) findings from her research on faculty feedback situations in Hong Kong, in which she criticises local teachers for having the tendency to over-mark and adopt overt correction that encourages students to passively accept teacher's comments or revision. In the situation of placement, I posit that this overt correction strategy seems inevitable when the novice lacks generic and communicative competences. Wayne simply did not have enough lexical resources to deploy when he completed the drafts, and yet it can be seen from the interview transcripts, in general, he is aware of the rationale behind and the subtleties of the teacher's revisions. Teacher comments, from this perspective, are consciousness-raising (Swales 1990; Widodo 2006). For the fieldwork instructor, helping Wayne to get the work accepted by the agency is her ultimate goal. In this respect, despite the strong view against grammar correction by some researchers such as Truscott (1996, 1999), and with the pressing timeframe and the goal-driven motive, her action of rewriting for Wayne seems justifiable in this context. However, I am not able to conclude if such an approach is deemed pedagogically effective in other situations.

As for feedback prompts, it is apparent that they are oriented to practice with a view to exerting effects on changing professional actions or approaches. In other words, the teacher's comments have an impact on Wayne's work-related practices and eventually on his writing, despite his low language proficiency. As a novice STWsw, it is crucial for Wayne to show a proactive manner in refining his professional practice; the chief means to reflect such a manner is by writing. The supervisor has played an indispensable role in drawing Wayne's into disciplinary practice, both discourse and professional, through providing specific and targeted comments.

In the next chapter, I will illustrate how roles are operationalised in the STWs' discourse practices in relation to their social identities.

7 Roles and Identities in Placement Practices

> Identity in practice is defined socially not merely because it is reified in social discourse of the self and of social categories, but also because it is produced as a lived experience of participation in specific communities. (Wenger 1998: 151)

After analysing genre-based practices and expert-novice interactions via feedback, this chapter intends to articulate the relationship between roles and identities in placement. I have started with an epigraph from Wenger (1998) with a view to highlighting the theoretical position taken on board in this chapter that *identity* in practice ties in with our participation in the social world and our representation of *self* in the course of reifying the practice. For decades, the question of 'who am I?' has been triggering discussions from various epistemological standpoints as the concept of *identity* spans fields as diverse as philosophy, social psychology, business, linguistics, to name just a few. In linguistics, for example, recent research on the negotiation of authorial presence has centred around the analysis of the choices of personal pronouns (e.g., Kuo 1998) and self-mentioning (e.g., Hyland 2001; Tang/John 1999), clustering mostly at the thematic positions of the discourse. The presence of 'I' in relation to 'others' is crucial to the understanding of the socio-political shaping of a written work as the positioning of oneself is often a matter of negotiation of authority and cultural capital available (Wardle 2004).

Despite the popularity of the term *identity* in linguistic research, the construct of *role* is foregrounded in this chapter because of the nature of this project which involves roles-transition/roles alternation (Ashforth 2001) in the context of placement training. In Chapter 4, I have identified three socially-determined identities aligned in the STWs, namely, student-professional, professional and student. Nevertheless, what seems to be more crucial to these STWs is their act of reifying their identities: they learn and they practise. In this respect, the construct of *roles* is more prominent and its operationalisation therefore needs to be scrutinised through texts.

The first section of this chapter is devoted to a textual analysis, i.e., a discursive construction, with the focus placed on processes used by STWs in their writing. Most of the previous studies on identities look at the subject position of a discourse or self-mentioning; the emphasis on *processes* in this study is more relevant as the functional roles these STWs take on in placement exert impact on how they perceive things and act on certain tasks. Although participant observation is not a feasible data collection method in this research as explained in Chapter 3, STWs' reflective writing provides a lens to reveal what actually goes on in placement. The second section illustrates the social context of writing that reifies identities and roles in practice. Given the hybrid status of these STWs, the purpose of this section is to bring to the surface the subtleties that STWs need to be aware of when engaged in writing tasks in the professional world. This chapter thus aims to answer the following research questions:
2. How do informants' roles influence their discourse practices in relation to their identities?

- 2a. *How are roles operationalised in placement?*
- 2b. *What and how linguistic devices are manipulated in constructing and reflecting the roles of the informants in texts?*

7.1. Quantitative analysis of processes

The major linguistic tool used in the analysis of STWs' role-based identity is transitivity, for its provision of descriptive labels to categorise participants and processes in a discourse. Although the discussion centres around processes, it is important to understand how the verbal groups mediate different participants involved. Such an analysis w assisted by the corpus analysis tool WordSmith 5.0 through generating concordancing lines for interpretation of usage and context of words. The Wordlist function of WordSmith was used to generate all the words of the texts which are arranged according to frequency.

Before analysing how processes (including nominalised processes) discursively reflect roles and construct identities, a quantitative analysis is needed to identify which processes deserve attention and thus merit a more in-depth contextual and grammatical analysis. Table 1 shows the 50 processes with the highest number of occurrences (per 10,000 words). An extended result table with processes with four occurrences or above per 10,000 words can be found in Appendix C.

*Process**	*No. of Occurrences*	*Process*	*No. of Occurrences*
Be	260	Show	14
Have	96	Attend	14
Do	75	Ask	13
Know	63	Serve	12
Learn	44	Assess	12
Need	41	Assist	12
Let	35	Observe	11
Work	33	Find	11
Think	31	Provide	10
Experience	30	Form	10
Give	30	Hope	10
Help	26	Plan	10
Use	24	Question	10
Try	23	Point	9
Feel	23	Develop	9
Change	19	Begin	9
Play	18	Inform	9
Understand	18	Like	9
Educate	17	Improve	9
Teach	17	Train	9
Join	16	Share	9
Want	15	Build	9
Make	15	Communicate	9
Order	14	Experiment	8
Discuss	14	Express	8

*The number of occurrences of each process includes its derivatives (e.g. nominal form, tensed form) with at least 1 occurrence per 10,000 words; the processes shown in the above table are in their base form.

Table 1. A list of 50 processes with the highest number of occurrences.

7.1.1. Selection of processes for further discussion: weeding-out procedures

After identifying the 50 processes with high frequency, elimination is a necessary step to take before the linguistic analyses. This is because some of the processes may only be used by one informant; insufficient lexical resources confine these STWs to a narrow range of vocabulary items and thus the same term may be used by a STW repeatedly which nevertheless boosts the frequency. For example, the process *hope* has ten occurrences per 10,000 words. However, this process can only be found from the texts written by one informant and therefore is not considered representative. To make the analysis more meaningful, it is important to identify those processes which are used by all the four main informants. Table 2 shows the processes which are not included in the analysis and the reason for exclusion.

Excluded Processes+	*Reason for Exclusion*	
Serve	NOT FOUND IN	Simon's texts
Hope		Candy, Eric or Simon's texts
Plan		Eric or Simon's texts
Question		Simon's texts
Point		Simon's texts
Develop		Eric's texts
Begin		Eric or Simon's texts
Inform		Eric's texts
Share		Simon's texts
Communicate		Simon's texts
Experiment		Candy, Eric or Simon's texts
Express		Simon's texts

* Including only those mentioned in Table 1.
+ Including all the derivatives.

Table 2. Processes excluded in the analysis*.

7.1.2. Results of quantitative analysis

The results show that, not surprisingly, the three processes (*be, have, do*) with the highest occurrences are those which can perform grammatical functions (e.g., as tense markers, voice markers and modality) in addition to their meaning-making functions as other processes. For example,

Example 1

(a) … At the placement, I feel that I was affected by the emotion… *(WR_TXT-WW-04)*

(b) … since the student worker had not experienced a normal child stage, hardly could the student worker understand the children… *(RF_TXT-CD-01)*

(c) … She does not like to socialise with other fellows… *(WR_TXT-CD-01)*

Example 2

(a) The group spirit is not very strong… *(WR_TXT-WW-04)*

(b) Since the student worker had to learn many administrative works… *(RF_TXT-CD-01)*

(c) The student worker found that it was very important for the group members to get a clear instruction before doing anything *(RF_TXT-CD-01)*

Example 2 illustrates how the use of 'be', 'have' and 'do' differs from that in Example 1. The 'is' in Example 2(a) shapes a relational relationship between the carrier (*the group spirit*) and the attribute (*strong*). As for (b), *had + to* suggests an obligation. *Doing* in (c) exemplifies the common usage of 'do' to mean engagement.

The quantitative analysis also reveals the nature of placement. Firstly, placement is a learning site, exemplified by a relatively higher occurrences of processes such as *know* (63/10,000 words), *learn* (44/10,000 words) and *experience* (30/10,000 words). For example,

Example 3 *(RF_TXT-CL-05)*

After the placement I know that working with different age group should use different respectful interaction.

Example 4 *(RF_TXT-CD-01)*

It was a very good experience that the student worker could learn from this project.

Apart from acting as the verb, nominalised processes such as *experience* in Example 4 are also important meaning resources to shape identities and roles.

On the other hand, placement is a work site. Processes reflecting this include *work* (33/10,000 words) and *help* (26/10,000 words). The following are some examples:

> Example 5 *(RF_TXT-CD-01)*
> It was the first chance for the student worker to <u>work</u> with a social worker.

> Example 6 *(RF_TXT-CL-02)*
> PTs <u>help</u> the patients to regain the maximal functions to deal with daily tasks.

Not only do these verbs show the functional role of the participants in placement, they also constitute the core meaning which signals the level of competence. For instance, *work with* implies collaborative efforts. If more contextual information is given, it should reveal a subordinating relationship and that the STW works peripherally alongside the social worker.

Further, placement is a site where reflection underlies actions. Mental processes such as *think* and *feel* thus share a significant proportion, with 31 and 23/10,000 words respectively. Consider the following two examples:

> Example 7 *(RF_TXT-CD-01)*
> Although the time for placement was much tight, the student worker <u>think</u> (thinks) that it was important for (to) hand in work on time.

> Example 8 *(RF_TXT-CL-03)*
> She just insisted her protocol. I <u>feel</u> that the discussion was governed by her.

In the above examples, the STWs recount placement experience construed through mental processes, a discourse feature which is characteristic of reflective writing. It is also common to have an evaluative stance built into the reflection, illustrated by *it was important* in Example 7. Another striking difference between the two lies in the participant of the action of reflection. The use of personal pronoun *I* in Example 8 appears to be the most typical choice of the subject position. *Student worker* (or simply worker) in Example 7 may seem unusual but this is common in social work discourse. Candy explains her choice of ‘student worker’:

Candy: Eh there are several ways of writing it. Student worker means student social worker but you won't write student social worker. Another way of saying is placement student. I have chosen student worker. I think students are students. I have the identity of student... many people use I but I think if I use I it's more like defending yourself. But because in this report I also wrote my own weaknesses so I used the third person to review what I have done I think it's better
(INT-CD-04)

Candy's use of 'student worker' is a dis-alignment from her *practice*-self and taking on a *reflective*-self. This discourse feature is also noted by Paré (2002) during his extensive fieldwork in a social service agency. He claims that this "disembodied presence [...] helps them (*the social workers*) reconcile the ideological conflict between their dual and contradictory role as advocate for the client and agent of the state" (2002: 65). The invisible 'self' constructs impersonality in this workplace genre, which has long been identified as largely an emotionally-neutral discourse. Taking a third-person approach, according to Candy, can sound more objective and be critical in evaluating her own performance although she could have used personal pronoun "I'.

Based on the quantitative analysis, the processes deployed can be classified into four types with respect to the context of placement (see Table 3): active involvement, passive involvement, collaborative teaching and learning, and reflective practice. These will be explained in relation to roles and identities of STWs.

Categories	*"Active" Involvement*	*"Passive" Involvement*	*Collaborative Teaching and Learning*	*Self-Appraisal / Understanding*
Processes	help*, observe*, assist*, work*, give, use, make, know, help, attend, change, understand, teach, join, discuss, show, ask, provide, assess, find, educate, form, ask, join, try, build, order, play	experience, make, give, let	learn, teach, discuss, ask, express, train, communicate, help, educate, improve	know, think, feel, change, understand, want, show, form, improve, find, like, need

Notes:
1. * Denotes attenuated involvement.
2. Some processes may be placed in more than one category. 'Understand', for instance, can be put under 'Self-Appraisal/Understanding' when it is used in "the student worker understood that different professionals had their own strength" or put under 'Active Involvement' when it is used in "I understand the needs of the clients" as part of the role-expectation.
3. "help" appears twice under the same category because it can be used to signal a full involvement as in "the student worker helped the clients take a bath" or attenuated involvement "the student worker helped the social worker to set up the program".

Table 3. A list of processes in relation to placement.

7.2. Textually derived interpretation of roles

The hybridised identity of a *student-professional* is a transient form of identity which is unique to the context of placement. The realisation of such an intermediate organisational identity can be seen from the STWs' representations in the genres they appropriate, how their competence as a professional and incompetence as a novice find its way into interaction in the workplace and what these apprentices perceive themselves their roles are, with the alignment of both identities. In other words, STWs' engagement in the professional practice influences how the genres are shaped.

In the following sections, I will derive from the processes the types of roles played by these STWs in placement, i.e., a textually derived interpretation. The associated grammatical structures provide functional interpretations of STWs' placement experience.

7.2.1. Attenuated active participation: playing a subsidiary role

Positioning between a learner and a practitioner, STWs' participation in the placement is often attenuated if not totally restrained. This peripheral participation is reflected in the frequent selection of material processes such as *assist, follow, help, and observe/look at.* Consider the following examples:

Example 9 *(RF_TXT-CD-01)*
... [ACTOR] the student (worker) [PROCESS: MATERIAL] assisted [GOAL] the social worker [CIRCUMSTANCE: PURPOSE] to accompany the students of Sha Kong Public Yuen Yick School to visit the Jockey Club Eduyount College

Example 10 *(RF_TXT-CL-02)*
[ACTOR] The student worker [PROCESS: MATERIAL] followed [GOAL] a social work(er) [CIRCUMSTANCE: PURPOSE] to hold a 'Life Growth Course' for primary 6 students

Example 11 *(RF_TXT-SN-01)*
[ACTOR/SENSER] I, in a group of 5, [PROCESS: MATERIAL] went to the hospital [PROCESS: MENTAL] to observe [PHENOMENON] the work of year 3 students. [ACTOR/SENSER] We had to [PROCESS: MATERIAL] follow [GOAL] one of the year 3 students [PROCESS: MENTAL] to look at [PHENOMENON] what he did and the way he used to treat the patient

Example 12^[18] *(RF_TXT-PE-01)*
[PROCESS: MATERIAL] observe [GOAL] measure calf size, [PROCESS: MATERIAL] observe [goal] Foley insertion and removed

18 ^ Denotes data from the supplementary corpus.

Example 13^ *(RF_TXT-PE-01)*
[PROCESS: MATERIAL] Assist [GOAL] in pouring milk into feeding bottle, for stomach tube

Example 14 *(RF_TXT-CD-01)*
[ACTOR] The student worker [PROCESS: MATERIAL] helped [GOAL] photographing and then [PROCESS: MATERIAL] observed [GOAL] the function

Such an attenuated participation is also construed by nominalised processes in circumstantial adjuncts:

Example 15 *(RF_TXT-CD-01)*
The student worker learnt how to have a better summer under the observation of the other colleagues' programs

The above examples illustrate that STWs' attenuated and subsidiary roles are chiefly realised through their engagement *with* a more experienced member of the professional community, either being articulated explicitly (e.g., *assisted a social worker*, *followed a social worker*, *observe the work of year 3 students* as in Examples 9, 10 and 11 respectively) or backgrounded (e.g., to observe the Foley insertion which is done *by a registered nurse*). What is foregrounded in Example 12 is the techniques acquired. STWs' peripherality of involvement is also further semantically reinforced and refined through what I call the secondary processes in the hypotactic verbal group complexes as *pouring milk* and *photographing* in Example 13 and Example 14 respectively, for these actions are often considered relatively immaterial.

7.2.2. Attenuated participation: playing a beneficiary role

Apart from actively looking at things and taking part in actions, STWs constantly passively experience things and processes. Not surprisingly, the verb most frequently appears in a placement text is the mental process *experience*, as a verbal group:

Example 16 *(RF_TXT-WW-01)*
[SENSER] The student worker [PROCESS: MENTAL] experienced [PHENOMENON] the effect of different methods of holding groups from the social worker and the volunteers

Example 17 *(RF_TXT-CD-01)*
During the placement, [SENSER] the student worker [PROCESS: MENTAL] experienced [PHENOMENON] the professional value of non-judgmental attitude

Rather than having direct involvements in goal-directed activities, the above examples are concerned with a higher level of knowledge building and consolidation grounded upon the conceptualisation of practical work. In other words, what is being realised by the mental process *experience* is not a physical but cognitive entity. Such a cognitive outcome is also commonly construed by nominalised processes:

Example 18
... these experiences save [BENEFICIARY] me time(s) to find the way in (to) the social work practice, in the real situation, you need to face the individual situation *(RF_TXT-CD-01)*

Example 19
... supervision gave [BENEFICIARY] me an opportunity to learn self-awareness *(RF_TXT-CD-01)*

Example 20
... this placement let [BENEFICIARY] me know how the health profession bring benefits to those kinds of patients and parents *(RF_TXT-SN-04)*

The nominalised processes *experiences*, *supervision* and *placement* in the above three examples perform metaphorically as if they were animate participants, or abstract rhetors, (Hyland 2000) of the material processes benefiting the recipient (the STWs) by providing them with opportunities to see the real world and understand the complex issues involved in professional work.

The above examples reveal the fact that STWs stress their role as beneficiary. This is mainly because of their access to tasks and resources which is often governed by the expert members in the organisation. On the one hand, the emphasis of 'beneficiary' is a way to show STWs' awareness of learning opportunities even without an active involvement; on the other hand, this creates a positive image of the organisation which offers training opportunities so that this kind of practice can continue.

7.2.3. Active participation: playing a sub-practitioner role

In addition to attenuated involvement in the workplace, some STWs also gain much greater independence and autonomy in handling clients as their professional counterparts. These are often expressed through active processes.

> Example 21 *(RF_TXT-CL-02)*
> [ACTOR] We really [PROCESS: MATERIAL] <u>help</u> [GOAL] the patients [CIRCUMSTANCE: MEANS] by our treatments such as ept modalities and manipulative therapy.
>
> Example 22 *(WR_TXT-WW-03)*
> [ACTOR] The worker [PROCESS: MATERIAL] <u>try</u> [GOAL] to help them ease the tension.
> →[PROCESS: MATERIAL] to help [GOAL] them ease the tension
> →[PROCESS: MATERIAL] ease [GOAL] the tension
>
> Example 23 *(RF_TXT-WW-04)*
> [ACTOR] The worker [PROCESS: MATERIAL] should <u>try</u> [GOAL] to improve the misbehavior in the group

What is intriguing about the three examples is the STWs' engagement in relation to their capacity as a 'sub-practitioner' in the placement. My use of the term 'sub-practitioner' implies an active involvement in the process but the nature of work involved is relatively indirect as compared with the work of a practitioner. In Example 21, the circumstantial adjunct *by our treatments such as ept modalities and manipulative therapy* encodes the background against which the process *help* takes place. The STW acknowledges the fact that the fundamental aspect of the physiotherapy work is the wide range of therapeutic and treatment methods. In other words, methods are foregrounded here insofar as the professional work of physiotherapy is concerned. Nevertheless, in this example, the STWp's use of the process *help* indicates a rather non-discipline-specific role taken. In addition, the use of inclusive *we* positions the STW within the professional community yet in a less authoritative way (as opposed to the stronger authorial pronoun 'I').

Examples 22 and 23 show a common grammatical structure, with the primary process (*try*) followed by another process (e.g., *help*). The use of *try* underscores the attempt being made in taking the action realised in the second/third process, which is a direct intervention, i.e., *ease the tension* and *improve the misbehavior*.

7.2.4. Collaborative participation: playing an active learner role

Learning sustains the continuity of disciplinary practices and forms the crux of the social structure of placement. It is thus not surprising to have a very high incidence of processes that shape the context of learning:

Example 24 *(RF_TXT-CL-04)*
[ACTOR] I [PROCESS: MATERIAL] have learnt [GOAL] the assertiveness skills through my placement

Example 25 *(RF_TXT-CD-01)*
...[CARRIER] the student worker [PROCESS: REL, ATTRIB] was [ATTRIBUTE] willing to ask help from the supervisor
→ ... [PROCESS: VERBAL] to ask [VERBIAGE] help [RECEIVER] from the supervisor

Example 24 shows that the STW benefits from his active participation in the placement through the use of *learnt*, a process which is frequently used by STWs in writing. As for Example 25, rather than simply shaping learning through a verbal process mediated by the choice of the verbal group *ask help*, the action is added with another layer by virtue of an attributive relational process construed by *was willing*. This implies the proactive engagement of the STW in the learning process.

Another process that is common in shaping the active learner role is reflected by the use of *understand*:

Example 26^ *(RF_TXT-PE-01)*
[SENSER] I [PROCESS: MENTAL] can understand [PHENOMENON] (that) the nurses and the health care assistance do not have enough time to have bathing for every client

Example 27 *(RF_TXT-WW-04)*
... [CARRIER] the daily dialogue to interview with children [PROCESS: REL, ATTRIB] is also [ATTRIBUTE] a good method to understand the need of the children.
→... [PROCESS: MENTAL] to understand [PHENOMENON] the need of the children

Example 28 *(RF_TXT-CD-01)*
... [ACTOR] the student worker [PROCESS: MATERIAL] had borrowed [GOAL] a lot of book to have a deeper understanding of this field and the skills for assessing and intervening the service target
→... [PROCESS: REL, ATTRIB] have [ATTRIBUTE: POSSESSED] a deeper understanding of this field and the skills for assessing and intervening the service target

By engaging with various participants and entities, STWs become enculturated into the way of doing things in the professional world. Such enculturation builds upon the scaffolding of cognitive awareness and realisation. Examples 26 and 27 construe learning via a mental process by means of the verbal group *understand* whereas the nominalised process *understanding* is used in Example 28 through a possessive attributive clause. The three examples show STWs' attempt to make sense of 'how things work' through participation and self-studying.

7.2.5. Collaborative participation: playing a 'facilitated' learner role

Apart from an active involvement in the learning process, the significant social 'others' around the STWs also play a critical role in their enculturation. The following examples illustrate how the STWs' learning is facilitated in placement:

Example 29 *(RF_TXT-CD-01)*
[ACTOR] Guidance from the colleagues and the supervisor [PROCESS: MATERIAL] was facilitating [GOAL] the student (worker) to learn more

→ … [ACTOR] the student (worker) [PROCESS: MATERIAL] to learn more
Example 30 *(RF_TXT-CL-04)*
Furthermore, [ACTOR] the CE [PROCESS: MATERIAL] teaches [GOAL] us how to learn to act assertively….
→ [ACTOR] us [PROCESS: MATERIAL] how to learn to act assertively

The above two examples share the same grammatical structure in that they both have at least two processes, with one acted upon by the expert member and one by the STW. In both examples, the learner role of STWs is made explicit with the use of the process *learn*, and the instructional role of the expert member is construed through the material processes *facilitate* and *teach* in Examples 29 and 30 respectively.

7.2.6. Reflective practice: playing a reflective practitioner role

As pointed out in Chapter 5, reflective practice is integrated into the professional and pedagogical practices of social work placement. Candy recognises the importance of reflective practice:

Researcher: What do you think about reflection?
Candy: I considered it much of a hassle before. Practice is practice. Why would I need to think that much? But after my first year of study there was a lot of impact on thinking. My own way of thinking turned out to be childish they kept exerting impact on you so in terms of thinking it got better. When I looked at a thing it is what it is. But after this process, I may think differently. There may be other factors, reasons not so simple as it seems. Reflection gives me an opportunity to look at the world
(INT-CD-04)

In physiotherapy, reflection is more explicitly realised as a tag-on component via reflective writing. After the placement, Carl and Simon were required to reflect on any aspects of their learning experience. The writing can be about a specific incident in the placement or a wider issue related to the placement (e.g., Carl relates his placement experience to the hospitalisation issues in Hong Kong). Whether reflection is an embedded or a tag-on component, training reflective practitioners is one of the most important missions of placement.

There are various lexico-grammatical structures which portray STWs' role of a reflective practitioner. Consider the following examples:

> Example 31 *(RF_TXT-SN-02)*
> Based on our expert knowledge, I [PROCESS: MENTAL] think we can also help the wheelchair users to reflect how the government and public about helping people with disabilities regain normal daily life activities...

> Example 32 *(WR_TXT-WW-03)*
> Time control is bad, always overtime and the conduction is not good. I [PROCESS: MENTAL] think that the worker should be more aware of the conducting skills

> Example 33 *(WR_TXT-WW-01)*
> At the placement, I [PROCESS: MENTAL] feel that I [PROCESS: MENTAL] was affected by the emotion...

> Example 34^ *(RF_TXT-PE-01)*
> I [PROCESS: MENTAL] want to improve it (*the performance*) so I need to enhance my confidence...

From the perspective of processes, the mental process is undoubtedly the most common grammatical form to characterise reflection in discourse. All the four examples shown involve STWs engaging in a self-dialogue, and yet they are realised in different stance marking (Biber *et al.* 1999).

In Example 31, the STW's reflection is encoded by an epistemic stance clause (*based on our expert knowledge*) and lexical verb (*think*) followed by the propositional content (*we can help the wheelchair users... daily life activities*). The two epistemic markers provide a very authorial context upon which the reflection is based. The use of *I think* in Example 32 is similar to the previous example in the sense that the basis of evaluation is made with reference to the previous sentence regarding the writer's skills of conducting the program.

While epistemic stance is chiefly conveyed in STWs' reflective writing via the lexical verb *think*, attitudinal stance is realised by a wider range of mental lexical verbs such as *feel,* and *want.* The attitudinal stance expressed in Example 33 is marked by a 'verb + *that*-complement' structure (*I feel that I was affected by the emotion*). As for Example 34, the mental verb *want* is followed by a to-complement clause. The lexical *want* reflects a strong determination to improve and the tone is further strengthened through "paratactic enhancement" (Halliday/Matthiessen 2004: 413) expressed by *so*, introducing the circumstance of cause ^ effect.

When discussing the rhetorical organisation of the social work session report in Chapter 5, I briefly mentioned the use of '*should* + verb structure' to indicate reflection. Here I will go into further detail regarding this rather common grammatical feature (21 per 10,000 words) found in the texts collected with respect to the context. The following shows some of the examples:

Example 35 *(RF_TXT-WW-01)*
The worker should make the teaching point more clearly.

Example 36 *(RF_TXT-WW-01)*
The worker uses a lot of the summarization skills and the question skills. However, I should put more effort of (on) the questioning skills.

Example 37 *(RF_TXT-CD-01)*
Student should not depend on teachers and teach from the university so much.

Example 38 *(RF_TXT-SN-02)*
Being a physiotherapist, it is important that we should have good knowledge in our own field but should also appreciate and (be) aware (of) other peoples' effort in promoting rehabilitation services in the society

Example 39 *(RF_TXT-SN-02)*
We need to train and teach them to use wheelchair effectively so as to enhance daily activities. It is important that we should have a clear picture of what difficulties they need to face and overcome in the real situation.

The use of the modulation *should* in Examples 35 and 36 presents a positive picture by phrasing the weaknesses as an obligation to improve (Yule 2008). For instance, the verbal group *should make* in Example 35 implies that the worker did not illustrate the teaching point clearly enough for the clients. Similarly, for Example 36, the negative polarity is implicitly realised through the connector *however* and the determiner *more*, implying that the practice needs to be refined.

Whereas the first two examples background the weaknesses, Example 37 makes explicit the STW's awareness of an inappropriate practice (i.e. too dependent on teachers) by expressing the obligation with a negative polarity '*should not + verb*' structure. The negation nevertheless strengthens the reflective nature of the discourse.

The use of *'should + verb'* structure in Examples 38 and 39 does not bear the implication of the need for improvement. Obligations construed here (e.g., *having good knowledge in the field, appreciating and being aware of other people's effort* and *having a clear picture of difficulties*) aim to reassure the readers of the STWs' own conception of good practices.

7.3. Contextual analysis of role-related practices

The analysis in the previous section goes from the discursive representation to understanding the broader context of writing. This section starts off with the social context of the written documentation accomplished by STWs in placement and ends with the implications of how it limits their lexico-grammatical choices with respect to roles.

The ultimate personal goal of the informants of this research is to gain a professional qualification in the field of study upon graduation. To qualify as a professional, one's performance and behaviour should live up to a very high standard of professionalism. Professionalism is a fuzzy terminology, the definition of which can vary across people and disciplines (Ephgrave *et al.* 2007). Based on the existing literature on professionalism (e.g., Thornby n.d.; Hilton/Southgate 2007), I attempt to come up with a rather broad working definition of it that is suited for my purpose of analysing placement discourse practices:

> Professionalism embraces an understanding and enactment of practices accountable to one's professional roles and ethics, and is judged against values and expectations agreed upon within the profession.

This definition highlights the conformity to normative behaviours and assessment which coincides with the standpoint of the Social Identity theory suggesting that "social identities are not only descriptive and prescriptive; they are also evaluative" (Hogg/Terry/White 1995: 260).

With reference to the above lines of argument, I will look at three aspects of student placement writing: (1) mastery of role-specific writing code, drawing attention to the highly specialised abbreviations, linguistic and paralinguistic representations; (2) recognition of role-boundaries, highlighting how discourse practice is influenced by the level of the writer's work-related competence and (3) embracing preferred representation of role-practices of the profession, with regard to the philosophical foundation of the professional practice.

7.3.1. Mastery of role-specific writing code

In some professions, especially the health professions, the use of abbreviations and paralinguistic signs in documentation are prevalent. Let us consider the following excerpt together with the type-up of relevant handwritten notes from Simon:

Example 40 *(WR_TXT-SN-05)*

Aggrav.
<u>P1</u>

- Walking – pain$^+$ during heel strike (probably due to knee extension). Immediate sharp pain to 7/10 but subsided immediately once off WB
- Any extension movement of the knee ↑ P_1
- P_2 ↑ when swelling ↑

....

Special Questions

- G.H. √
- Wt. Loss^0
- X-rays – nil
- Medication – pain-killers (slightly help)

<u>*Handwritten Notes*</u>

Knee extension → pain ↑ → sharp P9/10
Relief → stop extension
take off upwards

Walking → pain ↑ P7/10
Relief → resting
....

GH → good
Wt loss → no
X ray → b4
Medication → painkiller → relief pain
→ slightly have

Learning terminology of a profession does more than just understanding the meaning of roots, prefixes, suffixes and relevant morphological rules; communicating effectively using – including deciphering and producing – commonly known abbreviations and paralinguistic signs is as important. By comparing the handwritten with the final version, the transformation from textual representations to paralinguistic signs has been made transparent: from *good* to √and from *no* to *0* in superscript. The handwritten notes also reveal that the STWp is able to make use of relevant symbols to signify meaning, e.g., ↑ represents an increase. Abbreviations are also used for the ease of documentation, e.g., G.H. (General Health Status) and Wt. Loss (Weight Loss). These kinds of textual codes are reifications of institutional practices and ontological entities developed over time. They are reifications of invisible disciplinary boundary markers (see below on role boundaries) that invariably define professional roles and identities, separating in-group members (including but not limited to those in the same profession) from the out-groups. Pamela, a nursing student, also realises the functional value of learning medical codes for documentation during her placement work in the hospital:

> For more effective and convenient work, nurses always use symbol in documentation. It is new to me and that cannot learn from textbook. It is one of the key point that provide a smooth work. *(RF_TXT-PE-01)^*

In addition to using a specific writing code in documentation, another prevalent practice in medical documentation is diagram drawing. In Chapter 5, the placement text provides a human body diagram for the STWp to indicate the area of concern. However, towards the later stage of their placement, STWps are only given blank sheets of paper to document the consultation details. Consider the following example:

Example 41 *(WR_TXT-SN-03)*
PMH: - HT, on medication
- DM°, CA°, TB°, Allergy°,

XR: (L) hip no obvious #
Crack in greater trochanter

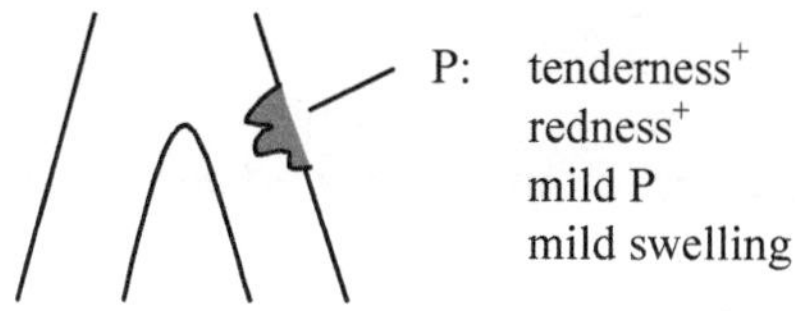

Example 41 shows Simon's hand-drawn diagram indicating the pain area, showing his awareness of an alternative form of representation available at his disposal which has a practical relevance to the work of a physiotherapist. Not only is the dimension of location important in a physiotherapist's documentation, other parameters represented in linguistic forms are crucial to enhancing the understanding of the diagram; for instance, physical (*tenderness*) and visual sensations (*redness, P, swelling*).

Disciplines such as social work, which require an elaborate description of clients rather than using technical terminologies, load the documentation with evaluative expressions supported by evidence.

> Example 42 *(WR_TXT-CD-01)*
> Ms. H is an introverted person. She does not like social with other fellows which result in not being used to tell other what problem she is facing. She is trend to hide her feeling in front of others. It makes her cannot present her own problems to others in that hardly can someone share her feeling.

> Example 43 *(WR_TXT-CD-01)*
> AA is the active group mate in the group, he often show the passion in each session, he is the core member in the group. Therefore, he is the only member, attend all session. He also shows the group leadership in the group, he let the group mate to finish the puzzle game and other experiment. In the activity of the Ying Cai School, he shows his responsibility of his duty, therefore, he is my assistant for the translation. At the end of the group, I shows the appreciate attitude for him.

Since I devoted a whole section to EVALUATION in Chapter 6, I will not undertake a detailed linguistic analysis here but I will mainly highlight the interaction between discourse and role. Although the evaluative lexis *introverted* and *active* are adjectives commonly used in daily English, they have become rather specialised in their own right in this context of writing. These specialised lexical choices come with them "rhetorical exigence" (Freedman/Adam 2000: 133) that warrant further intervention.

7.3.2. Recognition of role boundaries

As mentioned previously, *boundaries* are always an issue in professional disciplines. Boundaries are "real in the sense that [the] individual perceives them as such and acts as if they were real" (Ashforth 2001: 5). In other words, boundaries are products of our cognitive awareness. In the professional world, boundaries are crucial as they, even if they are yet to be institutionalised, order social environment and cue associated roles. Novices need to be able to recognise the very existence of boundaries and the associated role-expectations in order to discharge their duties in a legitimate way in an organisation. Boundaries are often socially constructed with reference to the level of competence and role expectations of respective professionals which in consequence have an influence on discourse practices. The following excerpt from the clinical record with teacher feedback prompts in bold exemplifies the presence of such boundary work:

Example 44 *(WR_TXT-CL-02)*

...
Functions:
...
Toileting: urination – catheterization
defecation – needs drugs
> *need assistance of nursing staff*

...

Short term goals:
...
Reduce depression √ *good point!*
↓
would be useful to state increase motivation to participate in rehabilitation program because "depression" is a diagnosis

The teacher's comments in italics clearly illustrate the importance of acknowledging professional work boundaries for the fact that a physiotherapy unit is not self-contained. The division of labour (e.g., *the assistance from the nursing staff*) is what makes the operation of a hospital efficient and is best for the client's interest. Likewise, in many other professional disciplines such as health sciences and social work, treating a client may involve the collaboration among many different professionals. As Dias *et al.* (1999: 32) point out, these disciplines rely on

> ideological practice to produce specialized professional discourse for managing and coordinating among themselves and other organizational professional and for connecting their work to that of psychologists, psychiatrists, nurses, teachers, police and occupational therapists.

This kind of "distributed cognition" (1999: 31) directs our understanding of the interplay between workplace practices and professional roles within the context of "culturally organized settings" (1999: 31) When planning the short-term goals to be achieved by the client, the STW writes *reduce depression* and the teacher's comment appears to emphasise that diagnostic descriptions should be avoided because 'diagnosis' is evidently a major role of a medical doctor. The primary role of physiotherapists is to give advice to clients on their rehabilitation programs. This is why the teacher suggests a revision that reflects the role within the work boundary of physiotherapy. The seemingly lay term *depression* which is very often used in the daily context has its meaning re-negotiated, re-contextualised and taken on a new identity within the discourse of physiotherapy – it has now become value-laden, role-specific and highly restricted in use (Lau 2006).

Related to the above point is the recognition of one's professional role. As shown in the previous example, the major role of a physiotherapist is to give professional advice on a rehabilitation program. In some of the STWps' documentation, this 'instructional' role is made rather explicit in the prescription:

Example 45 *(WR_TXT-CL-04)*
Rx: - ice pack for 15 min
- home ex. edu (ankle pump)
- advise ice Rx at home
+ elevation leg
- pamphlet given (OA care)
- SSB given (circum. 44cm)

Example 46 *(WR_TXT-CL-03)*
Rx: - massage on upper traplzius
- unilateral PA @ C5, 6
…
- education:
→ self stretch at upper trap

Example 47 *(WR_TXT-SN-02)*
Rx: - (R) ankle pump Exs x 5 times
- isometric ex of quad.
- deep breaking ex. x 5 times
- (L) bridging ex.
- education ~~of limited movn't of hip~~
on Rom allowed for (R) Hip Jt.[19]

Unlike medical doctors who prescribe mainly medication to clients, the above examples show that 'education' constitutes part of the major prescription which is construed through explicit verbal process *advise* in Example 45 and nominalised process *education* in Examples 46 and 47. In example 45, the instructional overtone is further implicated through passivisation *pamphlet given* regarding osteoarthritis care in addition to the noun phrase *home ex edu* (i.e home exercise education).

This role-related discourse practice is also seen in the suggested changes by the teacher to Wayne's proposal:

Example 48 *(WR_TXT-WW-01)*

[WFP1-52-O]	The influence of the social worker
[WFP1-52-OC]	The role of social workers

Researcher:	why the role but not influence?
Wayne:	mm my supervisor always remind me that in the first proposal in this group proposal I am not the social worker I am just a teacher teaching teaching and social work is different I plan to be teaching how to teach my use of influence directly to influence but here is the role how to use my knowledge to facilitate the people the children in this it is indirectly the group in the group let them have the experience to learn but in this influence I directly influence teach them too important role *(INT-WW-05)*

19 Teacher's revision

Example 48 shows the section heading in Wayne's proposal. In the first instance it seems the suggested changes are relatively trivial, from *influence* to *role* and from the singular form *the social worker* to the plural one *social workers*. However, the interview data explains how roles influence lexical choices. The use of *influence* has reflected the thinking of Wayne that he considers himself a professional social worker who wants to exert profound impacts or effect changes on the clients. This is further supported by his use of the definite article *the*. As pointed out by Wayne himself, he should have taken the *disguised* role of a teacher to facilitate the clients' participation in the program. The teacher's rewriting shows a distancing of Wayne's alignment to and taking on an objective stance to see the program's effects. The word *role* is relatively neutral which only underlies factual information such as the position and the involvements of the student worker. Also, the use of a plural noun *(social workers)* implies that the ideas can come from any social worker instead of a subjective, solitary opinion from a professional-to-be.

The taking on of disguised roles as a result of insufficient level of competence is also recognised by Candy. In her assessment report, she highlights explicitly her roles as an advisor, a resource person and facilitator rather than a social worker *per se*:

Example 49 *(WR_TXT-CD-01)*
Facilitator
Ms. H is not used to talk with others. It is quite difficult for her to start talking with others even if 10 minutes each day. She needs encouragement and appreciation especially in the beginning. Workers should encourage her ***to talk*** to others and to appreciate her when she can do it even a day. It will at the same time facilitate her ***to talk*** more in the future and build up a good relationship between Ms. H and others.

Advisor
Workers can try to analyze the people around her to assist her to find a significant person to share her feelings with. It is because some kind of people may not give the positive respond to Ms. H when she starts chatting with them. It is better for us to advise her ***to find*** some people can listen to her or give her some positive respond. If not, she may get frustration when she tries to share feelings to some people who are unaware, derogatory, immature or malicious.

Resource person and Facilitator

Ms. H may not find the information about the organizations easily. Workers can first tell her the mission and service area of the organizations for letting her knows more about the organizations in that it can help release her uncomfortable feelings. Workers can give her the address of the organizations or accompany her ***to go*** there in the beginning too. It may facilitate her to brave herself ***to seek*** help actively in the next time.

The supporting role of Candy is realised in the semantic properties of the primary processes as *encourage*, *facilitate, assist, accompany* and *advise* against the secondary processes, for which the actions exert a greater impact in the discourse in this case. The processes *talk, find, know, go, seek* acted by Ms. H lead to more tangible targets to achieve. In other words, these processes are the core activities depicted and foregrounded in the intervention plan.

7.3.3. Preferred representation of role-practice

To be a professional, in addition to embracing the institutional practices and norms of the discipline as mentioned above, it is also of utmost importance for him/her to understand the preferred representation of the profession. For instance, while most of the health professions rely mostly on quantitative data to reflect a client's health condition, e.g., blood pressure, temperature, some other professions may place strong emphasis on visual display (e.g., radiography) or qualitative descriptions (e.g., social work). Following these perspectives of 'professional practice', I attempt to trace how the roles and identities of *professionals* are reflected in the texts accomplished by the STWs.

In physiotherapy, for example, a number of tests have to be taken on the clients before a physiotherapist can prescribe the treatment plans. Test results are often represented and interpreted around numerical data. STWps thus need to be able to reproduce such features of rhetorical presentation in their clinical record.

Example 50 *(WR_TXT-SN-05)*
Main Problem

- see body chart
- P_1 – constant deep dull **(4/10)** with sharp pain to left medial keen **(9/10)** at terminal extension
- P_2 – tight sensation all around anterior knee **(5/10)**
- P_1 and P_2 related

The record written by Simon contains three numerical values (4/10, 9/10, 5/10), all of which denote the pain scale, ranging from 0 to 10. In other words, qualitative descriptions of pain have undergone re-contextualisation of representation which in turn contextualises interpretations with reference to a relative quantity. Presenting data in numerical forms not only shortens the reading time of other health professionals, it makes comparisons possible. The assignment of the numerical values also underlies important professional decisions which act as a reflection of institutional consensus across the board within and often outside a social structure, e.g., the understanding and interpretation of a numerical value should be the same between two health professionals. This has an important implication on the ensuing diagnosis and treatment plans.

This underlying disciplinary orientation is further proved by the teacher's feedback to the STW's work where qualitative descriptions should also be complemented by quantitative data as follows:

Example 51 *(WR_TXT-SN-06)*

Sensation	LUL	LLL	RUL	RLL
Tactile	√√	√√	√	√
Proprioception (JPS)	√√	√√	√	√
Proprioception (kinaesthesia)	√√	√√	√	√

*Simon's Notation: √√ - normal sensation; √ - sensation present but poor; X - absent

Be more quantitative XX/10 or XX/5

Standing

Reaching sideways: (L) Good (R) Fair Reaching forward: (L) and (R) good
Turning: Good

Turning 360° or how? *What do you mean by "fair"*

In Example 51, the extent to which the client has sensation for different limbs is presented in the tabular form. Simon develops his own way of indication and yet the teacher's feedback shows that the intermediate category (sensation present but poor) needs to be quantified. This further reinforces the preferred notation of representation; the use of numerical data provides more than just a descriptive category but a scaling device for assessment. The comment (*Turning 360° or how?*) that requires the STWp to frame his answer with regard to the degree of turning also indicates the inclinations towards quantitative data in the profession.

Whereas physiotherapy and social work (as shown in previous examples) orient towards quantitative and qualitative descriptions respectively, Pamela's clinical learning record, field notes taken during the placement and reflective journal, nevertheless, reveal noticeably the skill-based nature of the nursing profession. This is the case, for example, of one of her clinical record entries:

Example 52^ *(WR_TXT-PE-01)*

Day	*Date*	*Learning Activities*
3	16/2/2004	bed making, changing napkins, taking BP/P using sphygmomanometer & electronic BP machine, attend patient's need, i.e. pouring water, propped up, position patient by lifting up and turning left and right, observe H'stix taking, observe bathing, measure SaO_2, Assist in pouring milk into feeding bottle, for stomach tube. Rx mouth care with Thymolgargle explained, the use of O_2 apparatus (NC, mask) explained.

All the learning activities documented are not only related to the role-expectations of a student nurse but they are in fact the daily routines of a registered nurse. However trivial some tasks may seem, e.g., *bed making, changing napkins*, they nevertheless need to be handled properly and efficiently. As opposed to the use of processes as 'assist' and 'observe' exemplifying attenuated participation, some other activities are modified by processes which indicate direct involvement or "out on their own" (Anderson/Kiger 2008) such as *taking, changing* and *making.*

The accentuation of detail-mindedness and efficiency as the qualities of a nursing professional can also be traced through Pamela's reflective journal where she mentions:

> 1) Aware of actual condition
> Bed making is an example. From the textbook, a mitered corner is needed. However, it will be loosen if transfer client from one bed to another bed or move client upward. Therefore, the practice of Pok Oi Hospital will make a knot instead of making mitered corner....
>
> 2) Training the speed
> Moreover, I am not good at taking blood pressure by sphygmomanometer. During the practice in the real situation and practice several times for each placement, I aware that I have a sharp change in the speed of taking blood pressure. *(RF_TXT-PE-01)^*

Pamela's journal shows her awareness of attending to details such as transferring a client from one bed to another and being adaptable towards different hospitals' practices. Also, she realises the importance of improving her skills, with particular reference to efficiency, of taking blood pressure using professional equipment. All these recounts show Pamela's recognition of the foundation of the work role as a prospective nursing professional.

7.4. Concluding Remarks

In this chapter, I have demonstrated that the STWs' social identities, student-professional, student and professional are realised linguistically in various forms of role-related specificities. Analysing lexico-grammatical choices by STWs reveals that their hybrid statuses come with their special roles in the placement, one that inclines towards practitioners and one that inclines towards learners. Taking the practitioner role, STWs participate in various organisational tasks with various degrees of autonomy and engagement. More importantly, they reflect after they practice. As learners, STWs are inducted into the disciplinary practices through observation, assisting expert members and seizing learning opportunities. The placement work-related roles deduced from the textual analyses serve as an extension to the default roles of STWs, i.e., learner and practitioner, identified in Chapter 4.

I have then used the social context of roles as the starting point to investigate how roles influence discourse practice in placement. Similar to any professionals, STWs need to write based on the scope of work defined by their roles and the established practice in the profession. In addition, their discourse practice, such as lexical choices, is constrained by their level of competence.

One major theoretical argument derived from the two sections of analyses is that although "mutually sustaining" (Hall/Sarangi/Slembrouck 1999: 294; see also Stryker/Burke 2000; Ng/Feldman 2007), role is a more operationalisable and dynamic construct than identity. This is particularly relevant to this study where STWs learn by 'juggling' among various roles: ranging from being just an observer to a practitioner. Similar to identity, one's role is reflexive in relation to roles of others: from requiring assistance and guidance from peers and expert members to working independently on various tasks assigned.

The next chapter will conclude the whole study by summarising the major findings and highlighting how this empirical research enhances our understanding of learning to write in the workplace during placement.

8 Conclusion and Reflection

> [R]eflective practice [is …] a process that is undertaken in response to a positive or negative event that may be initiated consciously or subconsciously, that requires analysis to provide an answer or insight. (Chapman/Dempsey/Warren-Forward 2009: 167)

This chapter first summarises the major findings of the study with regard to the research questions set out in Chapter 1, and then highlights the ways in which this study illuminates the understanding of the discourse of learning to write professional genres in the context of placement and the linguistic aspects of a community of practice (CoP). The contributions of this study will thus be outlined in terms of theory, methodology and pedagogy. After that, I will state the limitations of this workplace research mainly with respect to data collection and then extrapolate from the findings to look at implications for further research.

8.1. Summary of major research findings

This section will begin by restating the constituents of placements. Then I will summarise the major empirical findings of this study in order to answer the research questions (RQs) set out in Chapter 1, which can be reinterpreted in two dimensions: (1) discourse of learning-to-write in placement and (2) construction and manifestation of the textually derived interpretation of roles in relation to STWs' social identities. At the end of this section, the concept of *practice* will be revisited in relation to these three dimensions.

8.1.1. The constituents of placement

This study argues for a more complex understanding and interpretation of the term *placement*: a theoretical conception that extends beyond recognising it as a static site for professional training. In this connection, this study has provided background information in regard to the constituents of placement. Drawing from textual analyses complemented with in-depth qualitative interviews, placement is conceptualised more functionally as a form of legitimate peripheral participation (LPP) within which re-contextualisation of various applications takes place. Placement, as an intermediate stage, is characterised by having hybridised features of academic discourse and professional discourse.

Text production plays a significant role in shaping the view that placement is socially and discursively constructed. As an artefact in the professional community, placement texts are produced in response to the rhetorical exigencies of various professional activities, for example, assessment of a client's conditions. On the other hand, placement texts show features of academic conventions and emphasise the demonstration of knowledge. Placement texts therefore have significant socio-political meaning as they shape subsequent social actions (e.g., STWp's advice on a home exercise program) and serve as an 'entry passport' that warrants a progression to the next academic stage.

Chapter 4 highlighted three defining characteristics of placement as a form of LPP, namely, the socio-cognitive nature of activities, the negotiated character of meaning and the relational perspectives of knowledge co-construction. These characteristics are based on the theoretical underpinning of CoP, a socio-cognitive concept that embraces aspects of participation, reification and identity. These aspects further imply an apprenticeship approach to learning in a professional context, involving interactions between expert members and novices. All this can be illustrated with an example cited in this study. Wayne, a social work student worker, participated in the design of a youth program helping street children learn some practical applications of science (see Chapter 6). His participation was not confined to organising activities to the clients; he had to document all his planning and session progress in various discursive forms (e.g., reports, proposals) which were then assessed by an expert member (e.g., a fieldwork instructor in this case). His lexical choices were very much governed by his identity, role, conventions and institutional requirements in the field.

8.1.2. Discourse of learning-to-write in placement

The second major component in this study is to investigate how STWs are inducted into disciplinary writing in placement and the relevance of learning the written documentation to the handling of other professional work. The following RQs are thus answered:

1. How do novices learn to adapt to discourse practices during their placement?

   1a. What kind of texts are produced in placement?
   1b. What are the roles of genres and practices in placement?
   1c. What social forces are imposed and how do they influence novices' discourse practices?
   1d. How do novice writers revise their texts produced and how are they drawn into disciplinary practices via making use of feedback from expert members?

The findings from the discussion in the analysis chapters clearly lead to the conclusion that learning to write professionally in placement is not a solitary act or involves formal, extensive training. The STWs acquire the written genres gradually through participating in various text-mediated activities in the community. Placement genres with a hybridisation of pedagogical and professional features are indispensable in drawing novices into the disciplinary practice. As explained in Chapters 5 and 7, through interacting with various placement genres and the concomitant lexico-grammar, novices learn the appropriate disciplinary methodologies, logical mode of thinking, preferred form of representation (e.g., qualitative vs quantitative descriptions, textual vs visual). The link between discourse practice and professional practice is made explicit. In section 5.2.1 of Chapter 5, for instance, I showed that the organisation of a physiotherapy text is rhetorical, which draws

STWps' attention to a logical sequence of consultation. This example clearly suggests a connection between genre and practice.

By making use of the feedback from the expert members in the process of textual production, the novices come to realise the appropriate discursive and evaluative stance (e.g. toning down of judgmental attitudes, objectifying subjectivity) adopted via lexico-grammatical choices, and categorise problems and issues accurately for ensuing interventions, practice-related specificities, as discussed in Chapter 6. Example 12 cited in section 6.3.3.1 of Chapter 6 illustrates a preference for presenting a positive image. Wayne's original phrasing '*... the street children will join the group and don't waste time...*' in his proposal was considered too negative and judgmental about the clients. The expression was revised by his instructor to '*to engage the street kids in some meaningful and productive learning activities*'. The rewrite appraises the activities positively and does not pass judgment on the clients.

Reflection through engaging in discourse practice is found to have played a significant role in placement learning as explored in Chapter 5. In the case of social work, reflection is embedded in discourse practice (e.g. completing the evaluation checklist in a session report) during placement. Reflective practice, in other words, forms the basis of social work placement and ties in closely with the on-the-spot professional work. As for Physiotherapy, reflection is rather implicitly linked to placement learning as a tag-on component (e.g., reflective writing done after the placement).

The discourse of learning-to-write cannot be understood without reference to 'social forces' underlying the placement structure. The word 'forces' is used metaphorically here to imply a tension between two competing yet overlapping discourses, academic and professional. Although working in a professional context, STWs' discourse practices are very much subject to the institutional requirements of academic discourse. This is exemplified by the facts that (1) English is used as the only recognised medium of documentation as part of the degree requirement and yet these STWs communicate with their clients almost exclusively in Cantonese, and (2) STWs are found to have looked for means to satisfy the linguistic demands from the academia (e.g., the inclusion of theories in writing) although they may not have seen the immediate relevance to their work.

8.1.3. Construction and manifestation of roles in relation to identities

Being both students and professionals, the STWs need to understand the fact that 'identity' is not just a descriptive label but comes with a schema of linguistic representations, which often tie in with the concept of role. In this regard, I have answered the following RQs:

2. How do informants' roles influence their discourse practices in relation to their identities?

    2a. How are roles operationalised in placement?

    2b. What linguistic devices are found and how are they manipulated in constructing and reflecting roles of the informants in texts?

Apart from direct involvement in discourse production, STWs also engage in observation and legitimate peripheral participation at the leading edge of learners' "zone of proximal development" (Vygotsky 1978). By interacting with capable peers, STWs learn their "identity and role" (Martin 2005: 143) in professional practices, which ultimately have an impact on the way they go about constructing and reflecting them-'selves' in writing as explained in Chapter 7. Placement provides an excellent platform where STWs learn to become aware of their hybrid identities (student-professional) and roles construed through linguistic choices. The different processes the STWs use in their writing reflect the different roles these novices have played in placement. Most important of all, STWs learn to define their boundaries of work within a joint enterprise by making use of appropriate lexical choices for their job descriptions and role-repertoires. Example 44 in Section 7.3.2 of Chapter 7 highlights the relationship between lexical choices and role boundaries. The STWp's use of the term *depression* is inappropriate because *depression* is diagnosis which is beyond the scope of a physiotherapist. Such a term is reserved for the use of medical doctors. Physiotherapists, and hence student physiotherapists, should recognise their role as an 'educator' when it comes to giving advice to clients. Examples 45 to 47 in the same chapter show the STWps' awareness of their proper role in the healthcare context by using *educate* in their documentation.

8.1.4. Revisiting the concept of practice

In Chapter 2, I outline four qualities of *practice* to signify its inherent social orientation:

- Practice is concerned with both the process and outcome;
- Practice ties in with professionalism, giving it a legitimate status;
- Practice relates to both individual and community;
- Practice is about engagement and experience to make meaning.

The term 'practice' has been invariably used in this volume, noticeably appearing in the title of all the last three main discussion chapters. It is necessary, therefore, to revisit the concept of *practice* in order to understand how it can be more contextually defined in relation to the research findings of this study. In other words, the operationalisation of *practice* is understood at a linguistic level. First of all, *practice* in this study is mediated by texts. Texts scaffold novices with the required structure and lexico-grammatical resources to practise appropriately in a given context. Through repeated operations, these genre resources are expected to become part of the internal knowledge which is readily retrievable in future practice. This conception coincides with the everyday saying "practice makes perfect".

Practice is governed by the status of participating members. Novices realise their role-expectations in the process of discharging their duties assigned by the expert members. Over time, novices are expected to acquire such an important aspect of professionalism to avoid performing tasks beyond the level a professional is entitled to. Practice, in this sense, is not a fixed entity but a construct that is subject to contestation based on the surrounding social conditions.

8.2. Contributions of this study

Following from the summary of the major research findings, this section highlights several ways in which this study can make a contribution to theory, methodology and pedagogy as a result of investigating professional learning.

8.2.1. Theoretical contributions

In terms of contribution to the theory of learning, this study brings to the surface the roles played by the deployment of linguistic resources at the initial stage of professional training. For example, Chapter 5 has shown that text designers induct novices into disciplinary practices through lexico-grammar (e.g., using complex nominal groups to present a given case). The linguistic construct of CoP is therefore made apparent.

In addition, while Wenger (1998) links identity to the social context of participation (e.g., full non-participation, peripherality), this study has also sought linguistic evidence to operationalise identity. The addition of the construct of roles is an important contribution to the understanding of theories of social learning and identity. In Chapter 7, I raised a theoretical argument that the construct of roles appears to be more operationalisable than identity in the present study which investigates STWs' active involvement in the joint enterprise through the textual analysis of processes and participants.

I have also introduced the term and framework of analysing 'genre-based practices' to encapsulate the fact that genre is inextricably intertwined with practice. A similar term "genre-aligned practice" was coined by Mavor and Trayner (2001) with a view to outlining a framework for designing ESP courses in line with the practices in the professional world. In other words, the motivation of the application of genre-aligned practices originates from the academic world and its ultimate effects thus also impact on the same place. Genre-based practices focus on the interactional nature of practice to produce effects on both academic and professional worlds. Figure 1 shows the differences between the two kinds of practices with respect to the bouncing effects generated.

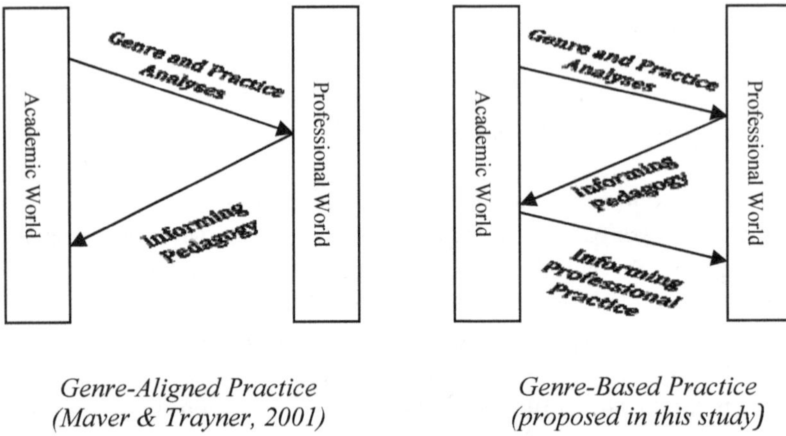

Figure 1. Bouncing effects of genre-aligned practices and genre-based practices.

8.2.2. Methodological contributions

I have proposed two linguistic means to gather information regarding the social context of writing. First of all, transitivity analysis has a role to play in reflecting how a participant is positioned in relation to other participants in an activity (as delineated in Chapter 7). Such type of analysis bridges the gap between the linguistic representation and professional practice (as explained in Chapter 5).

The second linguistic means adopted in this study is reflective writing. The value of keeping a reflective journal by the researcher has long been recognised in qualitative research literature (e.g., Ortlipp 2008). In this study, reflective writing is a data source which not only reflects the inner thought of the STWs, it also provides the recount of incidents critical to their learning experience. In this case, reflective writing is a text in its own right and at the same time shapes the social context of discourse production.

8.2.3. Pedagogical implications

In terms of pedagogical implications, this research has pointed out some fundamental concerns in designing professional training programs with "writing in the discipline" as an embedded component. It has found that there are disciplinary subtleties (e.g., some lexical items which are allowed to be used by certain professionals but not by others) which may not be readily apparent to language teachers. This study therefore provides empirical ground to support the advocate that the role of content experts cannot be overlooked. Their contribution to the design of English for Occupational Purposes is therefore indispensable by making language teachers aware of these subtle discrepancies of vocabulary meaning between daily and professional uses.

There has been research on placement learning but the informants in those studies are mostly native English speakers. The current study therefore adds another dimension to the demographics of informants who have to reconcile the conflicting linguistic demands (i.e., delivering professional services verbally in Cantonese yet English is used in documentation) and at the same time, wrestle with clients' problems which are always more complicated and unpredictable than cases practised at school.

8.3. Limitations of this study

8.3.1. Data collection

The limitations of this study are mainly concerned with data collection. As this is a piece of workplace research which intends to collect naturally-occurring data about the role of language in placement learning, the researcher's intervention at the data collection stage must be minimised. The risk of this is that the researcher might not have a complete control over the amount and the type of data collected. Even with a flawless research design and plan prior to data generation, the process is subject to change, as is shown by the feedback-revision data collected for this study. It is understandable that different teachers have different preferences for giving feedback. It was not until Wayne began working that I was informed that multiple drafting was adopted and that teacher's comments were abundant (while only verbal feedback was given by Candy's supervisor). This is why more attention was devoted to Wayne's data, and interviews were conducted more frequently during his placement.

Given the fact that the STWs in this study were all at the initial stage of their placement, the written tasks they could and needed to handle were restricted. Hence, the data collected may have been limited. Close readings of all the texts collected and in-depth qualitative interviews are therefore necessary.

8.3.2. Transferability of findings

As practice is a form of performance, subjectivities come into it. How learning proceeds depends a lot on the options available and the decisions STWs and expert members make. In this respect, aspects of learning are bound to have idiosyncrasies. The findings from this study thus need to be interpreted carefully as and when they are applied to other contexts.

8.4. Recommendations for further research

8.4.1. Longitudinal study

This study looks at the initial stage of placement across disciplines in order to make comparison more possible. However, I do not have enough empirical data to make a conclusion about the pedagogic effectiveness of any particular learning approach. A longitudinal study comparing the different learning approaches right before the STWs graduate will provide very rich data for helping design a well-structured professional training program. One possibility is to look at one discipline and to follow through a large group of STWs' learning trajectory from the first placement to the last one. If a larger sample size is available, other positivistic data collection methods such as questionnaire surveys can be adopted to yield quantitative information about STWs' perceptions and preferred learning approaches about placement learning.

8.4.2. Investigating the learning of other practices

Another extension of the current study is to investigate the learning of other practices, for example, counseling practice in social work, in addition to discourse practices in placement. I have already shown that discourse practices effect actions. A systematic analysis of the interaction of learning various practices will thus shed light on our understanding of specific stages of enculturation process and a wider context of professional growth.

8.4.3. Participant observation

Apart from the practical concerns stated above, the limitation with regard to the bodily and spatial enactment of 'practice' is also worth considering. Since practice is always situated in a local activity system, having informants recount their placement learning experience in interviews may lead to an oversight of some other resources or socio-cultural tools which play a part in STWs' participation. As mentioned in Chapter 3, participation observation was not used as part of data collection because access was not entirely feasible as nine participants were working at different organisations at the same time (mostly during the summer vacation). However, if only one discipline were investigated and the ethical issues were cleared, participant observation could be a useful data generation method providing important information about the social context and it could aid interpretation of linguistic data.

8.4.4. Using think-aloud protocol

It has been mentioned that think-aloud protocol was adopted in the pilot study but eventually was discarded in the main study. Although very labour-intensive, this method generates data which can more accurately portray a STW's revision process in light of the teacher comments. If teachers who are used to providing substantial written feedback are identified and student informants who are more able to verbalise thoughts participate in the research, the use of think-aloud protocol should provide a very insightful perspective regarding the negotiation of meaning.

8.5. Concluding remarks: learning in a textually-mediated world

In this chapter, I have delineated how my study makes a contribution to the body of knowledge related to social/implicit learning and professional training. The oft-neglected linguistic aspects are brought to the surface and operationalised.

With all the aspects and dimensions considered, this study has put forward a major claim that placement texts mediate between the appropriation of genre and practice, and between the realisation of identities and roles. In other words, placement learning is not just about skills training; it embraces learning of 'acting' and 'becoming' in a textually-mediated world and the 'acting' and 'becoming' are interconnected. Figure 2 presents a diagram summarising textually-mediated placement learning.

The actual learning scenario in placement is certainly more complicated than that presented in Figure 2, largely because of the presence of hybridisation and re-contextualisation of practices. This research has highlighted these two core characteristics which help differentiate placement from other learning settings.

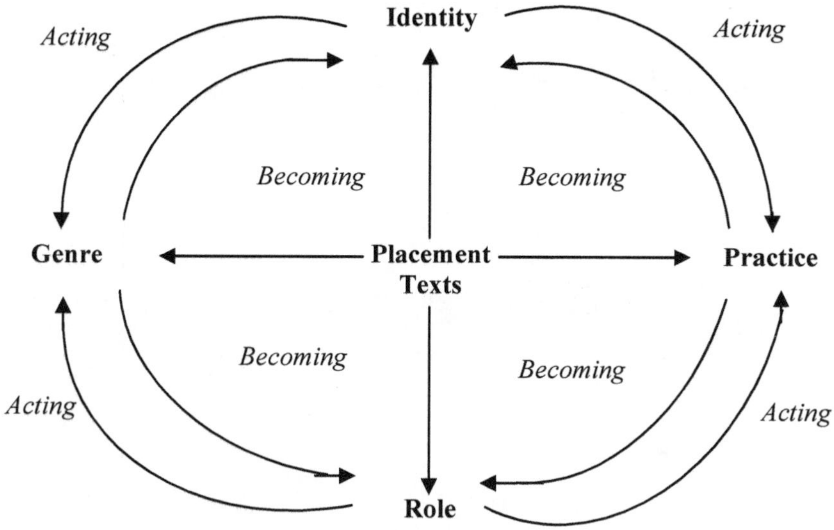

Figure 2. Textually-mediated placement learning.

In the course of acting and becoming in placement, negotiations naturally take place even though they seem to be controlled mainly by the expert members. A negotiation can happen internally within oneself but more often than not, this involves other members in the CoP. My study has already shown the significance of social others, including expert members, peers and clients along the STWs' learning path.

In conclusion, learning to become a professional in a textually-mediated world is a complex issue; the working definition of placement in Chapter 4 can now be reconsidered with a textual orientation. Negotiation, re-contextualisation and hybridisation are the three pillars of placement. They support and provide the structure to a student worker's learning experiences. Negotiation takes place in placement, even if it is merely about selecting relevant generic resources to go into the placement documentation. Re-contextualisation comes about even when it is just concerned with the choice of a vocabulary item that suits a STW's role. Last but not least, hybridisation occurs even if it is just a matter of recognising the textual features that dovetail discourse practice and professional practice.

References

Abbuhl, Rebekha 2005. *The Effect of Feedback and Instruction on Writing Quality: Legal Writing and Advanced L2 Learners*. Unpublished doctoral dissertation, Georgetown University, Washington DC.

Anderson, Evelyn / Kiger, Alice 2008. I felt like a real nurse – Student nurses out on their own. *Nurse Education Today*. 28/4, 443-449.

Andrews, Gavin / Brodie, David / Andrews, Justin P. / Hillan, Edith / Thomas, B. Gail / Wong, Josephine. et al. 2006. Professional Roles and Communication in Clinical Placements: A Qualitative Study of Nursing Students' Perceptions and Some Models for Practice. *International Journal of Nursing Studies, 43/7*, 861-874.

Arksey, Hilary / Knight, Peter 1999. *Interviewing for Social Scientist.* London: Sage Publication.

Ashforth, Blake E. 2001. *Role Transitions in Organizational Life: An Identity-based Perspective*. London: Lawrence Erlbaum Associates.

Askehave, Inger 2002. Drug Information for Laymen: Good or Bad Medicine. In Candlin, Christoper. N. (ed.) *Research and Practice in Professional Discourse*. Hong Kong: City University of Hong Kong Press, 279-292.

Axford, Beverley 2005. Entering Professional Practice in the New Work Order: A Study of Undergraduate Students and Their Induction Into Professional Work. *The Australian Educational Researcher, 32/2*, 87-104.

Baldock, John / Prior, David 1981. Social Workers Talking to Clients: A Case Study of Verbal Behaviour. *British Journal of Social Work.* 11/1, 19-38.

Bandura, Albert 1977. *Social Learning Theory*. New York: General Learning Press.

Bartlett, Harriet M. 2003. Work Definition of Social Work Practice. *Research on Social Work Practice.* 13, 267-270.

Barton, David / Hamilton, Mary 2005. Literacy, Reification and the Dynamics of Social Interaction. In Barton, David / Tusting, Karin (eds) *Beyond Communities of Practice: Language, Power and Social Context*. Cambridge: Cambridge University Press, 14-35.

Bathmaker Ann-Marie / Avis, James 2005. Becoming a Lecturer in Further Education in England: the Construction of Professional Identity and the Role of Communities of Practice. *Journal of Education for Teaching*. 31/1, 47-62.

Bazerman, Charles 1994. Systems of Genres and the Enactment of Social Intention. In Freedman, Aviva / Medway, Peter (eds) *Genre and the New Rhetoric*. London: Taylor and Francis, 79-101.

Bazerman, Charles / Little, Joseph / Bethel, Lisa / Chavkin, Teri / Fouquette, Danielle / Garufis, Janet 2005. *Reference Guide to Writing Across the Curriculum*. Retrieved March 20, 2009, from http://wac.colostate.edu/books/bazerman_wac/.

Beaufort, Anne 1998. Transferring Writing Knowledge to the Workplace, are we on track? In Garay, Mary Sue / Bernhardt, Stephen A. (eds) *Expanding Literacies: English Teaching and the New Workplace*. New York: SUNY Press, 179-200.

Bereiter, Carl / Scardamalia, Marlene 1987. *The Psychology of Written Composition*. New Jersey: Erlbaum.

Berkenkotter Carol / Huckin, Thomas N. 1995. *Genre Knowledge in Disciplinary Communication: Cognition/Power*. New Jersey: Lawrence Erlbaum Associates.

Bhatia, Vijay Kumar 1994. Generic Integrity in Professional Discourse. In B.L. Gunarsson/P. Linnel/B. Norberg (eds) *Text and Talk in Professional Context*. Sweden: ASLA, 61-76.

Bhatia, Vijay Kumar 2005. *Worlds of Written Discourse: A Genre-based View*. Cornwall: Continuum.

Bhatia, Vijay Kumar 2008a. Genre Analysis, ESP and Professional Practice. *English for Specific Purposes*. 27/2, 161-174.

Bhatia, Vijay Kumar 2008b. Towards Critical Genre Analysis. In Bhatia, Vijay Kumar / Flowerdew, John / Jones, Rodney, H. (eds) *Advances in Discourse Studies*. New York: Routledge, 166-177.

Biber, Douglas / Johansson, Stig / Leech, Geoffrey / Conrad, Susan / Finegan, Edward 1999. *Longman Grammar of Spoken and Written English*. London: Pearson Education Limited.

Biddle, B. J. 1986. Recent Development of Role Theory. *Annual Review of Sociology*, 12, 67-92.

Bitzer, Lloyd F. 1968. On the Classification of Discourse Performances. *Rhetorical Society Quarterly,* 7, 31-40.

Bjorklund, Anita 2002. Occupational Therapy Students' Paradigm: A Passage from Beholder to Practitioner. *Australian Occupational Therapy Journal,* 47, 970-1009.

Boud, David / Keogh, Rosemary / Walker, David 1985. *Reflection: Turning Experience into Learning.* London: Kogan Page.

Boyd, Evelyn M. / Fales, Ann W. 1983. Reflective Learning: Key to Learning from Experience. *Journal of Humanistic Psychology,* 23/2, 99-117.

Britton, James 1970. *Language and Learning.* Coral Gables: University of Miami Press.

Brown, James Dean 1995. *Understanding Research in Second Language Learning.* Cambridge: Cambridge University Press.

Bruner, Jerome 1986. *Actual Minds, Possible Worlds.* Cambridge: Harvard University Press.

Bulter, Christopher 2002. *Postmodernism: A Very Short Introduction.* Oxford: Oxford University Press.

Butt, David / Fahey, Rhondda / Feez, Susan / Spinks, Sue / Yallop, Colin 2000. *Using Functional Grammar: An Explorer's Guide.* Sydney: NCELTR.

Capucho, F./Oliveira A. M. 2005. Eu&I: On the Notion of Intercomprehension. In A. Martins (ed.) *Building Bridges: EU&I. European Awareness and Intercomprehension.* 11–18. Viseu: Universidade Cato'lica Portuguesa, Centro Regional das Beiras.

Carter, Michael 2007. Ways of Knowing, Doing and Writing in the Disciplines. *College Composition and Communication* 58/3, 385-418.

Carter, Michael / Ferzli, Miriam / Wiebe, Eric N. 2007. Writing to Learning by Learning to Write in the Disciplines. *Journal of Business and Technical Communication.* 21/3, 278-302.

Chafe, Wallace 1985. Linguistic Differences Produced by Differences Between Speaking and Writing. In Olson, David R. / Torrance, Nancy / Hildyard, Angela (eds) *Literacy, Language, and Learning: The Nature and Consequences of Reading and Writing.* Cambridge: Cambridge University Press, 105-123.

Chapman, Naomi / Dempsey, Shane E. / Warren-Forward, Helen M. 2009. Workplace Diaries Promoting Reflective Practice in Radiation Therapy. *Radiography.* 15/2, 166-170.

Chandler, Daniel 2006. *Semiotics for Beginners*. Retrieved March 7, 2009, from http://www.aber.ac.uk/media/Documents/S4B/sem04.html.

Cheng, Winnie / Mok, Desmond 2008. Discourse Processes and Products. *English for Specific Purposes.* 27/1, 57-73.

Chew, Kheng-Suan 2005. An Investigation of the English Language Skills Used by New Entrants in Banks in Hong Kong. *English for Specific Purposes.* 24/4, 423-435.

Coe, Richard / Lingard, Lorelei / Teslenko, Tatiana (eds) 2002. *The Rhetoric and Ideology of Genre*. New Jersey: Hampton Press.

Cohen, Louis / Manion, Lawrence / Morrison, Keith 2001. *Research Methods in Education*. (5th ed.). London: Routledge.

Connor, A. O. 2008. The Use of Reflective Practice on Critical Incidents, in Neonatal Setting, to Enhance Nursing Practice. *Journal of Neonatal Nursing,* 14, 87-93.

Cook-Gumperz, Jenny / Messerman, Lawrence 1999. Local Identities and Institutional Practices: Constructing the Record of Professional Collaboration. In Sarangi, Srikant / Roberts, Celia (eds) *Talk, Work and Institutional Order: Discourse in Medical, Mediation and Management Settings*. Berlin: Mouton de Gruyter, 145-181.

Cruse, Alan 2004. *Meaning in Language: An Introduction to Semantics and Pragmatics.* Oxford: Oxford University Press.

Davies, Janis 2006. The Importance of the Community of Practice in Identity Development. *The Internet Journal of Allied Health Sciences and Practice.* 4/3. Retrieved July 30, 2008, from http://ijahsp.nova.edu/articles/vol4num3/davis.pdf.

Davies, Mark 2004. Corpus of Contemporary American English. Retrieved February 22, 2009, from http://www.americancorpus.org/.

Denzin, Norman K. 1989. *The Research Act: A Theoretical Introduction to Sociological Methods*. (3rd ed.). New Jersey: Prentice Hall.

Devitt, Amy 2004. *Writing Genres*. Carbondale: Southern Illinois University Press.

Dias, Patrick 2000. Writing Classrooms as Activity Systems. In Dias, Patrick / Paré, Anthony (eds), *Transitions: Writing in Academic and Workplace Settings.* New Jersey: Hampton Press, 11-29.

Dias, Patrick / Freedman, Aviva / Medway, Peter / Paré, Anthony 1999. *Worlds Apart: Acting and Writing in Academic and Workplace Contexts*. New Jersey: Lawrence Erlbaum Associates.
Dias, Patrick / Paré, Anthony (eds). 2000. *Transitions: Writing in Academic and Workplace Settings*. New Jersey: Hampton Press, Inc.
Dudley-Evans, Tony / St John, Maggie Jo 1998. *Developments in English for Specific Purposes*. Cambridge: Cambridge University Press.
Eggins, Suzanne 1994. *An Introduction to Systemic Functional Linguistics*. London: Pinter.
Ellingson, Laura L. 2009. *Engaging Crystallization in Qualitative Research: An Introduction*. Thousand Oaks: Sage.
Emig, Janet 1977. Writing as a Mode of Learning. *College Composition and Communication*. 28, 122-28.
Engeström Yrjö 1999. Activity Theory and Individual and Social Transformation. In Engestörm, Yrjö / Miettinen, Reijo / Punamäki, Raija-Leena (eds) *Perspectives on Activity Theory*. Cambridge: Cambridge University Press, 19-38.
Ephgrave, K. S. / Ferguson K. / Sharp, W. J. / Woodhead, J. / George, T. / Markham, S. et al. 2007. Faculty Professionalism: Does it Vary by Discipline? *Journal of Surgical Research*. 137/2, 159-160.
Eribes, R. A. 1997. Foreword. In Pressman, Andrew *Professional Practice 101: A Compendium of Business and Management Strategies in Architecture*. New York: John Wiley and Sons.
Ericsson, K. Anders / Simon, Herbert A. 1993. *Protocol Analysis: Verbal Reports as Data*. London, The MIT Press.
Ethridge, Elizabeth A. / Branscomb, Kathryn R. 2009. Learning Through Action: Parallel Learning Process in Children and Adults. *Teaching and Teacher Education*. 25/3, 400-408.
Evans, Stephen 1999. The English Language Needs of Building Services Practitioners in Hong Kong. *Asian Journal of English Language Teaching*. 9, 41-57.
Eysenck, Michael W. 2001. *Psychology for A2 Level*. UK: Psychology Press.
Fairclough, Norman 1992. *Discourse and Social Change*. Cambridge: Polity Press.
Ferris, Dana R. 1995. Student Reaction to Teacher Response in Multiple-draft Composition Classrooms. *TESOL Quarterly*. 29/1, 33-53.

Ferris, Dana R. / Roberts, Barrie 2001. Error Feedback in L2 Writing Classes: How Explicit Does It Need To Be? *Journal of Second Language Writing*. 10, 161-184.

Flexner, Abraham 2001. Is Social Work a Profession? *Research on Social Work Practice*. 11/2, 152-165.

Flick, Uwe 1998. *An Introduction to Qualitative Research*. Thousand Oaks: Sage Publication.

Flower, Linda / Hayes, John R. 1980. The Cognition of Discovery: Defining a Rhetorical Problem. *College Composition and Communication*. 31, 21-32.

Flower, Linda / Hayes, John R. 1997. A Cognitive Process Theory of Writing. In Villanueva, Victor Jr. (ed.) *Cross-talk in Comp Theory: A Reader*. 251-275. Illinois: National Council of Teachers of English.

Flowerdew, John / Dudley-Evans, Tony 2002. Genre Analysis of Editorial Letters to International Journal Contributors. *Applied Linguistics*. 23/4, 463-489.

Flowerdew, John / Wan, Alina 2006. Genre Analysis of Tax Computation Letters: How and Why Tax Accountants Write the Way They Do. *English for Specific Purposes*. 25/2, 133-153.

Flowerdew, Lynne 2005. Integrating Traditional and Critical Approaches to Syllabus Design: The 'What', the 'How' and the 'Why?' *English for Specific Purposes*. 4/2, 135-147.

Fontana, Andrea / Frey, James H. 2000. The interview: From Structured Questions to Negotiated Text. In Denzin, Norman K. / Lincoln, Yvonna S. (eds) *Handbook of Qualitative Research* (2nd ed.) California: Sage Publications, Inc, 645-672.

Forey, Gail 2003. *Funding Proposal Submitted to Hong Kong Polytechnic University*.

Forey, Gail / Lockwood, Jane 2007. "I'd Love to Put Someone in Jail for This": An Initial Investigation of English in the Business Processing Outsourcing (BPO) Industry. *English for Specific Purposes*. 26/3, 308-326.

Fox, Steve 2000. Community of Practice, Foucault and Actor-network Theory. *Journal of Management Studies*. 37/6, 853-867.

Freedman, Aviva / Adam, Christine 2000b. Bridging the Gap: University-based Writing That Is More Than Simulation. In Dias, Patrick

/ Paré, Anthony (eds) *Transitions: Writing in Academic and Workplace Settings*. New Jersey: Hampton Press. 129-144.
Fretchling, Joy / Sharp, Laure (eds) 1997. *User-friendly Handbook for Mixed Method Evaluation*. Retrieved January 2, 2006 from http://www.ehr.nsf.gov/EHR/REC/pubs/NSF97-153/star.htm.
Galve, Ignacio Guillén 1998. The Textual Interplay of Grammatical Metaphor on the Nominalizations Occurring in Written Medical English. *Journal of Pragmatics*. 30, 363-385.
Garzone, Giuliana 2010. Actors, Identities and Roles in Professional and Academic Discourse: An Introduction. In Garzone, Giuliana / Archibald, James (eds) *Discourse, Identities and Roles in Specialized Communication*. Bern: Peter Lang, 15-29.
Gee, J. P. 2001. *An Introduction to Discourse Analysis: Theory and Method*. London: Routledge.
Gee, James Paul / Hull, Glynda A. / Lankshear, Colin 1996. *The New Work Order*. London: Allen and Unwin.
Gibbons, Michael 2005. Engagement with the Community: *The Emergence of a New Social Contract Between Society and Science*. Presented at Community Engagement Workshop, Griffith University.
Gilmore, Alex 2004. A Comparison of Textbook and Authentic Interactions. *ELT Journal*. 58/4, 363-374.
Glesne, Corrine 1999. *Becoming Qualitative Researchers: An Introduction*. (2nd ed.). New York: Longman.
Goffman, Erving 1971. *The Presentation of Self in Everyday Life*. Harmondsworth: Penguin.
Golafshani, Nahid 2003. Understanding Reliability and Validity in Qualitative Research. *The Qualitative Report*. 8/4, 597-607.
Gray, Bette 2004. Informal Learning in an Online Community of Practice. *Journal of Distance Education*. 19/1, 20-35.
Guba, Egon G. / Lincoln, Yvonna S. 2005. Paradigmatic Controversies, Contradictions, and Emerging Confluences. In Denzin, Norman K. / Lincoln, Yvonna S. (eds) *Handbook of Qualitative Research*. Thousand Oaks: Sage Publication, 191-216.
Hall, Christopher / Slembrouck, Stef / Sarangi, Srikant 2006. *Language Practice in Social Work: Categorisation and Accountability in Child Welfare*. London: Routledge.

Halliday, Michael A. K. / Matthiessen, Christian M. I. M. 2004. *An Introduction to Functional Grammar* (3rd ed.). London: Arnold.

Harper, Douglas 2001. *Online Etymology Dictionary*. Retrieved February 22, 2009, from <http://www.etymonline.com/index.php?search=practice&searchmode=none>.

Harris, Janet (n. d.). *Appraising Qualitative Research in Dentistry*. Retrieved March 21, 2009, from <http://www.cebd.org/index.aspx?o=1171>.

He, Ming Fang 1998. *Professional Knowledge Landscapes, Three Chinese Women Teachers' Enculturation and Acculturation Processes in China and Canada*. Unpublished doctoral dissertation, University of Toronto, Canada.

Henri, France / Pudelko, Béatrice 2003. Understanding and Analysing Activity and Learning in Virtual Communities. *Journal of Computer Assisted Learning*. 19, 474-487.

Herring, Susan C. / Schedit, Lois Ann / Bonus, Sabrina / Wright, Elijah 2004. Bridging the Gap: A Genre Analysis of Weblogs. *Proceedings of the 37th Hawaii International Conference on System Sciences*, 1-11.

Hesselgrave, David 2008. Enculturation and Acculturation: A Reading for Cultural Anthropology. Retrieved July 26, 2009, from <http://home.snu.edu/~hculbert/encultur.htm>.

Hilton, Sean / Southgate, Lesley 2007. Professionalism in Medical Education. *Teaching and Teacher Education*. 23, 265-279.

Hogg, Michael A. / Terry, Deborah J. / White, Katherine M. 1995. A Tale of Two Theories: A Critical Comparison of Identity Theory with Social Identity Theory. *Social Psychology Quarterly*. 58/4, 255-269.

(HKPolyU) The Hong Kong Polytechnic University. 2003. *University Prospectus 2003-2004*. Hong Kong: The Hong Kong Polytechnic University.

(HKPolyU) The Hong Kong Polytechnic University. 2006. *University Prospectus 2006-2007*. Hong Kong: The Hong Kong Polytechnic University.

(HKPolyU) The Hong Kong Polytechnic University. 2011. The Hong Kong Polytechnic University – About Work-Integrated Education.

Retrieved August 25, 2011, from <http://www.polyu.edu.hk/wieinfo/modx/index.php?id=75>.
Hood, Susan 2004. *Appraising Research: Taking a Stance in Academic Writing*. Retrieved February 21, 2007, from <http://www.grammatics.com/appraisal/hoodS-phd-links.htm>.
Hood, Susan 2006. The Persuasive Power of Prosodies: Radiating Values in Academic Writing. *Journal of English for Academic Purposes*. 5, 37-49.
Huckin, Thomas N. 2003. Specificity in LSP. *Ibérica*. 5, 3-17.
Hyland, Ken 2000. *Disciplinary Discourses: Social Interaction in Academic Writing*. Harlow: Longman.
Hyland, Ken 2001. Humble Servants of the Discipline? Self-mention in Research Articles. *English for Specific Purposes*. 20, 207-226.
Hyland, Ken 2002. Authority and Invisibility: Authorial Identity in Academic Writing. *Journal of Pragmatics*. 34, 1091-1112.
Hyland, Ken 2009. Writing in the Disciplines: Research Evidence for Specificity. *Taiwan International ESP Journal*. 1/1, 5-22.
Hyland, Ken / Anan, Eri 2006. Teachers' Perception of Errors: The Effects of First Language and Experience. *System*. 34, 509-519.
Hyland, Ken / Hamp-Lyons, Liz 2002. EAP: Issues and Direction. *Journal of English for Academic Purposes*. 1/1, 1-12.
Hyon, Sunny 1996. Genre in Three Traditions: Implications for ESL. *TESOL Quarterly*. 30/4, 693-722.
Iedema, Rick / Scheeres, Hermine 2003. From Doing Work to Talking Work: Renegotiating Knowing, Doing and Identity. *Applied Linguistics*. 24/3, 316-337.
International Federation of Social Workers 2005. Homepage. Retrieved March 4, 2009, from http://www.ifsw.org/
Ivanič, Roz 1997. *Writing and Identity: The Discoursal Construction of Identity in Academic Writing*. Amsterdam: John Benjamins Publishing Company.
Jerkins, Richard 2000. Categorization: Identity, Social Process and Epistemology. *Current Sociology*. 48/3, 7-25.
Johns, Ann M. 1997. *Text, Role, and Context: Developing Academic Literacies*. Cambridge: Cambridge University Press.
Jolliffe, David A. 1994. The Myth of Transcendence and the Problem of the Ethics Essay in College Writing Instruction. In Sullivan,

Patricia A. / Qualley, Donna J. (eds) *Pedagogy in the Age of Politics: Writing and Reading in the Academy.* Urbana: National Council of Teachers of English,183-194.

Jones, Chris 2008. Networked Learning – a Social Practice Perspective. Proceedings from 6th *International Conference on Networked Learning*, 616-623.

Jordon, Bill 2003. *Social Work, Mobility and Membership*. Retrieved 19 March 2009, from <http://www.socwork.net/2003/1/articles/ 394/index_html>.

Kärkkäinen, Elise 2003. *Epistemic Stance in English Conversation: A Description of its Interactional Functions, with a Focus I Think.* Amsterdam: John Benjamins Publishing Company.

Kell, Clare / Jones, Linda 2007. Mapping Placement Educators' Conception of Teaching. *Physiotherapy.* 93/4, 273-282.

Kember, David (ed.). 2001. *Reflective Teaching and Learning in the Health Professions*. Oxford: Blackwell Science.

Kember, David / Jones, Alice / Loke, Alice Yue / McKay, Jan / Sinclair, Kit / Tse, Harrison et al. 2001. Encouraging Reflective Writing. In D. Kember (ed.) *Reflective Teaching and Learning in the Health Professions.* Oxford: Blackwell Science, 113-125.

Kember, David / Wong, Frances Kam Yuet / Yeung, Ella 2001. The Nature of Reflection. In Kember, David (ed.), *Reflective Teaching and Learning in the Health Professions.* Oxford: Blackwell Science, 3-28.

Ketter, Jean / Hunter, Judy 2003. Creating a Writer's Identity on the Boundaries of Two Communities of Practice. In Bazerman, Charles / Russell, David (eds) *Writing Selves/Writing Societies: Research from Activity Perspectives* (E-book). Retrieved January 1, 2006, from http://wac.colostate.edu/books/selves_societies

Keys, Carolyn W. / Hand, Brian / Prain, Vaughn / Collins, Susan 1999. Using the Science Writing Heuristic as a Tool for Learning from Laboratory Investigation in Secondary Science. *Journal of Research in Science Teaching.* 36/10, 1065-1084.

Kress, Gunther / van Leeuwen, Theo 1996. *Reading Images: The Grammar of Visual Design*. London: Routledge.

Kroskrity, Paul V. 1993. *Language, History, and Identity: Ethnolinguistic Studies of the Arizona Tewa.* Tuscon: University of Arizona Press.

Kuo, Chih-Hua 1998. The Use of Personal Pronouns: Role Relationships in Scientific Journal Articles. *English for Specific Purposes.* 18/2, 121-138.

Langer, Judith / Applebee, Arthur 1987. *How Writing Shapes Thinking: A Study of Teaching and Learning.* Urbana, IL: NCTE.

Lau, Ken 2006. Learning in a Community of Practice: Investigating the Discourse of Learning-to-Write in Placements. *ESP Malaysia*, 12, 65-75.

Lau, Ken 2008. Cognitive Apprenticeship Approach to Teaching Cohesion in Writing. *ITL-International Journal of Applied Linguistics.* 156, 129-130.

Lave, Jean / Wenger, Etienne 1991. *Situated Learning: Legitimate Peripheral Participation.* Cambridge: Cambridge University Press.

Lee, Geraldine A. / Fitzgerald, Les 2008. A Clinical Internship Model for Nurse Practitioner Programme. *Nurse Education in Practice.* 8/6, 397-404.

Lee, Cynthia 2008. Interdisciplinary Collaboration in English Language Teaching: Some Observations from Subject Teachers' Reflections. *Reflections on English Language Teaching.* 7/2, 129-138.

Lee, Icy 1997. ESL Learners' Performance in Error Correction in Writing: Some Implications for Teaching. *System.* 25/4, 465-477.

Lee, Icy 2003. L2 Writing Teachers' Perspectives, Practices and Problems Regarding Error Feedback. *Assessing Writing.* 8, 216-237.

Legg, Miranda 2007. From Question to Answer: The Genre of the Problem-Based Learning Tutorial at the University of Hong Kong. *English for Specific Purposes.* 26/3, 344-367.

Lerner, Neal 2007. Laboratory Lesson for Writing and Science. *Written Communication.* 24/3, 191-222.

Lewis, Cynthia / Ketter, Jean 2004. Learning as Social Interaction: Interdiscursivity in a Teacher and Researcher Study Group. In Rogers, Rebecca (ed.) *An Introduction to Critical Discourse Analysis in Education.* New Jersey: Erlbaum Associates, 117-146.

Leydens, Jon A. 2008. Novice and Insider Perspectives on Academic and Workplace Writing: Toward a Continuum of Rhetorical Awareness. *IEEE Transaction on Professional Communication.* 51/3, 242-263.

Li, Florence So-Mui / Mead, Kate 2000. An Analysis of English in the Workplace: The Communication Needs of Textile and Clothing Merchandisers. *English for Specific Purposes.* 19/4, 351-368.

Li, Yongyan 2006. A Doctoral Student of Physics Writing for Publication: A Sociopolitically-Oriented Case Study. *English for Specific Purposes.* 25/4, 456-478.

Linde, Charlotte 1997. Evaluation as Linguistic Structure and Social Practice. In Gunnarsson, Britt-Louise / Linell, Per / Nordberg, Brengt (eds) *The Construction of Professional Discourse.* New York: Longman, 151-172.

Lock, Graham 2005. *Functional English Grammar* (7th ed.). Cambridge: Cambridge University Press.

Louhiala-Salminen, Leena 2002. The Fly Perspective: Discourse in the Daily Routine of a Business Manager. *English for Specific Purposes.* 21/3, 211-231.

Luk, Jasmine 2008. Assessing Teaching Practicum Reflections: Distinguishing Discourse Features of the 'High' and 'Low' Grade Reports. *System.* 36/4, 624-641.

Martin, Deirdre 2005. Communities of Practice and Learning Communities: Do Bilingual Co-workers Learn in Community? In Barton, David / Tusting, Karin (eds) *Beyond Communities of Practice: Language, Power and Social Context.* Cambridge: Cambridge University Press, 139-157.

Martin, James R. 1992. *English Text.* Amsterdam: John Benjamins.

Martin, James R. 2003. Beyond Exchange: APPRAISAL Systems in English. In Hunston, Susan / Thompson, Geoff (eds), *Evaluation in Text: Authorial Stance and the Construction of Discourse.* Oxford: Oxford University Press, 142-175.

Martin, James R. / Christie, Frances / Rothery, J. 1987. Social Processes in Education: A Reply to Sawyer and Watson (and others). In Reid, Ian (ed.) *The Place of Genre in Learning: Current Debates*. Geelong: Deakin University, 35-45.

Martin, James. / White, Peter Robert Rupert 2005. *The Language of Evaluation: Appraisal in English.* New York: Palgrave Macmillan.

Mason, Jennifer 2002. *Qualitative Researching* (2nd ed.) London: Sage Publication.

Mavor, Sally / Trayner, Beverly 2001. Aligning Genre and Practice with Learning in Higher Education: An Interdisciplinary Perspective for Course Design and Teaching. *English for Specific Purposes.* 20, 345-366.

Maxwell, Joseph 1996. *Qualitative Research Design: An Interactive Approach.* Thousand Oaks: Sage.

May, Nick / Veitch, Lin 1998. Working to Learn and Learning to Work: Placement Experience of Project 2000 Nursing Students in Scotland. *Nurse Education Today.* 18/8, 630-636.

Maynard, Douglas W. / Heritage, John 2005. Conversation Analysis, Doctor-Patient Interaction and Medical Communication. *Medical Education.* 39/4, 428-435.

McClure, Patricia 2008. *Making Practice-Based Learning Work* (E-book). Retrieved August 2, 2008, from <http://www.practicebasedlearning.org/resources/materials/docs/reflectiononpractice.pdf>.

McLeod, Susan H. 1989. Writing Across the Curriculum: The Second Stage, and Beyond. *College Composition and Communication.* 40, 337-343.

Mergel, Brenda 1998. *Instructional Design and Learning Theory.* Retrieved December 12, 2007, from <http://www.usask.ca/education/coursework/802papers/mergel/brenda.htm>.

Miles, Matthew B. / Huberman, A. Michael 1994. *Qualitative Data Analysis: An Expanded Sourcebook.* Thousand Oaks: Sage.

Miller, Carolyn 1984. Genre as Social Action. *Quarterly Journal of Speech.* 70, 151-176.

Miller, Carolyn 1994. Genre as Social Action. In Freedman, Aviva / Medway, Peter (eds) *Genre and the New Rhetoric.* London: Taylor & Francis, 23-42.

Myers, Greg 1989. The Pragmatics of Politeness in Scientific Articles. *Applied Linguistics.* 10, 1-35.

Myers, Greg 1990. *Writing Biology: Texts in the Social Construction of Scientific Knowledge.* Madison: University of Wisconsin Press.

Naumes, William / Naumes, Margaret 2006. *The Art and Craft of Case Writing* (2nd ed.). Armonk: M. E. Sharpe.

Nelson, Nancy 2001. Writing to Learn: One Theory, Two Rationales. In Writing as a Learning Tool: An Introduction. In Tynjälä, Päivi / Mason, Lucia / Lonka, Kirsti (eds) *Writing as a Learning Tool: Integrating Theory and Practice.* Dordrecht: Kluwer Academic Publishers, 23-36.

Ng, Thomas W. H./Feldman, Daniel C. 2007. Organizational Embeddedness and Occupational Embeddedness Across Career Stages. *Journal of Vocational Behavior.* 70, 336-351.

Norton, Janet Lynn 1997. Locus of Control and Reflective Thinking in Perspective Teachers. *Education.* 117, 404-410.

Ortlipp, Michelle 2008. Keeping and Using Reflective Journal in the Qualitative Research Process. *The Qualitative Report.* 13/4, 695-705.

Orlikowski, Wanda J. 2002. Knowing in Practice: Enacting a Collective Capability in Distributed Organizing. *Organization Science.* 13/3, 249-273.

Osterman, Karen F. / Kottkamp, Robert B. 1993. *Reflective Practice for Educators: Improving Schooling for Professional Development.* Newbury Park: Corwin Press, Inc.

Paré, Anthony 2000. Writing as a Way into Social Work: Genre Sets, Genre Systems, and Distributed Cognition. In Dias, Patrick / Paré, Anthony (eds) *Transitions: Writing in Academic and Workplace Settings.* New Jersey: Hampton Press Inc, 145-166.

Paretti, Marie C. 2006. Audience Awareness: Leveraging Problem-based Learning to Teach Workplace Communication Practices. *IEEE Transactions of Professional Communication* 49/2, 189-198.

Paretti, Marie C. / McNair, Lisa D. 2008. Introduction to the Special Issue on Communication in Engineering Curricular: Mapping the Landscape. *IEEE Transactions of Professional Communication.* 51/3, 238-241.

Parks, Susan 2000. Professional Writing and the Role of Incidental Collaboration: Evidence from Medical Setting. *Journal of Second Language Writing.* 9/2, 101-122.

Parks, Susan 2001. Moving from School to Workplace: Disciplinary Innovation, Border Crossings, and the Reshaping of a Written Genre. *Applied Linguistics.* 22/4, 405-438.

Phillips, Nelson / Lawrence, Thomas B. / Hardy, Cynthia 2004. Discourse and Institutions. *Academy of Management Review.* 29/4, 635-652.

Pogner, Karl-Heinz 2003. Writing and Interacting in the Discourse Community of Engineering. *Journal of Pragmatics.* 35/6, 855-867.

Pogner, Karl-Heinz 2005. *Discourse Communities and Communities of Practice: On the Social Context of Text and Knowledge Production in the Workplace.* Paper presented at the 21st EGOS Colloquium, Freie Universität Berlin, Germany.

Poon, Anita Y. K. 2004. Language Policy of Hong Kong: Its Impact on Language Education and Language Use in Post-Handover Hong Kong. *Journal of Taiwan Normal University: Humanities & Social Sciences.* 49/1, 53-74.

Poon, S. K. / Reed, Sue / Tang, Catherine 1997. Problem-Based Learning in Distance Education. *Proceedings of the 5th International Conference on Modern Industrial Training, Jinan, China.* 593-600.

Porpora, Douglas V. 1987. *The Concept of Social Structure.* New York: Greenwood Press.

Prince, Katie 1996. *Boring Records? Communication, Speech and Writing in Social Work.* London: Jessica Kingsley Publishers Ltd.

Quinn, Karen B. 1995. Teaching Reading and Writing as Modes of Learning in College: A Glance at the Past; A View to the Future. *Reading Research and Instruction.* 34, 295-314.

Rai, Lucy 2004. Exploring Literacy in Social Work Education: A Social Practice Approach to Student Writing. *Social Work Education.* 23/2, 149-162.

Richards, Janet C. 2006. Preservice Teachers' Professional Development in a Community of Practice Summer Literacy Camp for Children At-Risk: A Sociocultural Perspectives. *The Qualitative Report.* 11/4, 771-794.

Richardson, Laurel 2000. Writing: A Method of Inquiry. In Denzin, Norman K. / Lincoln, Yvonna S. (eds) *Handbook of Qualitative Research.* Thousand Oaks: Sage Publication, 923-948.

Richardson, Laurel / St Pierre, Elizabeth Adams 2005. Writing: A Method of Inquiry. In Denzin, Norman K. / Lincoln, Yvonna S.

(eds) *Sage Handbook of Qualitative Research.* Thousand Oaks: Sage Publication, 959-978.

Rogal, Sonya M. M. / Snider, Paul D. 2007. Rethinking the Lecture: The Application of Problem Based Learning Methods to Atypical Contexts. *Nursing Education in Practice.* 8/3, 213-219.

Russell, David R. 1991. *Writing in the Academic Disciplines, 1870-1990*. Carbondale: Southern Illinois University Press.

Russell, David R. 1997a. Rethinking School and Society: An Activity Theory Analysis. *Written Communication.* 14/4, 505-554.

Russell, David R. 1997b. Writing and Genre in Higher Education and Workplaces: A Review of Studies that Use Cultural-Historical Activity Theory. *Mind, Culture and Society.* 4/4, 224-237.

Russell, David R. 2002. *Writing in the Academic Disciplines: A Curricular History* (2nd ed.) Carbondale: Southern Illinois University Press.

Salager-Meyer, Francoise 2000. Procrustes' Recipe: Hedging and Positivism. *English for Specific Purposes.* 19/2, 175-187.

Sarangi, Srikant 2007. *Negotiating Identities/Roles in Professional Communication*. Plenary Speech Presented at the Discourse and Identity in Specialized Communication Conference, University of Milan.

Sarangi, Srikant 2010. Reconfiguring self/Identity/Status/Role: The Case of Professional Role Performance in Healthcare Encounters. In Giuliana, Garzone / Archibald, James (eds) *Discourse, Identities and Roles in Specialized Communication.* Bern: Peter Lang, 33-57.

Sarangi, Srikant / Roberts, Celia 1999. The Dynamics of Interactional and Institutional Orders in Work-Related Settings. In Sarangi, Srikent / Roberts, Celia (eds) *Talk, Work and Institutional Order: Discourse in Medical, Mediation and Management Settings.* Berlin: Mouton de Gruyter, 1-57.

Sarangi, Srikant / van Leeuwen, Theo 2003. Applied Linguistics and Communities of Practice: Gaining Communality or Losing Disciplinary Autonomy? In Sarangi, Srikant / van Leeuwen, Theo (eds) *Applied Linguistics and Communities of Practice.* UK: British Association for Applied Linguistics in association with Continuum, 1-8.

Sbisà, Marina 2001. Illocutionary Force and Degrees of Strength in Language Use. *Journal of Pragmatics*. 33, 1791-1814.

Scheeres, Hermine 2003. Learning to Talk: From Manual Work to Discourse Work as Self-Regulating Practice. *Journal of Workplace Learning*. 15/7/8, 332-337.

Schleppegrell, Mary J. 2001. Linguistic Features of the Language of Schooling. *Linguistics and Education*. 12/4, 431-459.

Schneider, Barbara / Andre, Jo-Anne 2005. University Preparation for Workplace Writing. *Journal of Business Communication*. 42/2, 195-218.

Schön, Donald A. 1983. *The Reflective Practitioner: How Professionals Think in Action*. New York: Basic Books.

Scollon, Ron / Scollon, Suzie Wong 2004. *Nexus Analysis: Discourse and the Emerging Internet*. New York: Routledge.

Scott, Mike 2007. WordSmith Tool 5.0 [Computer software]. Retrieved February 3, 2008, from <http://www.lexically.net/ wordsmith/ version5/index.html>.

Searle, John R. 2003. Social Ontology and Political Power. Retrieved June 28, 2006, from <http://www.law.berkeley.edu/centers/ kadish/searle.pdf>.

Smith, Dorothy 1999. *Writing the Social: Critique, Theory and Investigations*. Toronto: University of Toronto Press.

Smith, Mark / Jeffs, Tony 2005. *Informal Education: Conversation, Democracy and Learning*. Ticknall: Education Now.

So, Daniel Wing Cheong 1998. One Country, Two Cultures and Three Languages: Sociolinguistic Conditions and Language Education in Hong Kong. In Asker, Barry (ed.). *Teaching Language and Culture: Building Hong Kong on Education*. Hong Kong: Addison Wesley Longman China Ltd., 152-176.

Star, Susan / Griesemer, James 1989. Institutional Ecology, 'Translations' and Boundary Objects: Amateurs and Professionals in Berkeley's Museum of Vertebrate Zoology, 1907-39. *Social Studies of Science*. 19, 387-420.

Storey, Anne /Tsang, Sandra S. K. / Pao, Dora 2004. Written Communication in Social Work: Entering a New Discourse. Web Proceedings for *2nd Knowledge and Discourse Con-*

ference: Speculating on Disciplinary Futures. The University of Hong Kong.

Stryker, Sheldon / Burke, Peter 2000. The Past, Present and Future of An Identity Theory. *Social Psychology Quarterly.* 63, 284-297.

Stubb, Michael 2001. *Words and Phrases: Corpus Studies of Lexical Semantics*. Oxford: Blackwell Publishing.

Sutton, Lynette / Dalley, Jayne 2008. Reflection in an Intermediate Care Team. *Physiotherapy.* 94/1, 63-70.

Swales, John 1990. *Genre Analysis: English in Academic and Research Settings*. Cambridge: Cambridge University Press.

Swindell, Marian / Watson, Joshua 2006. Teaching Ethics Through Self-Reflective Journaling. *Journal of Social Work Values and Ethics.* 3/2. Retrieved February 26, 2009, from <http://www.socialworker.com/jswve/content/view/37/46/>.

Tajfel, Henri / Turner, John 1986. The Social Identity Theory of Inter-Group Behavior. In Worchel, Stephen / Austin,William (eds) *Psychology of Intergroup Relations.* Chicago: Nelson-Hall, 7-24.

Tang, Ramona / John, Suganthi 1999. The 'I' in Identity: Exploring Writer Identity in Student Academic Writing Through the First Person Pronoun. *English for Specific Purposes.* 18, S23-S29.

Taylor, Steven / Bogdan, Robert 1984. *Introduction to Qualitative Research Methods* (2nd ed). New York: John Wiley & Sons.

Thames, Agile 2002. Elder rehabilitation: Core Learning Objectives for Physiotherapy Students During Clinical Placement. *Physiotherapy.* 88/3, 158-166.

Thompson, Geoff 2004. *Introducing Functional Grammar* (2nd ed.). London: Arnold.

Thornby, Denise (n.d.). *Professionalism in the Workplace*. Retrieved February 17, 2008, from <http://www.esrdnet5.org/Education/Staff/scm_pres/professionalism.pdf>.

Truscott, John 1996. The Case Against Grammar Correction in L2 Writing Classes. *Language Learning.* 46, 327-369.

Truscott, John 1999. The Case for "The Case for Grammar Correction in L2 Writing Classes": A Response to Ferris. *Journal of Second Language Writing.* 8, 111-122.

Tsang, Nai Ming 2007. Orality and Literacy: Their Relevance to Social Work. *Journal of Social Work.* 7/1, 51-70.

Tseng, Wen-Shing 2001. *Child Development and Enculturation.* Elsevier Science and Technology Books.

Tsui, Amy / Edwards, Gwyn / Lopez-Real, Fran 2006. *Learning in Communities of Practice in School-University Partnership.* New Jersey: Lawrence Erlbaum.

Tusting, Karin 2005. Language and Power in Communities of Power. In Barton, David / Tusting, Karin (eds) *Beyond Communities of Practice: Language, Power and Social Context.* Cambridge: Cambridge University Press, 36-54.

Tusting, Karin / Barton, David 2006. *Models of Adult Learning: A Literature Review.* London: NRDC.

Tuzi, Frak 2004. The Impact of E-feedback on the Revisions of L2 Writers in an Academic Writing Course. *Computers and Composition.* 21, 217-235.

Tynjälä, Paivi / Mason, Lucia / Lonka, Kirsti 2001. Writing as a Learning Tool: An Introduction. In Tynjälä, Paivi / Mason, Lucia / Lonka, Kirsti (eds) *Writing as a Learning Tool: Integrating Theory and Practice.* Dordrecht: Kluwer Academic Publishers, 7-22.

Vygotsky, Lev 1978. *Mind in Society.* Cambridge: Harvard University Press.

Wardle, Elizabeth 2004. *Identity, Authority and Learning to Write in New Workplaces.* Retrieved April 10, 2009, from <http://enculturation.gmu.edu/5_2/index52.html>.

Weinreich, Peter 2009. 'Enculturation' Not 'Acculturation': Conceptualising and Assessing Identity Processes in Migrant Communities. *International Journal of Intercultural Relations.* 33/2, 124-139.

Wenger, Etienne 1998. *Communities of Practice: Learning, Meaning and Identity.* Cambridge: Cambridge University Press.

Wenger, Etienne / McDermott, Richard / Synder, William 2002. *Cultivating Communities of Practice.* Harvard: Harvard Business School Press.

White, Jonathan 2008. The Use of Reflective Writing in Exploring Students Experiences in Surgery. *Journal of Surgical Education.* 65/6, 518-520.

White, Peter. R. R. 2003. Beyond Modality and Hedging: A Dialogic View of the Language of Intersubjective Stance, *Text.* 23/2, 259-284.
Widodo, Handoyo Puji 2006. Approaches and Procedures for Teaching Grammar. *English Teaching: Practice and Critique.* 5/1, 122-141.
Williams, Brandon 2000. Collage Work as a Medium of Guided Reflection in the Clinical Supervision Relationship. *Nurse Education Today.* 20/4, 273-278.
Willis, Majorie 1996. *Medical Terminology: The Language of Health Care*. Baltimore: Williams & Wilkins.
Wiredu, Gamel Okoampa 2005. *Mobile Computing in Work-Integrated Learning: Problems of Remotely Distributed Activities and Technology Use.* Unpublished doctoral dissertation, University of London, London.
Woodilla, Jill 1998. Workplace Conversations: The Text of Organizing. In Grant, David / Keenoy, Tom / Oswick, Cliff (eds) *Discourse and Organization.* London: Sage, 31-51.
Woodward-Kron, Robyn 2004. 'Discourse Communities' and 'Apprenticeship': An Investigation of these Concepts in Undergraduate Education Students' Writing. *Journal of English for Academic Purposes.* 3/2, 139-161.
Yang, Ruiying / Allison, Desmond 2003. Research Articles in Applied Linguistics: Moving from Results to Conclusions. *English for Specific Purposes.* 22, 365-385.
Yule, George 2008. *Explaining English Grammar.* Oxford: Oxford University Press.

Appendix A. Excerpts from Pamela's PBL report

1) Introduction
Ah Ling is a 15-year-old girl who had a seizure at school and lost consciousness for a few seconds during her Physical Education lesson. She was sent to a nearby hospital. She needed to have close observation.

This case was chosen for further explored because epilepsy is the most common neurological condition. It may be a lifelong problem. In Hong Kong, there is no statistics on how widespread of this disease. However, in general, one in every 200-500 people has repeated epilepsy. On estimation, Hong Kong has about 30,000-60,000 people suffering from epilepsy (The Hong Kong Society for Rehabilitation, n.d.). The highest incidences are in childhood and in the elderly (Smith, Wallace, 2001). It follows a U-shaped curve in relation to age. The elderly and the children are the weak one that needs help. However, it does not means the other age groups will not have such disease. Epilepsy is no age, racial, social, sexual or geographical boundaries. Therefore, Ah Ling's case was chosen in an in-depth manner.

2) Learning Issue

In this report, Ah Ling had a seizure at school and lost consciousness for a few seconds. It is necessary to understand what seizure is and whether it is relevant to epilepsy or not.

Firstly, assuming Ah Ling is suffering from epilepsy, nurses should understand what epilepsy is.

Secondly, Ah Ling have lost consciousness for a few seconds, a physical examination about neurological signs and some diagnostic tests should be introduced to her. Assuming she have the chance for second seizure, nurses should know the prevention for further seizure and how to protect her during seizure.

Lastly, assuming Ah Ling is an epileptic, education on living with epilepsy can help her to rehabilitate. The main focus would place on the education because when a people was diagnosed a lifelong disease, the most concern is how to confront and overcome the difficulties that they may face in their daily life.

3) Assumption 1

Basic Knowledge on Epilepsy and Seizures for Reduce Anxious

Since it was the first time for Ah Ling to have seizures, she may feel anxious about the disease. Assuming Ah Ling is suffering from epilepsy rather than a single seizure, an explanation about epilepsy is necessary to reduce her anxious.

1) Definition of Epilepsy

In 2001, World Health Organization (WHO) stated that epilepsy is a neurological disorder that characterized by a tendency to recurrent seizures and it defined by two or more unprovoked seizures. Seizures may vary from the briefest lapses of attention or muscle jerks to severe and prolonged convulsions.

2) Physiology and anatomy of the brain

The brain is a highly complex structure. It composed of millions of nerve cells which is called neurons. The neurons are responsible for transmit nerve impulses when any stimulation is reach the threshold value. The seizure threshold value is a level of stimulation at which your brain will have seizure. People with epilepsy have a lower-than-normal seizure threshold, meaning that only slightly increased excitement will cause them to have a seizure (Freeman, Vining & Pillas, 1997). This level is mostly genetically inherited. However, many other factors can affect this level. For example, young age, high fever, chemicals, increased excitement and lack of sleep can also cause seizure.

4) Assumption 2

Nursing Process Help in Diagnosis and Promote Rehabilitate

Ah Ling was admitted into the medical ward, a nursing process should be proceeded to help in diagnosis of the type and the cause of her seizure.

1) Assessment

1.1) History taking

For Identifying Ah Ling's epilepsy, history taking must be done. Nurses should ask her about the feeling and the environment when she lost consciousness, it may be a cue for her to have an attack. Then, asking about her habit, including any sleep disturbance, any drug or alcohol taking and any underlying stress in her life and know more about her past health history because any head injury, infection, cerebro-vascular disease, metabolic disease (include severe renal failure, hypoxia and hyperglycaemia) or chance of pregnancy may induced seizure (Hall & Martin, 1997).

Idiopathic epilepsy most often begins before the age of 20-year-old. It is the genetic condition and often begins during puberty. Ah Ling is just 15-year-old. It is often no neurology abnormalities. Therefore, documentation of similar epileptic seizures or neurological symptoms of other family members may aid in the identification of Ah Ling's case. Ah Ling is too young that she may not remember what she has suffered from when she was an infant. Therefore, ask her family about her health history at that time is more suitable than ask Ah Ling herself.

Appendix B. Social work group skills checking list

Program Planning Skill 程序設計技巧		
Skills	Grading	Self-reflection
1/. Need Assessment Skill 需要評估技巧		
2/. Design of games and activities 遊戲/活動設計		
3/. Design of program material 教材或活動材料運用		
4/. Design of group task 小組任務設計		

Facilitating group processes 促進技巧		
Skills	Grading	Self-reflection
5/. Involving group members 協助組員投入 verbal invitation, minimal encouragement		
6/. Attending to others 專注技巧 non-verbal such as eye contact, body position and verbal behavior that convey empathy, respect, warmth , trust…		
7/. Expressing self 表達和自我披露 helping members to express their views and feelings, worker's self-disclosure in suitable moments		
8/. Focusing and clarifying skills 聚焦和澄清 focusing the group processes in a particular directions. This can be done by clarifying, asking a member to elaborate, repeating a particular communication, redirect the group if the interaction has been side-tracked by irrelevant issues, etc		
Data collection and assessment 資料整理和評估		
9/. Requesting information, questioning and probing skills 發問和探查、搜集		
10/. Analyzing skills 分析技巧 pointing out patterns, identifying gaps in the data, and establishing mechanisms or plan		
11/. Synthesizing skills 綜合技巧 providing feedback to members, describing patterns of the group's interaction		
12/. Summarizing skill 撮要 to present the core of what has been said and provide members an opportunity to reflect on the problem.		

Action/intervention skills 介入技巧 Helping group members to accomplish group tasks		
13/. Program Skills流程控制技巧 time control, flexibility, conducting and presentation skill		
14/. Cultivating positive group dynamics 促進正面的小組動力		
➢ Establishing positive group norms 建立正向的小組規範		
➢ Supporting group members 給予組員支持和鼓勵 develop and cultivate a supportive culture in the group, helping members respond empathetically to each other and validate and affirm shared experiences		
➢ Linking members' communication 協助聯繫組員 searching for a feeling link or an information link		
➢ Resolving conflicts 平息爭拗		
➢ Establishing relax and cheerful group atmosphere 製造融和及歡愉的氣氛		
15/. Problem-solving skills 問題解決和應變 to break down a complex problem or issue into manageable bit		
➢ Reframing and redefining 對關注的問題重新詮釋 helping members to view a problem from different perspectives and to find a creative solution		
➢ Group Resource Awareness 運用小組內部資源		
16/.Assertion of worker's role 確立工作員的角色 ➢ Directing 導向 helping members to participate in an activity, leading a discussion, sharing new information		
➢ Giving advice, suggestions and instructions 給予意見和指引		

➢ Providing resources 資料或資源提供		
➢ Modeling, role playing, rehearsing and coaching 給予示範，作為楷模		
➢ Disciplining 維持基本秩序		
17/.Fulfilment of group tasks 小組任務的完成		

Grading: (from: "1"-least satisfactory to "5"-most satisfactory)

Appendix C. Processes with the highest frequency

Sequence	*Processes with all derivatives found from the texts*	*No. of Occurrences per 10,000 words*
1	Is/was/are/were/being/been	260
2	Have/Had/Has/having	96
3	Did/Do/done	75
4	Know/knowledge/Known	63
5	Learn/learning/Learnt/Learned/	44
6	Need/Needs/Needed	41
7	Let	35
8	Work/Working/Works/Worked	33
9	Think/Thought/Thinking	31
10	Experience/Experiences/Experienced	30
10	Give/Gave/Giving/Given/Gives	30
12	Help/Helping/Helped/Helps	26
13	Use/Using/Used	24
14	Try/Tried/Trying	23
14	Feel/Feeling/Feelings/Feels	23
16	Change/Changed/Changes/Changing	19
17	Play/Playing/Played	18
17	Understand/Understanding	18
19	Education/Educate	17
19	Teach/Teaching/Teaches	17
21	Join/Joining/Joined	16
22	Want/Wants	15

22	Make/Making/Makes	15
24	Order	14
24	Discussion/Discuss	14
24	Show/Shows/Showed	14
27	Attend/Attendance/Attending	13
27	Ask/Asking/Asked	13
29	Service	12
29	Assessment/Assess/Assessing	12
29	Assistance/Assist/Assisted	12
32	Observation/Observe	11
32	Found/Find	11
34	Provide/Provides	10
34	Form/Forming	10
34	Hope/Hopes	10
34	Plan/Planning	10
34	Question/Questions/Questioning	10
39	Point	9
39	Development	9
39	Beginning	9
39	Information	9
39	Like	9
39	Improve/Improved	9
39	Training/Train	9
39	Sharing/Share	9
39	Build/Built/Building	9
39	Communication/Communicate	9
49	Experiment	8
49	Setting	8
49	Express/Expressing	8
49	Get/Getting	8
49	Operation/Operate	8
49	Hold/Held	8
55	Evaluation	7
55	Sense	7
55	Motivation	7
55	Control/Controlled	7
55	Lack/Lacking	7
55	Discover/Discovered	7
55	Write/Writing	7
55	Visit/Visiting	7
55	Promote/Promotion	7

55	Taking/Take	7
65	Behavior	6
65	Practice	6
65	Drop	6
65	Interaction	6
65	Support	6
65	Follow/Followed	6
65	Reflection/reflect	6
65	Focus/Focusing	6
65	Keep/Kept	6
74	Master	5
74	Report	5
74	Explain/Explained	5
74	Misbehavior/Misbehaviors	5
74	Interview	4
79	Analysis	4
79	Approach	4
79	Become	4
79	Face	4
79	Solve	4
79	Supervision	4
79	Talk	4

Index

Linguistic Insights

Studies in Language and Communication

This series aims to promote specialist language studies in the fields of linguistic theory and applied linguistics, by publishing volumes that focus on specific aspects of language use in one or several languages and provide valuable insights into language and communication research. A cross-disciplinary approach is favoured and most European languages are accepted.

The series includes two types of books:

- **Monographs** – featuring in-depth studies on special aspects of language theory, language analysis or language teaching.
- **Collected papers** – assembling papers from workshops, conferences or symposia.

Each volume of the series is subjected to a double peer-reviewing process.

Vol. 1 Maurizio Gotti & Marina Dossena (eds)
Modality in Specialized Texts. Selected Papers of the 1st CERLIS Conference.
421 pages. 2001. ISBN 3-906767-10-8 · US-ISBN 0-8204-5340-4

Vol. 2 Giuseppina Cortese & Philip Riley (eds)
Domain-specific English. Textual Practices across Communities and Classrooms.
420 pages. 2002. ISBN 3-906768-98-8 · US-ISBN 0-8204-5884-8

Vol. 3 Maurizio Gotti, Dorothee Heller & Marina Dossena (eds)
Conflict and Negotiation in Specialized Texts. Selected Papers of the 2nd CERLIS Conference.
470 pages. 2002. ISBN 3-906769-12-7 · US-ISBN 0-8204-5887-2

Editorial address:

Prof. Maurizio Gotti Università di Bergamo, Facoltà di Lingue e Letterature Straniere,
Via Salvecchio 19, 24129 Bergamo, Italy
Fax: 0039 035 2052789, E-Mail: m.gotti@unibg.it

Vol. 4 Maurizio Gotti, Marina Dossena, Richard Dury, Roberta Facchinetti & Maria Lima
Variation in Central Modals. A Repertoire of Forms and Types of Usage in Middle English and Early Modern English.
364 pages. 2002. ISBN 3-906769-84-4 · US-ISBN 0-8204-5898-8

Vol. 5 Stefania Nuccorini (ed.)
Phrases and Phraseology. Data and Descriptions.
187 pages. 2002. ISBN 3-906770-08-7 · US-ISBN 0-8204-5933-X

Vol. 6 Vijay Bhatia, Christopher N. Candlin & Maurizio Gotti (eds)
Legal Discourse in Multilingual and Multicultural Contexts. Arbitration Texts in Europe.
385 pages. 2003. ISBN 3-906770-85-0 · US-ISBN 0-8204-6254-3

Vol. 7 Marina Dossena & Charles Jones (eds)
Insights into Late Modern English. 2nd edition.
378 pages. 2003, 2007.
ISBN 978-3-03911-257-9 · US-ISBN 978-0-8204-8927-8

Vol. 8 Maurizio Gotti
Specialized Discourse. Linguistic Features and Changing Conventions.
351 pages. 2003, 2005.
ISBN 3-03910-606-6 · US-ISBN 0-8204-7000-7

Vol. 9 Alan Partington, John Morley & Louann Haarman (eds)
Corpora and Discourse.
420 pages. 2004. ISBN 3-03910-026-2 · US-ISBN 0-8204-6262-4

Vol. 10 Martina Möllering
The Acquisition of German Modal Particles. A Corpus-Based Approach.
290 pages. 2004. ISBN 3-03910-043-2 · US-ISBN 0-8204-6273-X

Vol. 11 David Hart (ed.)
English Modality in Context. Diachronic Perspectives.
261 pages. 2003. ISBN 3-03910-046-7 · US-ISBN 0-8204-6852-5

Vol. 12 Wendy Swanson
Modes of Co-reference as an Indicator of Genre.
430 pages. 2003. ISBN 3-03910-052-1 · US-ISBN 0-8204-6855-X

Vol. 13 Gina Poncini
Discursive Strategies in Multicultural Business Meetings.
2nd edition. 338 pages. 2004, 2007.
ISBN 978-3-03911-296-8 · US-ISBN 978-0-8204-8937-7

Vol. 14 Christopher N. Candlin & Maurizio Gotti (eds)
Intercultural Aspects of Specialized Communication.
2nd edition. 369 pages. 2004, 2007.
ISBN 978-3-03911-258-6 · US-ISBN 978-0-8204-8926-1

Vol. 15 Gabriella Del Lungo Camiciotti & Elena Tognini Bonelli (eds)
Academic Discourse. New Insights into Evaluation.
234 pages. 2004. ISBN 3-03910-353-9 · US-ISBN 0-8204-7016-3

Vol. 16 Marina Dossena & Roger Lass (eds)
Methods and Data in English Historical Dialectology.
405 pages. 2004. ISBN 3-03910-362-8 · US-ISBN 0-8204-7018-X

Vol. 17 Judy Noguchi
The Science Review Article. An Opportune Genre in the Construction of Science.
274 pages. 2006. ISBN 3-03910-426-8 · US-ISBN 0-8204-7034-1

Vol. 18 Giuseppina Cortese & Anna Duszak (eds)
Identity, Community, Discourse. English in Intercultural Settings.
495 pages. 2005. ISBN 3-03910-632-5 · US-ISBN 0-8204-7163-1

Vol. 19 Anna Trosborg & Poul Erik Flyvholm Jørgensen (eds)
Business Discourse. Texts and Contexts.
250 pages. 2005. ISBN 3-03910-606-6 · US-ISBN 0-8204-7000-7

Vol. 20 Christopher Williams
Tradition and Change in Legal English. Verbal Constructions in Prescriptive Texts.
2nd revised edition. 216 pages. 2005, 2007. ISBN 978-3-03911-444-3.

Vol. 21 Katarzyna Dziubalska-Kołaczyk & Joanna Przedlacka (eds)
English Pronunciation Models: A Changing Scene.
2nd edition. 476 pages. 2005, 2008. ISBN 978-3-03911-682-9.

Vol. 22 Christián Abello-Contesse, Rubén Chacón-Beltrán, M. Dolores López-Jiménez & M. Mar Torreblanca-López (eds)
Age in L2 Acquisition and Teaching.
214 pages. 2006. ISBN 3-03910-668-6 · US-ISBN 0-8204-7174-7

Vol. 23 Vijay K. Bhatia, Maurizio Gotti, Jan Engberg & Dorothee Heller (eds)
Vagueness in Normative Texts.
474 pages. 2005. ISBN 3-03910-653-8 · US-ISBN 0-8204-7169-0

Vol. 24 Paul Gillaerts & Maurizio Gotti (eds)
Genre Variation in Business Letters. 2nd printing.
407 pages. 2008. ISBN 978-3-03911-681-2.

Vol. 25 Ana María Hornero, María José Luzón & Silvia Murillo (eds)
Corpus Linguistics. Applications for the Study of English.
2nd printing. 526 pages. 2006, 2008. ISBN 978-3-03911-726-0

Vol. 26 J. Lachlan Mackenzie & María de los Ángeles Gómez-González (eds)
Studies in Functional Discourse Grammar.
259 pages. 2005. ISBN 3-03910-696-1 · US-ISBN 0-8204-7558-0

Vol. 27 Debbie G. E. Ho
Classroom Talk. Exploring the Sociocultural Structure of Formal ESL Learning.
2nd edition. 254 pages. 2006, 2007. ISBN 978-3-03911-434-4

Vol. 28 Javier Pérez-Guerra, Dolores González-Álvarez, Jorge L. Bueno-Alonso & Esperanza Rama-Martínez (eds)
'Of Varying Language and Opposing Creed': New Insights into Late Modern English.
455 pages. 2007. ISBN 978-3-03910-788-9

Vol. 29 Francesca Bargiela-Chiappini & Maurizio Gotti (eds)
Asian Business Discourse(s).
350 pages. 2005. ISBN 3-03910-804-2 · US-ISBN 0-8204-7574-2

Vol. 30 Nicholas Brownlees (ed.)
News Discourse in Early Modern Britain. Selected Papers of CHINED 2004.
300 pages. 2006. ISBN 3-03910-805-0 · US-ISBN 0-8204-8025-8

Vol. 31 Roberta Facchinetti & Matti Rissanen (eds)
Corpus-based Studies of Diachronic English.
300 pages. 2006. ISBN 3-03910-851-4 · US-ISBN 0-8204-8040-1

Vol. 32 Marina Dossena & Susan M. Fitzmaurice (eds)
Business and Official Correspondence: Historical Investigations.
209 pages. 2006. ISBN 3-03910-880-8 · US-ISBN 0-8204-8352-4

Vol. 33 Giuliana Garzone & Srikant Sarangi (eds)
Discourse, Ideology and Specialized Communication.
494 pages. 2007. ISBN 978-3-03910-888-6

Vol. 34 Giuliana Garzone & Cornelia Ilie (eds)
The Use of English in Institutional and Business Settings.
An Intercultural Perspective.
372 pages. 2007. ISBN 978-3-03910-889-3

Vol. 35 Vijay K. Bhatia & Maurizio Gotti (eds)
Explorations in Specialized Genres.
316 pages. 2006. ISBN 3-03910-995-2 · US-ISBN 0-8204-8372-9

Vol. 36 Heribert Picht (ed.)
Modern Approaches to Terminological Theories and Applications.
432 pages. 2006. ISBN 3-03911-156-6 · US-ISBN 0-8204-8380-X

Vol. 37 Anne Wagner & Sophie Cacciaguidi-Fahy (eds)
Legal Language and the Search for Clarity / Le langage juridique et la quête de clarté.
Practice and Tools / Pratiques et instruments.
487 pages. 2006. ISBN 3-03911-169-8 · US-ISBN 0-8204-8388-5

Vol. 38 Juan Carlos Palmer-Silveira, Miguel F. Ruiz-Garrido &
Inmaculada Fortanet-Gómez (eds)
Intercultural and International Business Communication:
Theory, Research and Teaching.
2nd edition. 343 pages. 2006, 2008. ISBN 978-3-03911-680-5

Vol. 39 Christiane Dalton-Puffer, Dieter Kastovsky, Nikolaus Ritt &
Herbert Schendl (eds)
Syntax, Style and Grammatical Norms: English from 1500–2000.
250 pages. 2006. ISBN 3-03911-181-7 · US-ISBN 0-8204-8394-X

Vol. 40 Marina Dossena & Irma Taavitsainen (eds)
Diachronic Perspectives on Domain-Specific English.
280 pages. 2006. ISBN 3-03910-176-0 · US-ISBN 0-8204-8391-5

Vol. 41 John Flowerdew & Maurizio Gotti (eds)
Studies in Specialized Discourse.
293 pages. 2006. ISBN 3-03911-178-7

Vol. 42 Ken Hyland & Marina Bondi (eds)
Academic Discourse Across Disciplines.
320 pages. 2006. ISBN 3-03911-183-3 · US-ISBN 0-8204-8396-6

Vol. 43 Paul Gillaerts & Philip Shaw (eds)
The Map and the Landscape: Norms and Practices in Genre.
256 pages. 2006. ISBN 3-03911-182-5 · US-ISBN 0-8204-8395-4

Vol. 44 Maurizio Gotti & Davide Giannoni (eds)
New Trends in Specialized Discourse Analysis.
301 pages. 2006. ISBN 3-03911-184-1 · US-ISBN 0-8204-8381-8

Vol. 45 Maurizio Gotti & Françoise Salager-Meyer (eds)
Advances in Medical Discourse Analysis: Oral and Written Contexts.
492 pages. 2006. ISBN 3-03911-185-X · US-ISBN 0-8204-8382-6

Vol. 46 Maurizio Gotti & Susan Šarcević (eds)
Insights into Specialized Translation.
396 pages. 2006. ISBN 3-03911-186-8 · US-ISBN 0-8204-8383-4

Vol. 47 Khurshid Ahmad & Margaret Rogers (eds)
Evidence-based LSP: Translation, Text and Terminology.
584 pages. 2007. ISBN 978-3-03911-187-9

Vol. 48 Hao Sun & Dániel Z. Kádár (eds)
It's the Dragon's Turn: Chinese Institutional Discourses.
262 pages. 2008. ISBN 978-3-03911-175-6

Vol. 49 Cristina Suárez-Gómez
Relativization in Early English (950-1250): the Position of Relative Clauses.
149 pages. 2006. ISBN 3-03911-203-1 · US-ISBN 0-8204-8904-2

Vol. 50 Maria Vittoria Calvi & Luisa Chierichetti (eds)
Nuevas tendencias en el discurso de especialidad.
319 pages. 2006. ISBN 978-3-03911-261-6

Vol. 51 Mari Carmen Campoy & María José Luzón (eds)
Spoken Corpora in Applied Linguistics.
274 pages. 2008. ISBN 978-3-03911-275-3

Vol. 52 Konrad Ehlich & Dorothee Heller (Hrsg.)
Die Wissenschaft und ihre Sprachen.
323 pages. 2006. ISBN 978-3-03911-272-2

Vol. 53 Jingyu Zhang
The Semantic Salience Hierarchy Model: The L2 Acquisition of Psych Predicates
273 pages. 2007. ISBN 978-3-03911-300-2

Vol. 54 Norman Fairclough, Giuseppina Cortese & Patrizia Ardizzone (eds)
Discourse and Contemporary Social Change.
555 pages. 2007. ISBN 978-3-03911-276-0

Vol. 55 Jan Engberg, Marianne Grove Ditlevsen, Peter Kastberg & Martin Stegu (eds)
New Directions in LSP Teaching.
331 pages. 2007. ISBN 978-3-03911-433-7

Vol. 56 Dorothee Heller & Konrad Ehlich (Hrsg.)
Studien zur Rechtskommunikation.
322 pages. 2007. ISBN 978-3-03911-436-8

Vol. 57 Forthcoming.

Vol. 58 Carmen Frehner
Email – SMS – MMS
294 pages. 2008. ISBN 978-3-03911-451-1

Vol. 59 Isabel Balteiro
The Directionality of Conversion in English: A Dia-Synchronic Study.
276 pages. 2007. ISBN 978-3-03911-241-8

Vol. 60 Maria Milagros Del Saz Rubio
English Discourse Markers of Reformulation.
237 pages. 2007. ISBN 978-3-03911-196-1

Vol. 61 Sally Burgess & Pedro Martín-Martín (eds)
English as an Additional Language in Research Publication and Communication.
259 pages. 2008. ISBN 978-3-03911-462-7

Vol. 62 Sandrine Onillon
Pratiques et représentations de l'écrit.
458 pages. 2008. ISBN 978-3-03911-464-1

Vol. 63 Hugo Bowles & Paul Seedhouse (eds)
Conversation Analysis and Language for Specific Purposes.
2nd edition. 337 pages. 2007, 2009. ISBN 978-3-0343-0045-2

Vol. 64 Vijay K. Bhatia, Christopher N. Candlin & Paola Evangelisti Allori (eds)
Language, Culture and the Law.
The Formulation of Legal Concepts across Systems and Cultures.
342 pages. 2008. ISBN 978-3-03911-470-2

Vol. 65 Jonathan Culpeper & Dániel Z. Kádár (eds)
Historical (Im)politeness.
300 pages. 2010. ISBN 978-3-03911-496-2

Vol. 66 Linda Lombardo (ed.)
Using Corpora to Learn about Language and Discourse.
237 pages. 2009. ISBN 978-3-03911-522-8

Vol. 67 Natsumi Wakamoto
Extroversion/Introversion in Foreign Language Learning.
Interactions with Learner Strategy Use.
159 pages. 2009. ISBN 978-3-03911-596-9

Vol. 68 Eva Alcón-Soler (ed.)
Learning How to Request in an Instructed Language Learning Context.
260 pages. 2008. ISBN 978-3-03911-601-0

Vol. 69 Domenico Pezzini
The Translation of Religious Texts in the Middle Ages.
428 pages. 2008. ISBN 978-3-03911-600-3

Vol. 70 Tomoko Tode
Effects of Frequency in Classroom Second Language Learning.
Quasi-experiment and stimulated-recall analysis.
195 pages. 2008. ISBN 978-3-03911-602-7

Vol. 71 Egor Tsedryk
Fusion symétrique et alternances ditransitives.
211 pages. 2009. ISBN 978-3-03911-609-6

Vol. 72 Cynthia J. Kellett Bidoli & Elana Ochse (eds)
English in International Deaf Communication.
444 pages. 2008. ISBN 978-3-03911-610-2

Vol. 73 Joan C. Beal, Carmela Nocera & Massimo Sturiale (eds)
Perspectives on Prescriptivism.
269 pages. 2008. ISBN 978-3-03911-632-4

Vol. 74 Carol Taylor Torsello, Katherine Ackerley & Erik Castello (eds)
Corpora for University Language Teachers.
308 pages. 2008. ISBN 978-3-03911-639-3

Vol. 75 María Luisa Pérez Cañado (ed.)
English Language Teaching in the European Credit Transfer System: Facing the Challenge.
251 pages. 2009. ISBN 978-3-03911-654-6

Vol. 76 Marina Dossena & Ingrid Tieken-Boon van Ostade (eds)
Studies in Late Modern English Correspondence. Methodology and Data.
291 pages. 2008. ISBN 978-3-03911-658-4

Vol. 77 Ingrid Tieken-Boon van Ostade & Wim van der Wurff (eds)
Current Issues in Late Modern English.
436 pages. 2009. ISBN 978-3-03911-660-7

Vol. 78 Marta Navarro Coy (ed.)
Practical Approaches to Foreign Language Teaching and Learning.
297 pages. 2009. ISBN 978-3-03911-661-4

Vol. 79 Qing Ma
Second Language Vocabulary Acquisition.
333 pages. 2009. ISBN 978-3-03911-666-9

Vol. 80 Martin Solly, Michelangelo Conoscenti & Sandra Campagna (eds)
Verbal/Visual Narrative Texts in Higher Education.
384 pages. 2008. ISBN 978-3-03911-672-0

Vol. 81 Meiko Matsumoto
From Simple Verbs to Periphrastic Expressions:
The Historical Development of Composite Predicates, Phrasal Verbs, and Related Constructions in English.
235 pages. 2008. ISBN 978-3-03911-675-1

Vol. 82 Melinda Dooly
Doing Diversity. Teachers' Construction of Their Classroom Reality.
180 pages. 2009. ISBN 978-3-03911-687-4

Vol. 83 Victoria Guillén-Nieto, Carmen Marimón-Llorca & Chelo Vargas-Sierra (eds)
Intercultural Business Communication and
Simulation and Gaming Methodology.
392 pages. 2009. ISBN 978-3-03911-688-1

Vol. 84 Maria Grazia Guido
English as a Lingua Franca in Cross-cultural Immigration Domains.
285 pages. 2008. ISBN 978-3-03911-689-8

Vol. 85 Erik Castello
Text Complexity and Reading Comprehension Tests.
352 pages. 2008. ISBN 978-3-03911-717-8

Vol. 86 Maria-Lluisa Gea-Valor, Isabel García-Izquierdo & Maria-José Esteve (eds)
Linguistic and Translation Studies in Scientific Communication.
317 pages. 2010. ISBN 978-3-0343-0069-8

Vol. 87 Carmen Navarro, Rosa Mª Rodríguez Abella, Francesca Dalle Pezze
& Renzo Miotti (eds)
La comunicación especializada.
355 pages. 2008. ISBN 978-3-03911-733-8

Vol. 88 Kiriko Sato
The Development from Case-Forms to Prepositional Constructions
in Old English Prose.
231 pages. 2009. ISBN 978-3-03911-763-5

Vol. 89 Dorothee Heller (Hrsg.)
Formulierungsmuster in deutscher und italienischer Fachkommunikation.
Intra- und interlinguale Perspektiven.
315 pages. 2008. ISBN 978-3-03911-778-9

Vol. 90 Henning Bergenholtz, Sandro Nielsen & Sven Tarp (eds)
Lexicography at a Crossroads. Dictionaries and Encyclopedias Today,
Lexicographical Tools Tomorrow.
372 pages. 2009. ISBN 978-3-03911-799-4

Vol. 91 Manouchehr Moshtagh Khorasani
The Development of Controversies: From the Early Modern Period
to Online Discussion Forums.
317 pages. 2009. ISBN 978-3-3911-711-6

Vol. 92 María Luisa Carrió-Pastor (ed.)
Content and Language Integrated Learning: Cultural Diversity.
178 pages. 2009. ISBN 978-3-3911-818-2

Vol. 93 Roger Berry
Terminology in English Language Teaching: Nature and Use.
262 pages. 2010. ISBN 978-3-0343-0013-1

Vol. 94 Roberto Cagliero & Jennifer Jenkins (eds)
Discourses, Communities, and Global Englishes
240 pages. 2010. ISBN 978-3-0343-0012-4

Vol. 95 Facchinetti Roberta, Crystal David, Seidlhofer Barbara (eds)
From International to Local English – And Back Again.
268 pages. 2010. ISBN 978-3-0343-0011-7

Vol. 96 Cesare Gagliardi & Alan Maley (eds)
EIL, ELF, Global English: Teaching and Learning Issues
376 pages. 2010. ISBN 978-3-0343-0010-0

Vol. 97 Sylvie Hancil (ed.)
The Role of Prosody in Affective Speech.
403 pages. 2009. ISBN 978-3-03911-696-6

Vol. 98 Marina Dossena & Roger Lass (eds)
Studies in English and European Historical Dialectology.
257 pages. 2009. ISBN 978-3-0343-0024-7

Vol. 99 Christine Béal
Les interactions quotidiennes en français et en anglais.
De l'approche comparative à l'analyse des situations interculturelles.
424 pages. 2010. ISBN 978-3-0343-0027-8

Vol. 100 Maurizio Gotti (ed.)
Commonality and Individuality in Academic Discourse.
398 pages. 2009. ISBN 978-3-0343-0023-0

Vol. 101 Javier E. Díaz Vera & Rosario Caballero (eds)
Textual Healing: Studies in Medieval English Medical,
Scientific and Technical Texts.
213 pages. 2009. ISBN 978-3-03911-822-9

Vol. 102 Nuria Edo Marzá
The Specialised Lexicographical Approach: A Step further in Dictionary-making.
316 pages. 2009. ISBN 978-3-0343-0043-8

Vol. 103 Carlos Prado-Alonso, Lidia Gómez-García, Iria Pastor-Gómez &
David Tizón-Couto (eds)
New Trends and Methodologies in Applied English Language Research.
Diachronic, Diatopic and Contrastive Studies.
348 pages. 2009. ISBN 978-3-0343-0046-9

Vol. 104 Françoise Salager-Meyer & Beverly A. Lewin
Crossed Words: Criticism in Scholarly Writing?
371 pages. 2011. ISBN 978-3-0343-0049-0.

Vol. 105 Javier Ruano-García
Early Modern Northern English Lexis: A Literary Corpus-Based Study.
611 pages. 2010. ISBN 978-3-0343-0058-2

Vol. 106 Rafael Monroy-Casas
Systems for the Phonetic Transcription of English: Theory and Texts.
280 pages. 2011. ISBN 978-3-0343-0059-9

Vol. 107 Nicola T. Owtram
The Pragmatics of Academic Writing.
A Relevance Approach to the Analysis of Research Article Introductions.
311 pages. 2009. ISBN 978-3-0343-0060-5

Vol. 108 Yolanda Ruiz de Zarobe, Juan Manuel Sierra & Francisco Gallardo del Puerto (eds)
Content and Foreign Language Integrated Learning. Contributions to Multilingualism in European Contexts
343 pages. 2011. ISBN 978-3-0343-0074-2

Vol. 109 Ángeles Linde López & Rosalía Crespo Jiménez (eds)
Professional English in the European context: The EHEA challenge.
374 pages. 2010. ISBN 978-3-0343-0088-9

Vol. 110 Rosalía Rodríguez-Vázquez
The Rhythm of Speech, Verse and Vocal Music: A New Theory.
394 pages. 2010. ISBN 978-3-0343-0309-5

Vol. 111 Anastasios Tsangalidis & Roberta Facchinetti (eds)
Studies on English Modality. In Honour of Frank Palmer.
392 pages. 2009. ISBN 978-3-0343-0310-1

Vol. 112 Forthcoming.

Vol. 113 Mihhail Lotman & Maria-Kristiina Lotman (eds)
Frontiers in Comparative Prosody. In memoriam: Mikhail Gasparov.
426 pages. 2011. ISBN 978-3-0343-0373-6

Vol. 114 Merja Kytö, John Scahill & Harumi Tanabe (eds)
Language Change and Variation from Old English to Late Modern English. A Festschrift for Minoji Akimoto
422 pages. 2010. ISBN 978-3-0343-0372-9

Vol. 115 Giuliana Garzone & Paola Catenaccio (eds)
Identities across Media and Modes: Discursive Perspectives.
379 pages. 2009. ISBN 978-3-0343-0386-6

Vol. 116 Elena Landone
Los marcadores del discurso y cortesía verbal en español.
390 pages. 2010. ISBN 978-3-0343-0413-9

Vol. 117 Maurizio Gotti & Christopher Williams (eds)
Legal Discourse across Languages and Cultures.
339 pages. 2010. ISBN 978-3-0343-0425-2

Vol. 118 David Hirsh
Academic Vocabulary in Context.
217 pages. 2010. ISBN 978-3-0343-0426-9

Vol. 119 Yvonne Dröschel
Lingua Franca English. The Role of Simplification and Transfer.
358 pages. 2011. ISBN 978-3-0343-0432-0

Vol. 120 Tengku Sepora Tengku Mahadi, Helia Vaezian & Mahmoud Akbari
Corpora in Translation. A Practical Guide.
135 pages. 2010. ISBN 978-3-0343-0434-4

Vol. 121 Davide Simone Giannoni & Celina Frade (eds)
Researching Language and the Law. Textual Features and Translation Issues.
278 pages. 2010. ISBN 978-3-0343-0443-6

Vol. 122 Daniel Madrid & Stephen Hughes (eds)
Studies in Bilingual Education.
472 pages. 2011. ISBN 978-3-0343-0474-0

Vol. 123 Vijay K. Bhatia, Christopher N. Candlin & Maurizio Gotti (eds)
The Discourses of Dispute Resolution.
290 pages. 2010. ISBN 978-3-0343-0476-4

Vol. 124 Davide Simone Giannoni
Mapping Academic Values in the Disciplines. A Corpus-Based Approach.
288 pages. 2010. ISBN 978-3-0343-0488-7

Vol. 125 Giuliana Garzone & James Archibald (eds)
Discourse, Identities and Roles in Specialized Communication.
419 pages. 2010. ISBN 978-3-0343-0494-8

Vol. 126 Iria Pastor-Gómez
The Status and Development of N+N Sequences in
Contemporary English Noun Phrases.
216 pages. 2011. ISBN 978-3-0343-0534-1

Vol. 127 Carlos Prado-Alonso
Full-verb Inversion in Written and Spoken English.
261 pages. 2011. ISBN 978-3-0343-0535-8

Vol. 128 Tony Harris & María Moreno Jaén (eds)
Corpus Linguistics in Language Teaching.
214 pages. 2010. ISBN 978-3-0343-0524-2

Vol. 129 Tetsuji Oda & Hiroyuki Eto (eds)
Multiple Perspectives on English Philology and History of Linguistics.
A Festschrift for Shoichi Watanabe on his 80th Birthday.
378 pages. 2010. ISBN 978-3-0343-0480-1

Vol. 130 Luisa Chierichetti & Giovanni Garofalo (eds)
Lengua y Derecho: líneas de investigación interdisciplinaria.
283 pages. 2010. 978-3-0343-0463-4

Vol. 131 Paola Evangelisti Allori & Giuliana Garzone (eds)
Discourse, Identities and Genres in Corporate Communication.
Sponsorship, Advertising and Organizational Communication.
324 pages. 2011. 978-3-0343-0591-4

Vol. 132 Forthcoming.

Vol. 133 Thomas Christiansen
Cohesion: A Discourse Perspective.
387 pages. 2011. 978-3-0343-0619-5

Vol. 134 Giuliana Garzone & Maurizio Gotti
Discourse, Communication and the Enterprise. Genres and Trends.
451 pages. 2011. ISBN 978-3-0343-0620-1

Vol. 135 Zsuzsa Hoffmann
Ways of the World's Words.
Language Contact in the Age of Globalization.
334 pages 2011. ISBN 978-3-0343-0673-7

Vol. 136 Cecilia Varcasia (ed.)
Becoming Multilingual.
Language Learning and Language Policy between Attitudes and Identities.
213 pages. 2011. ISBN 978-3-0343-0687-5

Vol. 137 Forthcoming.

Vol. 138 Maria Vittoria Calvi & Giovanna Mapelli (eds)
La lengua del turismo. Géneros discursivos y terminología.
365 pages. 2011. ISBN 978-3-0343-1011-6

Vol. 139 Ken Lau
Learning to Become a Professional in a Textually-Mediated World.
A Text-Oriented Study of Placement Practices.
261 pages. 2012. ISBN 978-3-0343-1016-1

Vol. 140–143 Forthcoming.

Vol. 144 Margrethe Petersen & Jan Engberg (eds)
Current Trends in LSP Research. Aims and Methods.
323 pages. 2011. ISBN 978-3-0343-1054-3

Vol. 145 Forthcoming.

Vol. 146 Rita Salvi & Hiromasa Tanaka (eds)
Intercultural Interactions in Business and Management.
306 pages. 2011. ISBN 978-3-0343-1039-0

Vol. 147–148 Forthcoming.

Vol. 149 Vijay K. Bhatia & Paola Evangelisti Allori (eds)
Discourse and Identity in the Professions. Legal, Corporate and Institutional Citizenship.
352 pages. 2011. ISBN 978-3-0343-1079-6

Vol. 150 Maurizio Gotti (ed.)
Academic Identity Traits. A Corpus-Based Investigation.
363 pages. 2012. ISBN 978-3-0343-1141-0

Vol. 151 Priscilla Heynderickx, Sylvain Dieltjens, Geert Jacobs, Paul Gillaerts &
Elizabeth de Groot (eds)
The Language Factor in International Business.
New Perspectives on Research, Teaching and Practice.
320 pages. 2012. ISBN 978-3-0343-1090-1

Vol. 152 Paul Gillaerts, Elizabeth de Groot, Sylvain Dieltjens, Priscilla Heynderickx &
Geert Jacobs (eds)
Researching Discourse in Business Genres. Cases and Corpora.
215 pages. 2012. ISBN 978-3-0343-1092-5

Vol. 153–157 Forthcoming.

Vol. 158 Bárbara Eizaga Rebollar (ed.)
Studies in Linguistics and Cognition.
301 pages. 2012. ISBN 978-3-0343-1138-0

FSC
www.fsc.org
MIX
Papier | Fördert
gute Waldnutzung
FSC® C083411

Kolibri 360 GmbH
Ferdinand-Jühlke-Straße 7
99095 Erfurt, Deutschland
produktsicherheit@kolibri360.de